Starring
Elvis

Starring

Elvis

Elvis Presley's Greatest Movies Stories and Photos

Edited by James W. Bowser

A DELL BOOK

Published by
Dell Publishing Co., Inc.
1 Dag Hammarskjold Plaza
New York, New York 10017

Dell ® TM 681510, Dell Publishing Co., Inc.

ISBN: 0-440-18241-7

Printed in the United States of America
First printing—October 1977

The assignment of editing a book about the movies of Elvis Presley wasn't one that I had expected, but, after the project was under way, I was glad that it had been given to me. Someone with a critical eye probably would have done a much more comprehensive job, but his or her reasons for selecting certain films to be included here might not have been as personal as mine. Criteria such as acting ability, directorial skill, camera technique, plot, dialogue, musical numbers, and film grosses at the box office are the material for most retrospectives. The judgment of an editor who never had known Elvis or who, perhaps, had not liked him as a performer—or as a person —would have to be based upon such standards. Mine was not.

I had met Elvis—just once, years ago at his first big press conference in New York City, and liked him at once. Already famous because of the army of fans who had sprung up around him almost overnight and the controversy over his influence on their morals, he tried to be a bit cocky but couldn't quite carry it off. He came across as the country boy who still couldn't believe that a roomful of big city reporters and columnists wanted to talk to him. "Sir" and "Ma'am"-ing us consistently no matter how barbed a question—because his parents had taught him always to be polite— he won me over. And, as a result, I went to see his movies, along with millions of other fans.

There were thirty-three in all, if one counts the two documentaries, *Elvis—That's the Way It Is* and *Elvis on Tour,* and they brought in hundreds of millions of dollars at movie houses all over the world. Some were good. A few were really bad. Most were entertaining, if one were an Elvis fan.

INTRODUCTION

If you weren't you probably shouldn't have been there in the first place.

The selection of the movies to be included in a book of this type has to be a personal one. Every fan has favorite Elvis films. Let me tell you why I chose mine and see if you agree. Chances are you will have plenty of opportunity to see them all again soon. TV stations have been showing them since August 16, 1977, when the "King of Rock 'n' Roll" died. The motion picture companies undoubtedly will rerelease everything in their storage vaults. The magic line *Starring Elvis* once more will be on marquees and fans will have a chance to pick their own "greatest" list. This is mine:

That *Love Me Tender* had to be included was obvious, being Elvis' first. He was as self-conscious as an actor as he had been as a new star being interviewed and, mentally, I've always connected him with the title song. *Loving You* is also closely linked to memories of Elvis, possibly because it was basically his own story—the poor boy who made it big but who still was happiest with down-home folks. He hadn't improved much as an actor, but there was a lot more music and it was in Technicolor.

Jailhouse Rock gave Elvis a chance to show the style that made him King of Rock. By *King Creole*, he was proving that he *could* act and seemed comfortable in the company of such true pros as Carolyn Jones and Walter Matthau. This is one of my favorites, followed by *Wild in the Country*. Somehow he appeared to be having fun just making that movie; it's been said he thought it was his best. Scenically, *Blue Hawaii* is terrific and, musically, second only to *Viva Las Vegas* in which he and Ann-Margret were perfectly paired, resembling the magic of a Fred Astaire and Ginger Rogers flick.

Elvis showed that he could handle comedy if given the chance in *Follow That Dream*. I never could believe him as a prizefighter in *Kid Galahad*, but who could resist a musical version of scores of earlier boxing movies? *Girls! Girls! Girls!* is pretty light when it comes to plot, but it gives Elvis a chance to Sing! Sing! Sing! *Roustabout* makes it with the help of a good cast that includes Barbara

Stanwyck, Leif Erickson, Pat Buttram, and Jack Albert-
son.

Finally a pair that are irresistible: *Harum Scarum* and
Charro! It is surprising it took so long for someone to
put Elvis in a costume in which he could be compared
to the earlier idol, "Sheik" Valentino, but in *Harum
Scarum* he hams it up in keeping with the tone of the
picture. *Charro!* gave Elvis a chance to do a Clint East-
woodlike role and he carried it off most of the time. And
did it while wearing—unheard of!—the same grubby duds
throughout.

That's the *why* of my "greatest." Yours will be different, I'm certain, but we'll both still be fans.

This book would not have been possible without the
efforts of many people and I thank them all. It would not
have existed without the efforts of one man and it is to
late to thank him for twenty-odd years of entertainment.
Starring Elvis is a beginning.

James W. Bowser

CAST

Clint Reno	ELVIS PRESLEY	Siringo	ROBERT MIDDLETON
Vance Reno	RICHARD EGAN	Brett Reno	WILLIAM CAMPBELL
Cathy	DEBRA PAGET	Mike Gavin	NEVILLE BRAND

LOVE ME TENDER

■ Vance Reno was big and all man, but for the moment he didn't believe he could take it. The girl he held tightly in his arms looked up at him with astonishment and something that was almost terror.

"I reckon you couldn't have knowed this," his youngest brother Clint had just said, "but me an' Cathy got married—'bout three months ago."

Vance stared with disbelief at his brother; he looked with bewilderment at his mother, who was watching with painful anxiety; he glanced at his other brothers, Brett and Ray, who for four long, agonized years had been his saddle companions and battlemates in Randall's Raiders, the famous Confederate cavalry regiment that had made life so miserable for the Federal forces in Arkansas, Louisiana and Mississippi. Vance, a lieutenant and squadron leader, had relied on Brett and Ray in more than one critical moment, but they could not help him now. They dropped their eyes.

Vance looked back at Cathy, a girl with fair skin and honey-colored hair, with well-remembered blue eyes and soft lips. The eyes were filling with tears now. Slowly, he released her.

"Married?" he repeated in a kind of trance.

"They told us you were dead," his mother said.

Vance knew that. The whole thing became sickeningly clear. He knew the Confederate Government had believed him to be dead—it had been one of those horrible mistakes that make war more terrible than it ordinarily is—and they had sent word home to his mother, his brother—and to Cathy.

"I don't know what we'd have done without Cathy, son —or her without us, after her folks died." Mrs. Reno was falsely cheerful. "We've all had mighty poor scratchin' to keep body and soul together, waitin' for the war to end."

"Waitin'," said Vance, still looking at Cathy. "Yes, that must've been hard." He breathed deeply, shrugged his great shoulders. "Well," he said, "congratulations, Clint. We always did want Cathy in the family. Didn't we, Ma?"

Mrs. Reno looked at him sadly. "Yes, son," she said. "Always."

That, then, was the homecoming of Vance Reno and

his brothers Brett and Ray, lately of the Army of the Confederacy. The shock was dreadful; worse, Vance thought, than the shock of the minnie-ball that had struck him in the fight over in Louisiana and had all but knocked the life out of him. He had recovered from that. Would he, he wondered, recover from this?

He had had high hopes for this homecoming to the old Reno farm in East Texas. Just before setting out on that homeward journey, he and Brett and Ray and what had remained of their squadron had captured a Federal paymaster's outfit, donned their captives' clothes, and tricked a Union major into handing over to them almost $13,000 in payroll money. After a battle that had taken off several of their number, they had escaped with this, and had divided it in a ruined farmhouse near the Texas line. There were only six, and it made a sizable stake for each of them.

This was before they had learned that the war was over. The news had struck them with stunning impact. It also had produced some misgivings as to whether they should keep the money. The three Renos were dubious at first, since the coup had been made after the war had—unknown to them—ended. The other three survivors of the squadron, Sergeant Gavin and Troopers Kelso and Fleming, had argued otherwise. Finally, even Vance came to see their point of view.

"We didn't steal this money," he said. "We took it in battle, fair an' square. We didn't know the war was over an' neither did the Federals. So it's still prize money."

That was the way of it. The three Renos rode west into Texas; the others made their way to their own homes.

Vance rode with his spirits high and his heart yearning. He was riding home to Cathy, whom he had loved always. For four years he had dreamed of Cathy. Her picture was in the gold locket she had given him, and every night he had taken it out of his leather wallet and had looked at it. The whole squadron knew Cathy well, because they had seen her picture so often and had heard Vance talk about her every day.

At the country store near their old home, the brothers

stopped to shave and clean up a little. They bought their
mother some odds and ends and Vance bought himself a
black broadcloth suit to be married in. He paid for this
and the other purchases with a twenty-dollar bill, one of
those from the Federal payroll money, much to the astonishment of the storekeeper. That was a mistake as it
turned out, but they didn't know that then.

They rode on toward the Reno farm and they swooped
down on it as they had in the days of their boyhood,
whooping and yelling like Indians, Vance the leader, as
always.

And now this. His little brother, who idolized him, and
who had been too young to go away to war, had married
the girl he loved—would always love.

It was hard for Vance to hide his feelings. But he did.
The supper was almost gay. And on the porch after the
meal, Clint took up his guitar and they sang as they had
sung in years before. But one song—it was the one that'd
had meaning for Vance and Cathy—he could not stand.

Abruptly, he rose and walked into the darkness to be
alone with his thoughts. He was standing there when he
heard Clint's voice.

"Vance, I know you an' Cathy used to be kinda fond
of each other. But you've got no hard feelin's against either
one of us now, have you?"

Vance had dreaded this moment, but he faced it. "Of
course not!" he said with emphasis.

"You really mean that, Vance?" asked Clint. All the
hero-worship of a younger brother was in his voice then.
"Down deep?"

Vance put his hand on Clint's shoulder. "Listen, Clint,"
he said earnestly, "did I ever lie to you?" And when Clint
shook his head, he hurried on: "I liked her, sure. We all
did. But I wasn't never in love with Cathy, if that's what
you mean. We was just good friends. An' that's how it still
is."

Clint believed him, as Vance had hoped, and went on
to the barn for some chore. Vance walked to the house—
and in the dark of the hall, near the stairway, Cathy stood
waiting for him. She had, he knew, been waiting for some
time. As he tried to pass her she stopped him.

Their faces and bodies were almost touching; the moment was painful to both of them. "You've got to let me talk to you," said Cathy. "Please let me try an' explain what—"

"There's nothin' to explain."

"Oh but there is! Just give me a chance to—"

They both started at the voice that came from the top of the steps. It was Brett. "Comin' to bed, Vance?" he asked quietly.

Vance went up the stairs. But, he knew, this was only the beginning.

Vance had buried the money he and Brett and Ray had brought back. It was in a stall in the barn. It would be used in good time; now they must work to set things right again. Young Clint had been overwhelmed by the place, with nobody but his mother and Cathy to help. The brothers were up before the sun these days, fixing fences, plowing, doing everything that should be done. But the tension between Vance and Cathy grew.

Vance was shoeing a horse in the barn one day. He was alone, and Cathy went to him.

"Won't you even try to understand?" she said.

"Nobody asks why a woman falls in love."

"But you do," she cried. "You ask me with every look. You've got no right to think I was faithless. I thought of you all day long and prayed for you every night. Then that letter came saying you were dead—and I didn't want to live *myself*. I loved you, Vance; with all my heart and soul I loved you dearly."

Vance stood up and moved away, looking out of the barn. "That's what hurts most, Cathy," he said. "I know—an' can't forget it."

"We've got to, both of us," said Cathy, "or we can't go on living here under the same roof. Why did you tell him there'd never been anything between us?"

Vance stared at her in surprise. "What'd you want me to tell him—the truth?"

"He already knows it," she said quietly. "I told him myself before we were married. If he's big enough to forget what's past, *you* can!" Cathy caught Vance by his arms, looked up into his face. "Oh, Vance, honey, try—for my sake—try to!"

Vance looked down into her stricken eyes. Then he tore himself away and hurried across the barnyard to the house, leaving her there, her head buried in her hands.

So they tried to forget, both of them. But it wasn't much use. In the still night Vance would lie there, thinking of Cathy in the next room with Clint. As for Cathy, there was the time Clint awakened and found her at the window, looking out into the night, tears streaming down her face. All the explanations she could make would not set his wondering mind at rest.

It was Vance who made the decision, and one night he went to his mother with it. "There's no other way, Ma," he said, "I've tried to hide it, but I can't stay on. Sooner or later Clint would see."

"He might guess it now, anyway," said Martha Reno.

"No he won't," said Vance. "I'll tell him I'm goin' out to California just for a few months, to look around. He'll believe it, an' the rest of you'll never tell him."

"When do you go?" asked Martha Reno. When he said he would leave the next day, she tried to protest. But he stopped her.

"The quicker the better," he said. "Tomorrow we'll all be goin' over to the raising of the new schoolhouse. I'll tell Clint and Cathy and ride out before they can try'n stop me."

"Clint thinks the sun rises and sets in you," said Mrs. Reno.

"I know, Ma," he said. "That's just why I'm goin'."

The schoolhouse raising was a big thing in the vicinity. People for miles around came to it. It was a worthy project, and besides that it gave them a chance for a real sociable time. The Renos went with the others, dressed their best— Cathy and Mrs. Reno in the buckboard with Clint driving the horse; Vance, Brett and Ray accompanying on horseback. The two latter, who knew of Vance's intention, were deeply disturbed; but they showed nothing.

The crowd at the schoolhouse site was gay. Clint, with some others, played his guitar and sang as people danced under the trees. Meanwhile Vance motioned to Cathy, and she followed him to the privacy of a clump of trees.

He told her, then, that he was leaving; he was going to California to work a ranch with an old army friend.

For answer she blazed: "That's not your reason! You're leaving because of me an' Clint."

Vance nodded. "Maybe so," he said. "I can't meet his eyes after what you told him."

Cathy was beginning to break. "*I* can't stay here," she cried, "facin' others, knowin' you've run away because of me—an' they knowin' it too!" She grasped his arms fiercely. "You can't go! You *know* how I feel! I—"

He cut her off hard. "Don't say it!" he ordered. "Even if it's true, *don't say it!* Now now—not ever!"

He pulled her hands from their almost painful grip on his arms. Cathy looked at him for a long moment. Then, almost hysterical, she turned and ran—and it was then that Clint saw her. He also saw Vance, and he was dumbfounded for a moment. Then he put down his guitar and hurried after his wife. He caught up with her but she broke from him and ran to a grove of trees at the rear of the schoolhouse site. He looked after her, puzzled, then turned back to where Vance was standing.

"What's wrong with Cathy?"

"I told her I was goin' away," said Vance. "An' I was comin' to tell you."

"Away? What do you mean?"

But Vance never had a chance to answer that. An old friend of the Renos, Marshal Galt, who represented the law in that part of East Texas, was calling out to Ray and Brett. Indicating a group of Federal troops and a civilian, he said, "these fellows want to talk to you and Vance."

There was more than a platoon of soldiers, led by a man in a major's uniform. Marshal Galt introduced him as Major Kincaid. The civilian, who turned out to be a Pinkerton detective working for the government, was Mr. Siringo. Siringo explained that he had been engaged by the government to recover property that was lost or stolen during the war.

"That's good news," said Vance. "We lost a lot of things 'round here. You want our list?"

"No," said Siringo. He was a good-looking man with a calm, intelligent face. "We've got our own."

The Pinkerton man went on relentlessly. He said that three of the Reno brothers, members of Randall's Cavalry, were part of a unit that had attacked the railroad station at Greenwood, Louisiana, had impersonated Federal officers and had taken a United States Army payroll amounting to $12,250 from an officer who was on the train. He said they had traced the Renos by the twenty-dollar bill one brother had given to a storekeeper. He said also that it might be possible that the Renos had not known the war ended around noon on the preceding day.

Vance turned to Ray and Brett. "You got any idea what he's talkin' about?" he asked.

Ray and Brett shook their heads. Clint scowled in bewilderment, and Mrs. Reno and Cathy looked on, afraid.

"Don't be foolish, Vance," said Marshal Galt. "I'd sure hate to see you get in trouble. So if you got the money, go on—give it up now!"

"I said we didn't steal any money, Ed," Vance said in a quiet voice.

"Well," said Siringo, "that's possible. But we mean to make sure. The Federal paymaster can identify the men who took the money from him."

Siringo might have been calm; the Major was not. He was angry about the boys' stubbornness, and showed it. "You're all three under arrest!" he snapped. "We're taking you to Tyler on tonight's train. Get your horses. . . ."

Back at the farmhouse, Clint raged that the whole thing was a frame-up. "But what'll they do to Vance?" Cathy asked him.

"Clap him in some stinkin' prison most likely an' keep—" He broke off, staring at his wife. "Why did you just say Vance?" he asked, the memory of the scene at the schoolhouse crossing his mind. An old jealousy flared in his breast. "We're worried about all three of 'em—ain't we?"

It might have been a crisis, but they heard horses outside. Clint grabbed Vance's old service revolver and rushed to the porch. Three men on horseback lingered at the edge of the lamplight that glowed from the farmhouse door. It was Gavin, Kelso and Fleming, the other members of the payroll-raiding party.

"We're friends o' your brothers," said Gavin. "Any of 'em around?"

"No," said Clint. "Why?"

"Some Federal men lookin' for 'em."

"You're too late." Clint's voice was bitter. "They arrested all three of 'em this mornin'—on some lyin' charge—an' took 'em away."

"Where'd they take your brothers?" asked Fleming.

"Into town," Clint said. "An' tonight they're goin' on the train to Tyler, to stand trial."

"Let's get goin'," said Gavin.

"Wait!" Clint called. "I'm goin' with you!"

Martha Reno and Cathy would have held him back, but Clint would not be stayed. He rode off with Gavin and the others. . . .

Meanwhile, Vance and his brothers, with the Major, Marshal Galt, and Siringo, were on their way. They sat in humiliation, manacled to the seats of the railroad car, their captors facing them. Siringo and Vance were isolated from the others.

"I don't want to send you boys to prison," said Siringo. "Tell me you'll give me the money back, and I give you my word we'll drop the charges—forget the whole thing." He paused, then resumed: "If they identify you tomorrow you'll get ten years. And even if they let you go you'll be watched for the rest of your life. The money'd do you no good."

Vance thought hard. He realized also that Siringo was honest in his offer. He knew all at once that the peace and security of himself and his whole family depended on his decision.

"We—" He paused, then went on: "We haven't got all of it—only our shares."

The other four men of their party could not hear them. And none of the group noticed the two tall men who moved down the aisle of the swaying car, their faces indistinguishable in the light of the dim oil lamps—Gavin and Kelso, who had hopped the train at a water stop some miles back. Nor could the brothers or their captives know that at that moment Fleming, his gun drawn, was creeping over the tender to take care of the engineer and fireman.

"Who's got the rest?" continued Siringo, his thoughts on the payroll.

"I don't know," said Vance loyally. "I'm ready to do what you say, but we can't give you any more'n we've got."

"Then," said Siringo bluntly, "we've got no deal."

The Pinkerton man froze as he felt the muzzle of Gavin's gun in the back of his neck. "Set still, mister," said Gavin. "Don't make no moves." Across the aisle, Kelso had given the same orders to Major Kincaid and Marshal Galt. The three Reno brothers looked up in speechless surprise. "Vance," Gavin ordered, "get his gun an' his keys. Unlock those cuffs."

Before he quite realized what he was doing, Vance did as directed. Gavin unlocked the manacles from the Renos and fastened Siringo, Kincaid and Marshal Galt to the seats instead. As he did, the train ground to a stop. The engineer, confronted by Fleming's gun, also was obeying orders. Throughout the coaches people started to their feet in alarm, and women screamed in fear. But they quieted as Gavin's warning shot through a window told them that if they made a suspicious move they would be in real peril.

Vance, as if aware for the first time of what was going on, started to reason with Gavin. But the Sergeant shoved him down the aisle. "Get goin'!" the gunslinger snarled. "It's all set."

Still bewildered, the Renos ran with the others down the aisle to the platform. They jumped from the train and scrambled up the bank into the woods just as bullets from the armed baggage guard cut the branches and leaves around them.

The escape had been well timed. Standing in a little clearing were seven horses—those of Gavin, Kelso and Fleming, and three mounts for the Renos. Clint Reno was already on the seventh horse.

"What the devil're *you* doin' here?" demanded Vance of his youngest brother.

"Git mounted!" yelled Gavin. "Git outa here!"

They did, but down the road Vance pulled up. "Get off the road," he said. "We're goin' to settle this here and now." And when they were in the deep woods: "I could've made a deal with Siringo—but now he'll be gunnin' for us."

Gavin, Kelso and Fleming—even Clint and the other two Renos—looked at Vance in amazement. The three ex-Troopers glowered. This wasn't what they had expected.

"I led you fellers through four years o' fightin' an' I never once steered you wrong, did I?" Vance continued. "So you ought to know that nobody hates givin' up more'n I do. But these Federal men'll hound us 'til we're all dead or behind bars."

"So you did take the payroll!" cried Clint. "Why didn't you tell me the truth?"

"We felt we had a right to it, Clint—as spoils of war."

"What's changed your mind?" asked Gavin. His tone was dangerous.

"Siringo. He offered to forget the whole thing if we surrendered the money. An' I got a hunch he'll *still* do it, in spite o' the train holdup. Nobody was hurt; nobody was robbed."

Brett and Ray were for Vance's plan; Gavin and the other two Troopers angrily rejected it. They were keeping their shares, they said; the Renos could do as they pleased. They turned their horses to go, but were stopped by Vance's cold voice.

"Hold on!" he said and when they looked, they saw that his gun was drawn. "This deal with Siringo's only good if we turn in *all* the money." He turned to Ray and Brett. "Get it! And their guns." And when they had done this: "Now I'm goin' back and get our shares. I'll meet you right after daylight, at Hanna's Mill. Brett, that means you and Ray, too."

Gavin, Kelso and Fleming were looking at him murderously, but also with a kind of respect. They hated him in that moment for ruining their plans, but they were remembering the way he'd commanded them during the war. Grudgingly, they had to admire him.

Vance turned to Clint: "Nobody knows you're in on this, so you ride into town. Tell Siringo I'll come in with the money tomorrow mornin'. Then you come to the Mill an' give us his answer."

Almost before Vance had finished, his baby brother was on his way. Vance turned his horse and galloped off toward their home.

But it was not as simple as that. When Vance reached the hilltop overlooking the farm, he stopped in dismay. In the familiar yard between the house and the barn were Federal troopers, and he could make out the figure of Major Kincaid. He turned and galloped back the way he had come. At a decaying log cabin a mile or so from the Reno farm he stopped and knocked. An old man, a long-time friend of the Renos, came to the door.

"Jethro," said Vance. "We're in bad trouble. But it may work out if you'll help us."

"Of course I will," Jethro said, and Vance told him where the money was hidden. He knew that Jethro would not arouse suspicion, even if seen. Sending his old friend for the cache, he waited impatiently for his return.

But it was not Jethro who returned. It was Cathy.

"What're you doing here?" demanded Vance uneasily.

"I've brought the money." She explained that the troops had been searching the place and that she had intended to ride out to warn Vance and his brothers that Kincaid meant to leave a guard waiting for them. But in the stall she had come upon Jethro, who'd explained the plan, and Cathy had decided to bring the money herself. She'd thought she could get away with it more easily. In that she had been right. They had permitted her to go.

"Where are the others?" she asked, when she had explained.

"Waitin' for me," he said. "We're goin' to give it back, Cathy. Then they'll let us go free—we hope."

"They've got orders to shoot you on sight!"

"Then I've got to get to Siringo first. Clint rode into town to tell him I'd come. So give me the—"

They heard horses. Then, through the woods, they saw Federal troopers—perhaps twenty of them, led by Major Kincaid—galloping along the road. The troopers spied them and began firing immediately.

Cathy's horse bolted of its own accord; Vance's followed. The chase led through woods and up and down hills, but the terrain was familiar to the oldest Reno and not to the troopers. He and Cathy managed to outdistance their pursuers, at least temporarily. They reached the edge of a large swamp.

"If we can cross this swamp," said Vance, "there's a place beyond where we can hide. You willin' to try it?" And when she nodded: "Then follow me close."

The swamp was fetid; it crawled with unseen things. Hanging vines that might have been snakes brushed their faces and when Cathy turned her horse slightly to avoid one, its feet slipped into the deadly mire of quicksand. The animal stumbled forward, throwing Cathy herself into the morass.

Vance was off his horse and after her in an instant. He reached her and managed to swing her to his shoulder, but the added weight caused him to sink dangerously. It might have been a frightful end for both of them if Cathy's mare, instinctively flailing its hooves toward firm ground, had not managed to reach it. When she did, she began to pull herself out and Vance, holding to the stirrup of Cathy's saddle, pulled himself along.

On the mossy bank beside the morass, they fell, exhausted. Vance's arm was still around his brother's wife. They lay there for a moment, their faces close, their eyes searching each other. And then, with a kind of sigh, Cathy kissed him—at first gently, then savagely, with all the pent-up hunger she had known for him, and Vance responded. . . .

Later, while Vance reconnoitered, Cathy washed her clothes, wrapped herself in saddle blankets, and hung up her garments to dry. Vance came back and gazed at her.

"After you've given the money back," she asked, "will you still go away?"

"Even farther now."

"It won't help, Vance. We'll never forget each other."

The man was silent for a moment. Then he sighed. "We know that, Cathy. But nobody else must ever know it." He looked at her with such yearning that she began to weep. But he did not go to her.

Meanwhile, at Hanna's Mill, Brett and Ray Reno and

the three other Troopers from Vance's squadron were waiting. Gavin, Kelso and Fleming seemed reconciled to their
loss now and Brett and Ray had returned their guns to
them. But the morning was well along and Vance hadn't
come back. They were muttering their impatience when
Clint rode up.

"You seen Siringo?" asked Brett. "What'd he say?"

"He agreed," said Clint, "but he says you got to take a
chance comin' in. Major Kincaid don't trust you, an' he
can't get word to him." He looked around. "Where's
Vance? He shoulda been here by now."

Gavin's eyes were hard. "That's what we figure," he
said.

Clint had other news. He had seen old Jethro and had
learned that Cathy had ridden out with the money to meet
Vance. "She's my wife," he explained.

They were surprised. "*Your* wife?" asked Gavin. Kelso
added, "She was *Vance's* girl."

Clint's face tightened. "What else did Jethro tell you?"
Brett said hastily.

Clint looked slowly from Gavin and the others to his
brothers. "That's all he knows," he said.

"Didn't Cathy come back home?"

"No." Clint's voice was hoarse.

"They coulda rode a long ways by this time," said Gavin
bitterly.

"What d'you mean by that?" snapped Clint.

"He's got *all* the money now," said Gavin. "Didn't you
know he was crazy 'bout your wife?" Gavin smiled crook-
edly. "It's time somebody opened your eyes, kid. He
wanted her—an' now he's run off with her."

"An' with our money!" snarled Kelso.

"They prob'ly had it all figured out," said Gavin. He
began to laugh mirthlessly.

As he did, Clint's face contorted with surrender to jeal-
ous rage. He whirled his horse, dug spurs into it and galloped down the road, heedless of Brett Reno's cry for him
to wait. Brett turned to Ray with alarm. "We've got to find
'em before he does," he said, and the two brothers took off
in pursuit.

Suspiciously, Gavin and his two henchmen followed.

"They could *all* be in on this," said the Trooper.

Vance and Cathy had left the swamp, and had found a cave in the rocky hills, to which the brothers had gone on hunting trips when they were boys.

"Clint'll be waitin' for me at the Mill," said Vance, taking his leave of Cathy.

"But what'll you do if he's not?"

"Go into town an' give 'em back the money. You stay here and I'll send somebody for you by nightfall."

But even as he was leaving her, Clint, now accompanied by Gavin and his henchmen and followed apprehensively by his two brothers, was riding with murder in his heart. Brett and Ray looked at the youth with amazement and worry. "If he does find 'em he won't even wait to listen, Brett," said Ray. "He's half crazy now."

Brett agreed. "But Vance ain't runnin' away," he said. "Chance is they're just hidin' out 'til—" He paused, as the sudden hunch struck him. "Hold on! I got an idea where they might be." They reined their horses in and nodded to Clint and the three Troopers. "Let 'em ride on." Suddenly, they whirled their mounts and rode in the direction of the well-remembered cave, where they found Cathy.

Swiftly, she explained what had happened, telling them that Vance had gone to Hanna's Mill to meet his cohorts, but that he meant to go on into town if they weren't there. That was good news, but there was still the matter of Clint.

"Clint thinks you ran off with Vance," said Brett. "He thinks you've left him for good." He explained about Gavin's men. "They think Vance took the money—an' you —to clear out. We tried to reason with him, Cathy, but he won't listen. He's out of his mind with jealousy."

"An' if he finds Vance now," said Ray, "there's no tellin' *what* he'll do."

Cathy was already on her mare. "Where is he?" she begged tensely. "Let me talk to him. . . ."

The tragedy of errors was soon made complete. Vance, riding to do precisely what the government wanted him to do, was sighted by Major Kincaid and his troops.

Promptly they fired on him and gave pursuit. Cathy, meanwhile, riding with her two brothers-in-law, had come upon Clint with the other three. For a moment they all sat their horses motionless, as Clint stared at his wife with bitterness. Cathy met his stare, dismounted and walked toward him.

"Where is he?" demanded Clint.

"Do you believe what these men told you, Clint?" asked Cathy quietly.

"Nobody *had* to tell me!" he snarled. "I reckon I've always known it. This just showed me plain."

"Wait, Clint. Hear what I've—"

But he would not wait. His bitterness flooded out of him: the memory of her tears that night by the window; the day before at the schoolhouse, when she had broken from him; other times he had been tortured by doubt. "Say I'm lyin'!" he almost screamed at her. "Say he warn't your lover!"

He was off his horse now and advancing toward her. Brett tried to stop him, but Clint threw his brother aside with maniacal strength. He grabbed Cathy by the throat and began to slap her face. "You love him!" he shouted insanely. *"You love him!"*

He knocked Cathy down—would have thrown himself upon her—but Brett and Ray were on him now, holding him, while Gavin and his henchmen looked on cynically.

Brett left Clint to Ray and went to help Cathy up. "Get away from here before he goes *clean* crazy," he whispered to the girl. "Ride back to where we found you an' wait for Vance, in case he returns. Warn him what's happened, an' to stay there 'til we come."

Cathy nodded. She looked sorrowfully at Clint, then turned and rode off. "I've sent her back home," Brett said to Clint. "Now you're goin' with us into town. Get mounted."

But Gavin had other ideas. He had drawn his gun and was covering Brett and Ray. "They're lyin' to you, Clint," he said. "She's headin' back to him, wherever he's hidin' out. You do what you want. We're trailin' her."

Clint was ready to believe him. The inflamed mind knew

no reason. "You're right," he said. "They're still tryin' to throw us off." He mounted quickly and rode after Cathy.

"Get their guns," growled Gavin. Riding to Brett and Ray, Fleming took their revolvers. "Now," continued Gavin, "you can ride to the Mill—or to Hades—far's we're concerned. Just don't foller us!" And he and the other two rode away after Clint.

Left alone, the two weaponless brothers breathed deeply. Ray was the first to speak. "We've got to find Vance!" he said. "But where?"

"Let's try the Mill," said Brett.

Vance was at Hanna's Mill and had been wondering where his partners had gone. He was appalled by what they told him. "First," the eldest brother said, "we've got to get rid of *this*." He handed Ray the money. "Take it an' ride into town, fast. Give it to Siringo. Tell him what's happened." He and Brett were going to try to get back to the cave, to which Brett had sent Cathy, ahead of Clint and the pursuing Troopers. "You bring what help you can. Now get movin'!"

Ray wheeled and rode for town. Vance and Brett rode off for the cave. On the way, Vance said he would talk to Clint; Clint respected him, and would listen to him, Vance insisted. He would not believe Brett's warning that Clint had changed.

They did not make it to the cave before Clint and the Troopers. These four were all down the slope, conferring.

"All we got to do now is wait for 'em to come down," said Kelso.

"Yeah," said Fleming. "Money an' all." Clint laughed —a frightening sound. "That's your business," he said. "Just leave *him* to me."

"What's keepin' 'em up there?" asked Kelso.

"Maybe," said Fleming, leering at Clint, "they're restin'. Waitin' for nightfall."

Clint's mouth twisted into a snarl. "I been waitin' long enough," he said, and started up the slope. The others followed.

But when they reached the top all they saw was a startled Cathy. "Where is he?" demanded Clint.

"I—I don't know, Clint. I—"

"You're lyin'! Where's he hiding'?" He wrenched her arm cruelly and she cried out. "You're tryin' to protect him!" he shouted.

"Let her alone, Clint. That ain't helpin' us none. He wouldn't've left her here 'less he was comin' back. So we just set here 'til he walks in."

That Gavin was right was shown minutes later, when they saw Vance and Brett ride into view. They hid down the slope, and Vance's voice came up to them.

"Clint," it said, "can you hear me, Clint?" The rocky hillside was still. Up above, on the ledge, the men listened. Clint glowered, and Cathy watched him in terror. "I know what you're thinkin'," Vance's voice went on. "But you got it all wrong. Clint—*dead* wrong. All Cathy did was bring me the money. There's nothin' between us. I swear it!" He paused, and Cathy could hear Clint's horse breathing. "I was goin' away, Clint. An' I'm still goin'—for good! But I had to square things with Siringo first. An' I've *done* it."

"He couldn't have," whispered Gavin. "He ain't had time to get into town an' back. He's workin' a scheme to draw us out."

"I'm comin' up, Clint," said Vance's voice.

"He's lyin' to you 'bout the money," Gavin said, worried now. "He's still got it on him. He only came back for her—an' she *knows* it!"

Clint darted a raging glance at his wife and turned back, his revolver pointed at the advancing form of his brother. Vance was climbing slowly among the boulders. "Clint, listen to me," he was saying. "Ray's gone in to take Siringo the money. That'll give us clean hands—*all* of us —unless one of you loses his head now an' adds killin' to it."

Gavin was impatient. "What's stoppin' you?" he hissed at Clint. "Can't you see he's just stallin', workin' closer 'til he can jump us? He's prob'ly got Ray an' Brett workin' 'round behind us. Go on. You asked for him, *take him!*"

"Why don't you answer me, Clint?" Vance was asking. "I only came to tell you our trouble's over. We can go home with nothin' to fear."

"Go on!" snarled Gavin. "Take him now—or I'll take him myself!"

Whatever had been going on in Clint's mind overwhelmed him then. The shot rang from his gun, clear in the morning air. Vance staggered slightly, a look of surprise on his face, and then fell. Cathy screamed, and Gavin shouted, "Come on, let's get the money and get outa here!" With Kelso and Fleming he ran down the slope to where Vance lay. Snatching the gun from his holster, he turned Vance over roughly to search his pockets. Vance, though conscious, was helpless to defend himself.

Up above, Clint cried out, aghast at what he had done. The horrible sight of the three Troopers manhandling his wounded brother brought back all the love and loyalty that had been overshadowed by his jealousy. "Get away from him!" he yelled. He fired a warning shot and started down the slope. But he stiffened, poised there as if in some kind of strange dance, as Gavin's bullet tore into his chest. Then he pitched headlong down the hill, to lie a few yards from Vance. Cathy, not heeding the possible danger from the murderous trio, now ran toward the two stricken brothers.

Brett came into view, climbing the slope. Gavin turned toward him in fury; he and his men had found no money. Whatever he had in mind, however, he did not carry out, for across the valley below them he and the others beheld the Federal troops. They were headed by Major Kincaid and Ray, and with them were Marshal Galt and Siringo. Gavin, Kelso and Fleming were cut off from their horses!

They scrambled up to the ledge, but there was no fight left in them. Despairing they threw down their guns and gave up.

But the group down the slope were not interested in the scene above them. Cathy held her dying husband in her arms, while he called for his brother Vance. Painfully, the older Reno rose and walked to where Clint lay. "I'm right here, Clint," he said.

"I—I—didn't mean to do it, Vance. I—"

His voice failed, but his eyes did not. They pleaded for understanding.

"I know you didn't," said Vance. "You don't have

to tell me. Everything's goin' to be all right, Clint."

The boy smiled, and looked from Vance to Cathy. "Sure," he said, his voice only a whisper. "I know. Everything's right for all of us now."

Which was the way Clint Reno died—in his wife's cradling arms, with his brothers standing by him.

In later—and happier—years, they remembered him only with charity and love.

Adapted from the 20th CENTURY FOX CINEMASCOPE
   Production
Copyright 1956 by 20th CENTURY FOX FILM CORP.
Produced by DAVID WEISBART
Directed by ROBERT D. WEBB
Screenplay by ROBERT BUCKNER
Based on a story by MAURICE GERAGHTY
Adapted for SCREEN STORIES by JEAN FRANCIS WEBB

CAST

Deke Rivers	ELVIS PRESLEY	Susie Jessup	DOLORES HART
Glenda Markle	LISBETH SCOTT	Carl Meade	JAMES GLEASON
Tex Warner	WENDELL COREY	Jim Tallman	RALPH DUMKE

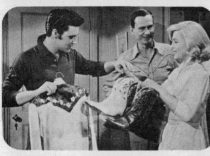

LOVING YOU

■ My name is Glenda Markle. I realize it doesn't mean a thing to you, but there are a few people who know it. On Madison Avenue, mostly, in the big publicity offices. Mention Glenda Markle and they'll say, "Oh sure—one of the smartest gals in the business. Good looking, too. Used to make a fortune around here a couple of years ago. Coulda sold ice boxes to the Eskimos. . . ."

Man, they should have seen me the day I met the kid. Me, Glenda Markle, a flop and a failure, trying to sell an ex tonic peddler named Tallman to the voters of a certain state—which shall be nameless because I might want to go back there some day—as their next governor. And brother, I'd tried everything. Take that very day, for instance. We had a rally on, so I planted a poster on every hitching post in forty miles. I set up free lunch—popcorn (soggy), peanuts (stale), pigs' feet (let's not even discuss *them*). I hired a hillbilly band—the same band that had tagged Tallman all over the state so I could hire them. It happened to be led by a guy named Tex Warner.

Once this guy's name had been Walter Warner and the band he led had worn tuxes instead of Levis and they didn't have to follow anyone around. That was at the same time that I was married to Walter, hereafter known as Tex. Complicated? I'll explain. Like Tex always says, once he and I were engaged—but it didn't work out, so we got married. That didn't work out either, so we got divorced. And you know something funny? That wasn't working out either . . .

Well, never mind all that. The point is, this rally was dying on its feet. No one was listening to Tex, much less Tallman, and I was hunting around in the crowd for a gimmick—something in the way of local talent I could stick up on the bandstand, to get a little attention.

Finally, I spotted these two cowboys unloading a case of beer. Tex and the boys were hitting a hot one then, and one of the cowboys was shaking it up a little along with the beat. I strolled over.

"Want to dance for us, cowboy?" I asked. "We could use a home-town touch."

He stopped dead, turned purple and gulped. "I can't dance, ma'am," he said. Then his eyes lit up and he jerked

his head toward his friend. "You want *singin'*, *he's* your
man. He sings up a storm."

So I turned around and got my first real look at the kid.
Yup, Deke Rivers. I didn't know his name then, and I
didn't care. He wasn't much to look at—faded khakis,
tousled hair—but there *was* something about the face. And
I wasn't in any mood to quibble. "We could use a good
storm about now," I muttered, and the dancing cowboy
and I started hauling the kid off toward the platform.

I thought he'd die on the spot. "He's kiddin', lady," he
kept wailing. But the other one grinned at me.

"Just give this cat a guitar, ma'am," he said, "and then
stand back."

I don't know who boosted him onto the platform. Next
thing I did know, Tex was saying to him. "So you sing?"
and the kid was shuffling his feet and mumbling, "I just
fool with it."

Tex nodded. Local talent was nothing new to him. But
he reached out to Skeeter, the guitarist, borrowed his box,
handed it to the kid, and pointed out at the audience.
"They're all yours, son," he said.

Well, the kid stood there and stared at the crowd. For
a minute I felt sorry for him; they were a tough bunch,
and they weren't on his side. Then his pal shouted up,
"Get with it, Deke! One for the money, two for the
show—"

A change came over the kid's face. He set his jaw and
gritted his teeth, and I noticed that those sweet, lonesome-
puppy-dog eyes of his could spark. Then he slung the guitar over his shoulder.

"—three to get ready, and go, cat go!" his friend hollered.

And, cat, he went.

He stomped his foot. He shook his head. He wiggled
his pelvis, tossed his arms, and lit into that song like he
was going to take it apart. After a minute, I shook myself and looked around. And you know what I saw? The
crowd, moving. The women shoving their way up to the
bandstand, craning their necks for a better look at him.
The men tapping their feet and nodding.

I tell you, right then—I knew. I didn't know just how

big the kid was going to get. I didn't know exactly what he was going to mean to every kid in the country. I won't say I could have predicted it all. But I'm a publicity woman, and a good one—Tallman to the contrary—and I knew at least this: that kid was going to be my ticket back to Madison Avenue. He was going to lift Tex out of this political freak show and change his name back to *Walter* Warner. That kid was going to be worth a million bucks, cold cash.

And I was going to arrange it all.

Tex would have let him walk right off, of course. Sometimes I think Tex isn't so bright. Sweet, yes—a darn sight sweeter and nicer than I am. Nice enough so that even when he hit the bottle and lost the band and his rep and me along with it—even then, when I couldn't live with him, I never stopped loving him. Nice enough so that when he went on the wagon and started over with this hillbilly bit, I headed for the hinterlands to be near him— on a strictly business basis, of course. That's how much I love him, how nice he is.

But he can't pick a winner the way I can.

No, Tex shoved the kid off the platform the minute he shut his mouth, tossed the guitar back to Skeeter, and shouted, "Now I'd like you to meet our own little singin' sweetheart, Sweet Susie Jessup." Then, while Susie went into *The Yellow Rose*, Tex came down to me and said, "Another chorus and they'd have started throwing things at him."

I thought of the eyes on those women, eating the kid up. "Yeah," I said. "The key to their room."

Then I went looking for Deke.

I found him bawling his pal out for making a fool of him. A riot, huh? He didn't know any more than Tex did, what he was.

But I did.

"What's your name?" I asked him.

"Deke," he said. His voice sounded cautious. "Deke Rivers."

"I like the way you sing," I said. "You've got—something. I don't know what it is. Ever think of doing it for a living?"

He gave me a funny look. "Everybody *thinks*. Thinking and doing, that's two different things."

Well, that was true enough. "How much do you make delivering beer?" I asked.

He reared back. "How much do you make doing what *you* do?"

I started to laugh. He was no dope, this kid. I liked him better every minute. "I'm a public relations counsel— a press agent—and I don't make enough to suit me." I looked at him. "How'd you like to come with me—with Tex Warner's band?"

He nodded thoughtfully. "In St. Jo, Missouri, one time, a man said he'd pay me to sing in a show. After I sung, the man ran out on me and took my guitar with him."

I grinnned. "Then what more have you got to lose?"

"A steady job," he said firmly. "First one I've had in a year. I aim to keep it. Eighteen a week and tips. Twenty-six dollars last week."

"You're on your own?"

He nodded again. "That's why I gotta hang onto something steady. Some day, I aim to have me a place of my own—a farm."

"This could be steady," I told him. "Fifty a week to start." But I was watching the eyes. I knew what the kid's answer would be.

"No," he said slowly. "I think I'll stay here." He looked at me. "But thanks a lot."

I didn't push. "Think it over," I said. "You've got until eight o'clock tomorrow morning. We'll be leaving from the hotel."

I watched him as he drove away. Then I found a phone and dialed the number I'd seen on that case of beer. "Hello," I said. "Hi-way Liquors?"

I hoped they'd fire the kid gently.

I was the only one in the bunch who wasn't surprised when Deke's jalopy pulled up the next morning. I hadn't told anyone he was coming with us. Not Tex nor Susie. Not even Tallman. All I'd told *him* was goodby. I'd wanted to add *good riddance* but I didn't. He hadn't paid me in three weeks, but I'm a lady.

Besides, I had better things to do: Tell Tex I had a

gimmick that would head us up again. Make him sign an agreement that I handled the money this time. I ran the show. It wasn't the easiest thing, getting him to give in. It wasn't the easiest thing, keeping from just turning my life over to that big dope again. He kissed me, and when Tex kisses me I go weak, remembering, wanting. . . .

But I came out of it. And when I did, I remembered why we were out in the middle of nowhere, instead of on top of the heap, and I knew that this time we had to play it my way—hard and fast and pointed in only one direction. Up.

So anyway, Deke showed up. Late, bewildered, blurting out, "I wasn't gonna come, but I got fired this morning. Somebody complained I was late making a delivery."

"Maybe it's all for the best," I said innocently.

He nodded worriedly, "Y'all still want me with you?"

"Us-all do," I said. Then I called, "Oh Tex! You remember Deke Rivers?"

Tex did, all right. He gave me a fishy look and muttered, "So this is the gimmick!" He gave the kid a quick nod and pulled me aside. "You're not putting this kid on the stage with my outfit," he hissed.

But I was way ahead of him. "You're right," I said. I'm not."

And off we went. . . .

I got to know a lot about Deke Rivers in the next few days. Maybe not as much as every high-school girl in the country knows about him now, but still—a lot. That his folks were dead and he didn't want to talk about them. That he had the shirt on his back and his jalopy and nothing else. That nothing small ever riled him up; that he could get along with anybody. That he started really liking me when he found out I knew my way around a car motor better than he did. That he came to trust me gradually, and that once I had his trust, his life was in my hands.

But it wasn't his sweetness I was putting to work.

Like I told Tex, I *wasn't* going to put the kid on stage with him—not at first. I was bringing him up slowly, seeing what he could do, figuring all the angles. None of the big towns would touch Tex, but I got him booked into every two-bit hick burg in the state, playing one-night stands. And every night just around eleven o'clock, Tex would step up to the mike and say, "Now, friends, we got a little extry surprise for you. They tell me that one of Longhorn County's own (or Sunrise County, or Battle-field County) has got a different way with a song—an' if we can persuade the boy, he'll come and do a little number for us. So how 'bout a hand for Longhorn County's Deke Rivers?"

Then Deke would come up from the audience and climb onto the stage and borrow Skeeter's guitar. And while Tex and Susie and the boys took a break, he'd rip into a song and we'd all watch the crowd go crazy. If anyone muttered, "I don't remember seeing him around here," I'd wander over and drop a word about how he worked across the river, or just got back from the Army. Then I'd station myself where I could give the kid a smile and a wink if he seemed nervous. He always looked for me in the crowd.

But gradually he wasn't nervous any more. Gradually he got to look like he belonged up there, holding those crowds in the palms of his hands, cuddling the women with his eyes. Until finally one night, Tex, who'd been watching him, too, called Deke over after the show and said, "Beginning tomorrow you start right on stage with the rest of us."

Deke sucked in his breath. His face went white and then red. He looked at us with such gratitude that I—Glenda the hard-boiled—felt almost guilty. He still didn't know that he was the one keeping this show on the road. Then Skeeter said, "What's more, kid, from now on you're not borrowing my box. Susie!"

And Susan handed Deke a guitar—a present from Tex.

"Gee," the kid said. His voice was shaky. "Mr. Warner —all of you—I—"

For a minute I thought he was going to cry. . . .

I guess it was around then that Susie fell in love with him.

I should have seen it coming. I suppose they were made for each other. She was a pretty kid, cheerful and helpful

—used to spend her evenings darning socks and sewing
on buttons for the boys. And Deke—well, every girl within a hundred miles was in love with him by now. Why
should Susie be any different?

But I didn't like it. Oh, don't glare like that. I'm not
the wicked stepmother, you know; I don't go around pulling the wings off flies. But my whole life, and Tex's, too,
was riding on this boy's undulating torso. Let him start
dreaming about firesides and kiddies and we were all sunk.
I knew darn well that Deke's dream of a farm of his own
had just been temporarily shelved—not lost. And Susie
was a farm girl herself; she didn't want to stay in this
racket forever, either.

So when Deke walked into band practice one morning
wearing a big grin over the brightest green sport shirt in
four states, and announced that Susie had picked it out
(the shirt, not the grin), I wasn't exactly overjoyed.
"Where'd you get that?" I demanded.

"Here"—Deke was beaming—"at Monkey Ward's."

"I'll bet you had to get there early before they were all
gone," I said sarcastically.

Deke stared at me, surprised. "I thought you'd like it,
Miss Markle."

I patted his cheek. "Sure, I like it," I said coldly, "for
street wear. But onstage I want them to see that face."

All right, so I felt like a louse. But the important thing
wasn't how I felt. The important thing was that I knew
that as soon as I walked out of the room, Deke Rivers
would take the shirt off. And probably never put it on
again. I told you he trusted me.

That night, while Deke was delivering a quickie about
"I'm a lonesome cowboy," and the girls in the audience
were squealing like a batch of stuck pigs, he came to a
line that went: "If ya don't call me, Mama, I ain't comin'
home." And a girl stood up in her seat and hollered,
"What's your number, honey? *I'll* call you!"

The audience howled. Deke flushed, tumbled, lost his
beat, and just did manage to finish the song. The audience
gave him more applause than ever, loving him, loving that
girl. I loved her, too—though she'd cost me five bucks

for that bit of jubilation. But I was the only one who knew it.

The next week. *I* bought Deke a sport shirt. He flipped when he saw it. "You went out and—uh—'s real nice of you, Miss Markle," he stammered.

"Can't you call me Glenda?" I said.

He turned purple. "Sleeves look kinda short," he mumbled.

"Not too," I said, watching him.

"Maybe Susan could let them out a couple of inches," he said.

Well, that did it. "Maybe she could." I snapped. "You seem to be spending a lot of time with her lately."

He shrugged. "Well, Susan—I can talk to her."

"You can talk to me. In school I got *A* in conversation."

Deke looked away. "Well, with you it's different, ma'am. I mean, it's more like—well—business with you."

"What kind of business?" I said impatiently. "I got you a job, because you make my job easier. It's that simple."

Deke nodded. "I was talking about that with Susan. She thinks *you* think I'm liable to—kinda make good."

"Make good?" I said. "Deke, I figure you to zoom right up to the top. And when you do, you're gonna find yourself *surrounded* by Susans—by a lot of people who're going to want to glom onto you, try to take advantage of you—"

"I don't think Susan's that kind," he cut in.

I shrugged that off as a bad try. "Okay, it may not be Susie—but sharpies you never heard of'll move into your life and cut your pockets off."

Deke looked up at me. "I sort of imagined *you'd* see that doesn't never happen."

I played it careful. "By that time, you might not even want me around."

"That's not so," he said earnestly. "Why, if it wasn't for you—"

"You don't owe me anything," I said. "Finding you was just part of my job for Tex. If he wanted to fire me to-morrow that'd be the end of it. You work for Tex, not for me."

"But *you're* the one who's been working for *me,*" Deke

said. "If I ever get anywhere, I'll have you to thank. I'm not much on business deals, but it appears to me we oughtta have some kind of agreement—I mean, somethin' legal, in writin', between you and me."

Whew, I thought. "Deke," I said, "I wouldn't want you to think I'm one of those people trying to take advantage of you. So I'm delighted to hear you talk like this." I reached into my purse and pulled out a paper. "In fact, I've been carrying this around waiting for you to—"

Deke grinned. "I know. Mike Harris, the lawyer who typed it up back in Delville—he told me. You got a pencil?"

Did you ever feel like the rug was pulled out from under your feet? He was way ahead of me all the time. Deke Rivers, that kid from nowhere—two steps ahead of Glenda Markle, and grinning! Absolutely shaken, I pulled out a pen and watched him sign the contract without even reading it. He knew what I wanted—fifty per cent—but he still trusted me. All right, I thought, one good turn deserves another. I held up the shirt. "I think if she lets it out about an inch, it'll fit," I said.

Besides, I wasn't scared of Susie any more.

In fact, I wasn't scared of anything. With the contract tucked away in my suitcase, I went into action. There was no holding me back—or Deke, either. Shall I give you a list of the things I did? Well, I paid a couple of older women to say, in the middle of a mob of screaming girls, that they didn't like Deke. The pictures of the fight that followed made every morning paper for miles around. I—but that's enough. That was the gimmick that got us the big break, so why fill you in on all the little ones? Just let me add one thing: Maybe I did make things happen a little. But you can't make pay dirt out of an empty space; working for Tallman had taught me that. Nothing I did would have mattered a hoot if Deke hadn't had what it took to get there on his own. All I did was speed up the process.

Tex didn't take it that way. When I told him we had a date in Amarillo, he thought I'd personally given him back the world he'd lost. "Amarillo! Bless you, baby!"

he gushed, and paced up and down the room. "This is the giant step back! We've hit the city. Maybe not Chicago or New York—but it's a city! They got sidewalks, cops who wear shoes! A city! We're bound to get good enough notices to jump us to Fort Worth, Dallas; then it's only a step to St. Louis." Every time he paused for breath, he kissed me. "Then comes Chicago, New York, radio, television—"

He was still kissing me when I got my senses back and called a halt. "You're giving me too much credit," I told him. "I didn't do this for you. It was Deke. You can kiss *him*."

"Sure," Tex said largely, "I appreciate the kid. He's gonna be our featured vocalist."

I sat back. I knew this was going to hurt, but there wasn't any way to put it so Tex's pride would be saved. "Uh uh," I said slowly. "The manager of the Grand Theatre is booking Tex Warner *and* Deke Rivers. Equal billing. That's the way it has to be."

He took it hard. I guess it sounds silly, but anyone in show business knows how much a thing like that can hurt —a seasoned performer having to split the kudos with a Johnny-come-lately. But there wasn't anything we could do about it, even if I'd wanted to. It was worth it to me to hurt Tex's feelings now. We'd make up for it later, when Deke hit the real big time and we hit it with him.

Anyway, Tex survived it. Give credit to that nice streak in him, I guess. An hour later he was telling the kid about it as if it were his own idea; showing him the jazzed-up cowboy suit I'd bought for Deke, as if he'd picked it out himself. And half believing it, too.

As for Deke, it was a shame we had the bus to take us from place to place. He could have walked to Amarillo on air.

He didn't know what he was in for, in Amarillo. Well, neither did I. I wasn't even in on the kill, so to speak. But I got the story from Skeeter.

It seems Skeeter and Deke stopped in at the bar and across from the Grand. They sat down in a booth. Skeeter got a beer, Deke got a plate of ribs and a glass of milk— and they never even noticed the high-school kids come in.

They didn't know it was their regular hangout.

But the kids noticed them. At least, one of the girls did. She'd seen Deke somewhere *en route*, and she must have started raving about him there in the grill. Because a few minutes later Deke looked up and a boy was standing over him, saying, "Hey, you! Cowboy! There's a chick over there wants you to sing."

Deke didn't know quite what to think. "Well, I don't—" he began.

But Skeeter knew. He cut in fast. "That's right neighborly, young fella. But you tell the lady that Mr. Rivers will do four shows a day, right across the street, starting tomorrow."

"She doesn't like to wait," the boy said coldly. He looked at Deke. "She wants to hear you sing right now."

Skeeter didn't like it. "Maybe you don't understand, fella." He stood up. "Mr. Rivers don't sing in saloons. Now go on back and drink your malted."

That did it. The boy knocked Skeeter onto the floor, the manager ran over babbling about show folks causing trouble, and Deke made up his mind what to do.

"No," he said. "There's no trouble. Would you mind if—if I sang a little song for the folks?"

So he sang for them. And because he was Deke and didn't know how to do less than his best, he gave them the full treatment—guitar, dancing, everything. Everyone went nuts except Skeeter. Skeeter sat there watching and wondering. Was Deke yellow? Scared to fight? He wasn't scrawny—not by a long shot. But scared—who knew?

Then the song was over. Deke put down his guitar. He walked over to the kids' booth. The girls were babbling about how wonderful he was, but Deke wasn't listening. "What do you do for a living, buddy?" he asked the boy.

The boy stared up at him. "I'm with my Dad. Auto accessories. Why?"

"I get *paid* for singin', as a rule," Deke said calmly. "I figure now you oughta do whatever you do—for me. So how 'bout you comin' out and fixin' up my car with some seat covers?"

The boy snickered. "What color you want, cowboy? *Yellow?*"

So Deke grabbed him by the collar, pulled him to his feet, and commenced to lay him out.

That's how Skeeter got his answer to whether Deke was too scared to fight—in spades. And the next day the pictures of Deke behind bars ran with headlines. It was the other kid who got fined, and rightly, for starting the fight. Deke got off with a clean bill of health—and more free publicity than I could have bought him in a month of trying. We played to packed houses every show. We had lines of kids going round and round the block, waiting for tickets.

The only one who didn't like it was Deke.

But Deke didn't like what happened five days later, either.

There was a girl in his dressing room.

Her name was Daisy, and it turned out that she was the one who'd started the ruckus in the first place, wanting to hear him sing in the café. It turned out she'd ditched her boy friend and had been at every show Deke had done. It turned out she'd talked so much about him that her friends had dared her to go sneak in and kiss Deke. And it turned out she didn't come out of her little hiding place until Deke was half undressed.

Well, the poor kid tried to get his shirt back on, but she had her arms around him. He tried to talk to her, but she was trying to kiss him. He put up such a good fight that finally the girl stepped back and snapped, "You *are* afraid! You don't sing scared—but you *are!*" She raised her head and looked him straight in the eye. "You're a phony!"

So what did Deke do? Well, I'll tell you. He did the only thing a man could do. He grabbed her and he kissed her—but good.

And that was when I walked into the dressing room with a battery of newsmen and cameramen behind me— and I don't mind saying, it caught me just a little bit off guard.

You see, I hadn't planned that one. I didn't know anything about it.

But by the next morning, the whole area knew. And the box-office figures did what we thought they couldn't do: they went *further* up. And a place called Freegate, just seven miles out of Dallas, offered their Civic Hall—in case Mr. Rivers would like to do a one-man concert.

And Deke turned on me and accused: "Well, that's how you're selling me! Monkey in the zoo! That's what you want, isn't it?"

Everyone's entitled to make a couple of mistakes. I made mine right then, I suppose. I should have seen how fed up Deke was becoming, how dead serious he was about hating the kind of reputation he was getting. But, listen, I was busy. Things were popping all over the place.

Tex was letting half the band go—and Susie with them. It killed him to do it, especially to Susan, but he didn't have much choice. Offers were pouring in for Deke—but all they'd pay for was a small combo behind him. They weren't interested in a pretty girl with a pleasant voice when they could have Deke Rivers. So there was that to take care of.

And then there was Project Cadillac, my brain child—the gimmick that was going to land Deke in the headlines in every paper in the country. Not the state, not the area, but the whole USA. We were going to borrow on Tex's life insurance—the one piece of security we had—and buy us a Cadillac convertible the likes of which is seldom seen—white, with red upholstery. And as far as Deke and the rest of the world knew, it was going to be a little remembrance to him from a rich, anonymous widow who said Deke Rivers reminded her of the son she'd never had.

Talk about human interest—the paper didn't exist that wouldn't print that story!

So I took off for Dallas to set up the deal on the car, and Tex said goodbye to Susie and the boys he was letting go and gave everyone a week off between dates.

That's how it happened I wasn't around to prevent Deke's driving Susie home to her parents' farm. But by the time Tex joined me in Dallas, I had heard, and I was steaming.

"Whose brilliant idea was it to send him to Farming-dale?" I demanded.

"It was my idea," Tex said calmly. "At least up there they're not going to be taking pictures of him like this!" He threw a paper on the coffee table in my hotel room. I glanced at it. Deke, bare chest and all, kissing that girl on the front page.

"That's pretty darn good publicity," I snapped.

"I don't think so. I like him," Tex said. "I don't want to see you hurt him."

Oh, for cryin' out loud! "When I bring him back from Susan's in that red-and-white custom job," I said slowly, with emphasis, "they'll forget all about this."

Tex gave me a funny look. "I doubt it. You can't fight sex with horsepower."

"Who's *fighting* sex?" I asked. "It sells cold cream, steam engines, shampoo—it can sell singers, too."

"*And* press agents," said Tex.

"I beg your pardon!" I gasped.

Tex pounced on me. "I'll tell you why I sent Deke with Susan: that boy needs to spend some time with a sweet kid who's nuts about him."

"What are you," I said, still shaken, "a marriage broker?"

"I'm a realist, honey," Tex said coldly. "Deke is *nuts* about you. Just mention your name and his eyes pop like bubble gum." He shrugged. "My head may be full of tapioca, but I'm still in love with you." Tex walked to the door.

For a minute I just watched him go. But when he was halfway out the door, I heard my voice saying, "Walter—" And when he turned around, somehow or other, there I was with his arms around me, murmuring, "I'll get the car first thing in the morning."

I never could resist that big dope.

So it wasn't until late the next day that I got to Farm-ingdale. And by then it was—well, maybe not *quite* too late. Maybe not quite. But by then Susan's dad had given Deke umpteen lessons in contour plowing. Susan's ma had stuffed him so full of homemade goodies he could hardly move. Susan had told him she wasn't going to be

with the band any more and it was pretty clear Deke was
in no mood to say goodbye permanently.

Well, I couldn't blame him. They'd gone to every two-
bit carnival across the state together. They'd held hands
on the roller coaster, and now I suppose they'd kissed in
the moonlight on the farm. And Susie was a sweet kid. But
I had myself to think about—and Tex, too, since he
wouldn't think for himself.

So I pulled up in front of the farmhouse in that come-
to-glory Caddie, and I honked the horn. "Deke!" I called.
"Hey, Deke!"

The house door opened, and about ten heads stuck
themselves out. Among them were Deke's and Susan's,
and even from that distance, I didn't like the soft glow in
Deke's eyes. I waited until they all got around me and
the Caddie, and then until they stopped exclaiming over
it. "Hope you don't mind my barging in like this, Susan,"
I said sweetly, "but I had to show Deke his present."

Deke stared at me, then at the car, then at Susan.
"Mine? How? Why?"

I laughed. "You've all got to hear it," I said. "When
Deke was appearing in Amarillo, some woman, the widow
of an oil man—"

I gave them the whole bit, and before they got over it
I added, "I'm afraid we'll have to leave right away. Better get your things, Deke."

There were protests all around. I watched Deke nervously. Finally he said, "Well—" and headed for the
house. His shoulders were drooping, but he went. I
breathed a sigh of relief. Only at the door he turned
around and said, "Susan, wanna give me a hand?"

I watched them go in together. A few minutes later
they were out again with the valise and guitar. Deke muttering, "It sure is hard to say goodbye. I never had much
practice." He stopped, and looked around longingly.
"Makes it kind of tougher to leave the farm. I mean, as
long as you were coming along— You know what I
mean."

"I'll be here," Susan said softly. "I'll always be here."

I felt terrible all the way back to Dallas.

But not nearly as bad as I felt when we pulled up in

front of the Freegate Civic Hall and found Tex and Skeeter and the Freegate sheriff arguing in front of a mob of angry kids around the box office. One look and I knew why. There was a big sticky banner smacked across the window: SHOW CANCELED.

The publicity, it seemed, had backfired.

The women's clubs thought Deke Rivers was a bad influence. They'd deluged the mayor with telegrams, letters, petitions. They'd dug up the pix of Deke in that brawl, Deke getting kissed, women fighting over Deke. They'd managed to close the show.

But they hadn't managed to shut me up. I left them standing there—Deke upset and bothered, Tex shouting at the sheriff—and I took off for a phone. I've never had a really bad break yet that I wasn't able to switch into a bonanza. Five minutes on long distance to New York and I had done the impossible—I'd talked an old friend on a coast-to-coast TV network into turning a half hour over to The Freegate Issue. Freedom of speech, freedom of song, freedom of a boy to make good his own way—it was a natural. The men with the cameras would be out the next day. We had it made! We were in!

I was in the middle of celebrating when Tex walked into my room and threw himself onto the couch. "I just had a long talk with young Mister Rivers," he said slowly.

I looked up. "What's the matter with him?"

Tex shoved his hands in his pockets. His voice took on a drawl. "Well, ma'am, he just ain't happy, Miss Glenda, ain't happy at all. This ruckus down at Civic Hall, the kind of pictures they've been puttin' in the papers, all this talk goin' round— Deke figures he'd be lots happier just jockeyin' a tractor over at the Jessup farm." He sat up and let me have it: "He's about to quit, Glenda."

I went to find Deke. I found him—packing. The guitar was on his bed. "Aren't you going to pack the guitar, too?" I asked. "It's yours now."

He straightened up and looked at me anxiously. "Oh—ah—Tex told you, huh?"

I glared at him. "How do I feel when you go to *Tex* to tell him you're walking out? You don't come to me, you go to him!"

"I guess I just couldn't face you," Deke muttered. "Not after all the hard work you've done."

I pulled out a hankie. "Well, thanks for that much, anyway." I said into it, and turned away.

Deke stared at me, horror-stricken. Then he crossed the room, pleading, "Somethin's been happenin', Miss Glenda. I've been changin' every minute. All this fake and phony! The clothes I been wearin', the car I been drivin'—"

I looked at his troubled face. "What's phony about all that? You've made something of yourself!"

"I'm not so sure I like what I've made," Deke said, "I never meant for people to say I'm a—well, they got it sounding like folks should be ashamed just listenin' to me sing. I wanted to make people proud of me, to have friends, to stop bein' alone."

"Deke," I said quickly, "you're talking like a child. You've got nothing to be ashamed of. You heard that crowd tonight: *they* were all for you. *They* wanted to hear you."

"And why were they there?" Deke said bitterly. "On account of those stories in the paper. And that's not right, either."

"What you're really saying is, it's all my fault."

Instantly he was beside me. The words came tumbling out. "Oh no! You've been just wonderful to me. Outside of Susan, you're the only one ever had faith in me. That's why I feel so bad. I've let you down."

I had him then, right in the palm of my hand. And suddenly I couldn't stand myself. I let that silly hankie drop to the floor. I said, without thinking, "No, Deke, no you haven't."

"You tried to help me," he said. "You knew how it was with me—crawlin' all my life. Crawlin' and runnin'. You got me to thinkin' maybe I didn't have to crawl and run no more. But it ain't so. Tonight showed me it ain't so. I'm scared again, real scared."

And without knowing what I was doing, just because he was sweet and young and so unhappy, I took him in my arms and I said, "You have no reason to be scared; not any more. I'll help you. You're going to be all right."

And then he kissed me.

I walked out of that room plenty troubled. But I had hold of myself again. If the only way I could keep Deke around for the show was to let him think I— Well, then, that was how it had to be. Just for a little while. After all, it wasn't my fault. I hadn't planned it like that. I swear I hadn't. And tomorrow I'd see that he understood.

Only tomorrow never came. That afternoon Deke told Tex that he and I were in love! And Tex, that dope, he got mad and let Deke have it—right between the eyes. The whole bit about him and me—engaged, married, divorced—nobody out here knew that. He gave it to the kid, and then, blazing mad, he told him that all I wanted, all I ever wanted, was a meal ticket, and Deke was the best one around. He left the kid reeling, not knowing where to turn or who to believe.

And then it was my turn. Tex walked in on me and told me off. What can I tell you about that scene? The things that he said to me—that he'd never really thought of himself as my *ex*-husband before, but now he liked the idea? That he was through, getting out, leaving me? That I'd do anything for a buck, or a thousand bucks? And what he didn't say, his eyes said—louder and clearer.

Oh, I tried. I tried to tell him that all I did was kiss Deke; that he needed reassurance; that I never meant him to think—what he thought. That I loved Tex, always had, always would. That this whole bit with Deke was really just for Tex, just to get him going again.

But he wouldn't believe me; he wouldn't listen. He didn't give a darn any more. He turned around and walked out on me, and this time I couldn't call him back.

This time I was all alone when, two minutes before show time, they came and told me that Deke Rivers had taken off in his old jalopy and he wasn't coming back.

I had thirty minutes to find him and bring him back. Thirty minutes while people went nuts and the network fumed and the show began. Thirty minutes while Tex and Susie and all the kids and women who knew Deke and loved him filed in front of the cameras and the mikes and ad-libbed, talking about Deke. Thirty minutes while the irate women of Freegate got their chance to tell the world that Deke was no good.

Thirty minutes to bring him back and get him before those cameras—or let the country laugh in my face, and Tex's, and most of all, Deke's.

Deke didn't know Susie was here for the show. He'd head back to her if he went anywhere. So I climbed into the Cadillac and pointed it in the direction of the Jessup farm. I took off at about ninety per.

I found his old jalopy parked on a shoulder. Deke under it. It had broken down miles out of town. He crawled out, dusted off his hands, and looked at me with eyes I'd never seen on him before. Cold and hurt and angry.

"You're a regular bloodhound, ain't you?" he said.

But there was something in *me* that had never been there before, too. Something equally hurt, and very tired, and very, very miserable.

"Deke, please," I said, "I've had enough for one night. Just tell me—where did you think you were going?"

"If I could lie like you," he said bitterly, "maybe I could figure out an answer."

I sighed. I knew how he felt. He thought he'd had friends—and now he thought they'd all turned into nothing but leeches. He thought he'd even had a lover—and she was the worst of them all. Well, I had no lie that would patch that up. I had nothing to give him but the truth—nastier and harder than lies, but the truth.

"You tired of lies?" I said. "See that car? Tex hocked his life insurance to buy that. There is no oil widow. The pictures in the paper, the kids fighting over you, the yelling from the audience—I started it all. I even had you fired in the first place so you'd come with us. That's my job."

He stared at me. His mouth trembled. "Why didn't you tell me none of this last night?"

All of a sudden, to my horror, I was fighting tears. "Last night I still had Tex." I took a deep breath. "And whatever I let you believe, that was as much a part of my job as dreaming up a car or planting stooges in an audience—or anything else I had to do to make you worth something to us and to yourself." I looked at him—me, Glenda Markle, pleading with a kid. "One thing I didn't lie about is your future, Deke. It's waiting for you on that stage, right now, in Freegate. You don't need my gimmicks any more. You're about to make it on your own!"

I saw the struggle going on in him. I knew he couldn't believe me so easily—he'd believed me before. He shook his head. "It's not *my* future you care about," he said desperately. "It's *yours*. It's what I can do for you. You don't care about me, *or* about Tex—or anybody but yourself."

It hurt. Oh, friend, it hurt good. Worse than Tex's telling me off. Worse than anything on this mortal earth. And it hurt that bad because maybe, just maybe, it all was true.

So I did the only thing I *could* do to prove it wasn't so. To prove it not just to the kid, but to myself—because not even *I* could walk around for another fifty years believing that. I couldn't have lived with myself—and it looked like I wasn't going to have anyone else to live with.

I took out the contract—the one the kid had signed months ago, turning over half his earnings to me in return for services rendered—the little piece of paper that was worth at least a cool million bucks any day of the week.

And I tore it in half.

"Here's your contract," I said. I handed him the papers. "I don't even want half of it." I looked at him standing there covered with car grease, and I saw belief coming back into his eyes. I saw him start to look like the Deke Rivers I knew. "The only one you owe anything to now is yourself," I said. "And Susan—or somebody like her." Then I took Deke Rivers by the hand and led him back to that red-and-white Caddie. "You've got fifteen minutes to get in front of that camera and find out if you've even got a future."

You know the rest. You saw that TV show—everybody did. You know that Deke sang as he'd never sung before. You know that a nation full of teen-age girls and boys rose up and told the world that they loved Deke Rivers, that he spoke for them—for all the lonesomeness, all the hurt, all the happiness and wild jubilation they ever felt. You know that they took him to their hearts and made him the biggest singer—anywhere. You know the rest, all right.

What you don't know, maybe, is me. My name is Glenda Warner. That's right—Warner. My husband is Walter Warner, the big band leader. He makes enough now so that I could stay home and raise kids if I wanted to. And sooner or later I will, too. Only right now I'm kind of busy. I manage a kid I know. I keep him from falling off the top of the world, where he's been sitting for a while. His name is Deke Rivers.

Adapted from the PARAMOUNT VISTAVISION Production
Copyright 1957 by PARAMOUNT PICTURES, INC.
Directed by HAL KANTER
Produced by HAL B. WALLIS
Screenplay by HAL KANTER and HERB BAKER
Color by TECHNICOLOR
Adapted for SCREEN STORIES by
BARBARA MAYER RIBAKOVE

CAST

Vince Everett .... ELVIS PRESLEY   Teddy Talbot .... DEAN JONES
Peggy Van Alden .... JUDY TYLER   Sherry Wilson .. JENNIFER HOLDEN
Hunk Houghton ... MICKEY SHAUGHNESSY
Mr. Shores .... VAUGHN TAYLOR

JAILHOUSE ROCK

■ Vince Everett was a free man again. But not the same spirited kid who'd been sent away on a manslaughter rap. That younger Vince, who'd driven a construction company skip loader and had hit the beer spots on paydays, had died even before the trial. Knowing that his unintended punch had killed a barfly who'd picked a fight with him, knowing that the fires in him could burst loose and rub out a man, was a grim thing. Yet the change in him only started there.

Partly, it was the floggings a sadistic warden meted out. Partly, it was being cellmates with Hunk Houghton, in whose underground jailhouse empire cigarettes were coin of the realm and any man who couldn't pay got no privileges. Partly—mostly—it was having found out that he could sing.

There'd been a prison show on television. Sort of a smoke screen to hide some of the rawer features of prison life from the State Legislature's visiting committee. And Hunk—who used to do hillbilly guitar in vaudeville before they sent him up—had coached Vince in a number.

He'd sensed at the time that the listeners liked him. But only today, only when he was set to leave, had the warden given him the mass of fan mail that had poured in after the telecast. Holding it back—not letting a con feel he could do anything important—had given the warden kicks.

All the way on the train, Vince read letter after letter: *I thought you sing real cool . . . My name is Marijane If you ever come to Riverport, give me a blast. . . .* They were from young girls, mostly. Something in the hurt, savage passion of his music had gotten through to them.

Vince still was mulling over those letters when he got to the town Hunk had spoken about. He checked into a cheap room in a crummy hotel.

"Where's the nearest pawnshop?" he asked the drab who made his bed.

Her wet old eyes squinted. "Gonna buy yourself a diamond ring, son?"

"Honey, I'm gonna buy a guitar and sing love songs to you! . . ."

Hunk had said Vince could get a job at the Florita dive

any time. Hunk had written a letter to Sam Brewster, the owner—an old buddy of his. And if you didn't deliver, you weren't any buddy of Hunk's.

Vince had signed a paper agreeing to do a partnership act with Hunk when he was released in five more months. If Vince hadn't signed, Sam Brewster never would have been mentioned between them.

The Florita was good-sized, and garishly lit with miles of neon tubing. Vince went inside and ordered a beer and watched a tired stripper work her routine with a three-piece combo for music. A girl came in. Vince regarded her with cool curiosity. When the stripper bowed out to bored applause, the girl took pencil and notebook from her purse. Deftly, she removed an inner plate from the juke box and copied figures off the counters. One of the bartenders said, "How's your boy doing, Peg?"

"Large." She grinned. *Crying to the Stars* got eighty-four plays."

As she turned back, she found Vince's steady gaze fixed on her. She flushed. "Tell me what you see," she snapped.

Vince's voice was bored. "I saw you puttin' down figures. I wondered what they were. So don't get any fancy ideas about yourself."

"Well! Buy me a fresh drink, and I'll tell you about the figures."

"Buy your own drink and tell me."

"All right." She looked as if she were trying to figure what made a character like him tick. "I'm in exploitation. The record business. I work for Mickey Alba. I plug his records with disc jockeys, juke boxes, stores—" She broke off as a sad-faced man wandered up. Sam Brewster, she told him.

"I'm Vince Everett," Vince said. "You got Hunk Houghton's letter?"

Brewster shrugged. "You want a job, huh? Start whenever you want to."

"Can those guys—the combo—play with me when I sing?"

"What sing?" Brewster belched. "You're a barboy. Make setups, bring ice. This place ain't no hobby, kid. Hunk taught you a couple of songs? So be the life of your next party. You wanta job here, it's barboy."

As he walked off, the girl said. "Hunk Houghton? Seems familiar."

"An old hillbilly singer. I met him in the pen." Vince grabbed up his guitar and vaulted to the runway. "Ladies and gentlemen! I'm not part of the show, so pay me no mind at all!" He began to strum and sing.

They took him at his word. They didn't pay him any mind at all. They kept on talking, drinking, laughing, as if Vince Everett didn't exist. In frustrated fury he broke off midway, jumped down, strode to the booth of one particularly loud-mouthed customer and, with a swing that smashed the guitar, swept bottles and glasses from the table. Then he stalked out.

He was halfway up the block before the girl caught up with him. "That was quite a temper tantrum!" she murmured. "I didn't think you were very good back there, Vince."

He glared. "Well—my career started and finished with one song."

"I don't know why. Did you ever listen to yourself? Make a tape recording. Maybe you can hear what's wrong."

"I haven't even got a guitar."

She had a million-dollar smile. "I'll borrow one for you. . . ."

Her name was Peggy Van Alden. She was twenty minutes late at the recording studio, next morning. But she brought a borrowed guitar with her—and the trio from the Florita, to give him some free background.

The first time through, he sang the song the way Hunk had taught him. In the sound booth, the engineers read comic books.

"Man!" Vince moaned, when they played it back. "Ain't that pitiful?"

"Then put your own emotions into the song. Make it fit *you.*"

"This guitar—it bothers me. I'll just go through the motions." He was on his feet. "Let's do it again, boys. Get smoke into it."

The play-back of the second tape was a little like Columbus discovering America. Even the bored engineers took notice. The trio swung with his beat. The violence and passion and rebellion in him poured out.

Peggy was breathless at the end. "Wonderful, Vince!"

He nodded. "It's good enough for a record. Let's go ahead."

"It's—not that easy. You have to sell a record company the idea—"

"You know the business. So cut us in on the loot."

Because Peggy's hit singer Mickey Alba was with Geneva Records, she took Vince there first. Their repertoire man, Jack Lease, listened condescendingly to the tape and promised to play it to New York long-distance. That was the best he could do, even as a favor. So they left the tape in his hands.

Peggy called Vince's hotel next day with bad news. Lease had said that the man in New York didn't go for the tape. The only thing left to do was to try other labels. If he'd meet her at a restaurant that night—

He was late turning up at the restaurant. But he didn't apologize. "I been sleeping," he told her indifferently. "You eat yet?"

Peggy glared at him. "You might at least ask me what's happened! I sold the record to Royal Records, that's all!"

Vince gave her a glance. "Okay. You sold it. That's your job. I make the records, you sell 'em. What's Royal Records? Never heard of 'em."

"It's fairly new." Peggy couldn't hold back the glow. "They're crazy about it! Let's celebrate, Vince. Then we'll drive out and see my parents."

They had a big dinner, and Peggy paid for it. When they got out to the handsome Van Alden house in the suburbs, a party seemed to be in progress.

"Not a bad pad," Vince admitted. "What's your old man do?"

"He's a professor. At Bertrand College."

The party was small but gay. Vince resented it—suspecting, despite their pleasant manners, that these people disapproved of him. He took pains to shock them with

frequent references to his jail term. They countered by
playing progressive jazz recordings, since music was his
job. People asked him questions, he couldn't even be
certain were in English. Altered chords, dissonance,
atonality—who were they kidding?

He made a rude answer to one fluttery lady and
stalked out of the house to stunned silence. When Peggy
caught up with him, she was blazing.

"Well! I hope you're satisfied. You insulted my father
and my mother. It's unforgivable! I—I think I'm going to
just *hate* you!"

"No, you ain't." A hard smile flicked his lips. "You
ain't gonna hate me." He grabbed her and kissed her hard
and long.

She struggled. He waited for the resistance to weaken
before he let her go. Then, without a backward look, he
swaggered off. . . .

They had to meet again, of course, for business reasons—to get their platter for Royal spinning. But it wasn't
until the date it was set for release, when they were entering a record shop together, that he could gruffly ask her to
apologize to her mother for his loudmouthed behavior.

At the counter inside, when they mentioned the title,
a clerk said the new record was selling the largest. But
when the shiny new discs were set on the counter for
wrapping, Peggy went rigid. Mickey Alba's name was on
them, and Geneva's label.

Those next ten minutes were a revelation to Vince. In
a booth, they listened to Mickey Alba sing. The same ar-
rangement, background, phrasing—the entire attack was
Vince's own. He listened aghast.

"The dirty thief! He stole my style, my—everything!"

Peggy nodded wearily. "Lease copied your tape and
gave it to him. We can forget about our Royal record,
Vince. It's gone."

Vince paid a brief, painful visit to the Geneva offices.
Bland and smooth, Lease pointed out that anyone could
record a published number. Rage and frustration built up
in Vince. But he couldn't do a thing.

He was lying on his hotel bed later, staring at nothing,
when Peggy came in wearily.

"In the pen," Vince growled, not looking at her, "they're Cub Scouts compared to Jack Lease! Well—we make another record."

"The same thing might happen all over again," Peggy protested.

"We'll start our own record company. We'll find out the details from a lawyer. You don't have to own a factory. You can contract for pressings."

"But Vince! You can't just go out and start a company!" She was struggling to believe him. "Of course, I know about distribution—b-but—"

"Sure you do! And exploitation! What do you say? You with me?"

It was her moment of decision, and she knew it. "I—yes, I am. I'll quit my job tomorrow."

"We need a lawyer with an eye to the buck."

"I know a retired one. But Mr. Shores is cold-blooded —he has the first dollar he ever earned."

"Sounds like my man," Vince said. "Interested only in money. When can we see this Mr. Shores?" He ignored her hurt look. What *could* be as important as money?

She took him to the lawyer's house that same evening.

Mr. Shores was a cold-eyed little man, about as emotional as a turtle. As he talked about corporation papers and registering their trade mark, Vince felt he'd met real kinfolk.

"How'd you like to come out of retirement and be my manager?" he offered, although Peggy looked hurt. "Peg and I are going to earn some money now. When we get it, we'll make another record and be in business. Mr. Shores, I'll make you rich."

Shores spoke in his dust-dry voice. "I am already rich."

"You'll be richer! Good night!"

Cutting their second record—the first for Laurel label —was only the beginning. Vince watched in fascination the job of processing—transferring his work from tape to master record, setting up the master as a mold, actually pressing the copies. He and Peggy put the new labels in place themselves; personally wrapped them, addressed them, mailed them. After that, they hit the road in Peggy's convertible to tour the record shops and make deliveries. Kansas, Oklahoma, Texas—

She had connections among the disc jockeys, and she used them for all they were worth. At first the men were cool. But in one city a guy named Teddy Talbot, who was in love with Peg or something, played the piece low, at her urging, in back of his dog food commercial. The station got enough complaints about not being able to hear the new singer with the new style, so that Talbot apologized on his program and played the number again.

The reaction was good enough so that a record shop featured the platter at an autographing party. That meant an order for five hundred records, and a crowd at the store.

Among them, to Vince's amazement, was Mr. Shores, the lawyer. Coldly, he told Vince that he had acquired confidence in the young singer's earning capacity, and was now prepared to manage him for ten per cent of the company plus five per cent of Vince's earnings.

After cutting him down to nine and four, Vince discovered that the lawyer had anticipated him and had already drawn up papers to those amounts. He was delighted to sign. A brain like Shores' was exactly the thing to have behind you.

That night, full of good spirits, he knocked at Peggy's hotel door dressed for a big evening. He found her wearing a sensational number.

"I just checked the record shop," he informed her. "We sold four hundred and twenty-five copies! We got a hit, kid! Stick with me, I'll put diamonds in your teeth."

"Nice," said Peggy.

"You look sexy tonight. You read my mind when you put on that dress." He took her into his arms and kissed her. "Tonight's the real celebration. Soft music, loud champagne."

"I like the idea," she said, somewhat weakly. "B-but not tonight. I have a date with Teddy Talbot."

"But I had it all planned. Reservations at the local night swamp."

"Well, you should have made reservations with *me*." She looked hurt, almost angry. "I still have a life of my own, you know."

"This is one night I didn't think you'd let me down."

"Vince, you told me yourself that money was all you were interested in. I will not be subject to your beck and call. I—" She broke off to answer a knock on the door, and let Talbot in. Vince watched in frustrated disgust as they set out together, two laughing people, to paint the town. A cold film settled over his eyes as he watched the door close.

Beginning with the success of that first sleeper record, Mr. Shores had plenty of business to manage. Vince Everett was a name on its way up. When Vince had a club date these days—and the clubs weren't joints like the Florita—he had his own trio to back up the passionate, fierce songs he belted.

They cut new records, and Laurel sales continued to mount. The adolescents of a nation found Vince's singing style right down their alley. Mr. Shores, who continued to prefer Sibelius, deducted a flashy red convertible from Vince's tax for *business transportation*. But he couldn't risk claiming that all the parties his boy threw were for business.

One thing—since that night in Joplin, Vince never again asked Peggy to go out anywhere with him. He'd made contact with a cute little torch named Laury Jackson, and he nibbled her ear at the parties Peggy wasn't asked to attend. Once—because Peggy had just heard that Vince was signed to do a big TV spectacular back east—Peggy did attend, on her own hook, to congratulate him. She got an eyeful of the nibbling act.

Vince grinned coldly, taking Peggy aside. "Laury can sing up a real storm. I'm taking her with me to New York City."

"In that case," Peggy said icily, "I don't think I'll go."

"Oh? Were you planning to go? Got nothing to do with records." The cold look deepened. "Like you said in Joplin, it's strictly business."

"Let's keep it that way!" She whirled toward the door.

He followed her, the mask cracking, a look of appeal in his eyes. But before he reached the door, it opened— and Hunk Houghton stood there, beaming.

"Remember me?" he boomed, his voice as loud as his

plaid jacket. Before Vince could recover, Hunk had turned to Peggy. "I'll bet you're the gal started the record company with Vince, I'm the bird got old Vince started. Yeah, I taught that boy plenty."

"You'll find just how *well* you taught him," Peggy said thinly, over the shrill din of the party. "Good night!"

Vince might have followed her then, but Hunk barred the way. "Well, boy, so you made it! I read about you and I'm proud of you. I knew the minute you opened your mouth in cell block twenty-one you had talent. What are your plans for me, boy?"

"Well, I ain't exactly got any." Vince wavered. "What do you want?"

"What we agreed. To go in business together. I can see you're a single. So forget the double. Just work me into your show—that TV show."

Vince recoiled. "Hunk, you're crazy! Times have changed. You might fall on your face. *I* tried your style; I laid a bomb."

"You ain't me. Look, kid, I want just one good shot. You can give it to me on that TV show. I been thinkin' about it—for eighteen years."

So Vince took Hunk east with him. At the dress rehearsal for the big telecast, where Vince's own *Jailhouse Rock* number was a smash hit, the producer threw out Hunk's single after four minutes' listening.

The show itself was a sensation. But back at their hotel afterward, while Hunk swilled whisky like water, Vince wasn't happy.

"I got calls and wires from everybody in the country!" he complained. "But not her, not Peg. I bet she didn't even tune in on me. Okay, Babe, you wait for me to call you!"

Hunk had a different problem. Jail was behind him, but it looked as if nothing were ahead. "One flop ain't a man's life. I'll—"

"I warned you," Vince said bleakly. "You wouldn't listen. What're you gonna do now? I'll be honest: I ain't gonna put the brakes on my career now. I don't want you

in my troupe. You're not good enough." He saw the older man wince. "It's been a long time, Hunk. Music changes."

Hunk snorted. "I'll be in show business when they don't remember your name! And ain't you forgettin' something, boy? It's a legal contract. Fifty-fifty."

Vince smiled—the same hard smile that Hunk was smiling. "No, Hunk, it ain't. I turned Mr. Shores loose on that contract. It's not worth the ink it took. You should have checked with a lawyer, Dad."

"I—I always figured it was a contract of good faith more'n legal."

Having seen the shrewd smirk shaken from the older face, Vince still bore in. "That what you figured? When you knew about the fan mail I got in the can—and didn't tell me? Let's level. You did me a favor, then tried to rob me. So I'm gonna honor that contract—provided I don't hear no more jazz about good faith. But not for fifty per cent. For ten." His eyes narrowed. "Check my airplane reservations, Hunk."

There was silence. Hunk was thinking.

"A punk like you might just get lucky enough to make a million dollars a year," he mused. "Ten per cent of a million, that's a hundred thousand. You're gonna have the most expensive flunkey in show business." He picked up the house phone and got the desk. "Gimme airlines reservations. . . ."

After that television show, the floodgates opened wide. The biggest clubs in America wanted Vince Everett. New York. Chicago. Las Vegas. Florida. Receipts doubled and redoubled. Mr. Shores was really busy. His only regret was that Laurel Records wasn't pressing any new platters. It seemed that the forty per cent stockholder and the sixty per cent stockholder wouldn't communicate.

Finally, there was only one phase of the entertainment industry left to conquer. So they signed an exclusive contract with Pacific Studios and moved into a mansion in Beverly Hills, with a limousine and two convertibles in the garage and gaudy hangers-on crowding the bar and swimming pool.

Laury was left behind in the East. Somehow, she didn't give Vince a charge any more. But the first thing he said as he walked into his new mansion sounded almost breath-less. "Any telephone calls for me?"

"She ain't called, Vince," his man said. He didn't mean Laury.

Well, there were plenty of girls beside Peggy Van Alden! His leading lady in the movie Pacific had lined up for him was a bomb named Sherry Wilson. Sherry was bored, at first, at the studio's directive that they were to be seen around in public together. But the first day on the set there was a kissing scene. What happened when Vince put his mouth on hers was something that had the crew bug-eyed and the director ogling his wrist watch in sheer disbelief. After that, Sherry was like Vince's shadow.

He threw one of his big whingdings for a housewarm-ing. Everyone invited turned out to see the new singing sensation. The only eyes in the crowd that didn't watch him with a glow, when he got up to sing, were the jaun-diced eyes of Hunk Houghton—and the even warier ones of two sad but aristocratic Basset hounds that Vince had bought and put in Hunk's charge.

"I didn't see you applauding," Vince said out of the side of his mouth, as Hunk pushed by with the dogs. "You didn't like me?"

"You come a long ways since cell block twenty-one. But you haven't hardly touched ground at all. Walked most of the way on somebody else."

Vince's eyes took on a mean glitter. "Getting bitter, old buddy?"

"Not me. I just want you to enjoy it while you got it. You won't be up there long. The people who buy the tickets—sooner or later, they'll spot you for a phony."

Vince stiffened. "Ten per cent of nothing'll be nothing, cell mate."

Sherry drifted up to him, pouting because he'd been neglecting her. Bored, wishing that she'd fade, he quieted her by nibbling her neck and telling her she was a doll. When he looked up, his heart almost stopped beating. In the doorway, studying him stonily, stood Peggy! He rushed to her, yelling her name in his elation. "Peg! Sweetheart! I thought you'd never come!"

"Hello, Vince," she said quietly.

"I kept wondering if you missed me like I missed you—"

"There's always the telephone, Vince. It would have been nice if you'd called. I came about the record company. Isn't it about time you cut a few sides? Nobody gets too big for records. Not even Crosby."

"Records?" He stared at her, and the elation drained from him. Slowly, the old mocking mask reassembled itself on his face. "That why you came? Sure, I'll make records. Set a date." He turned away fast.

He was still stalking his party in a glum mood when Mr. Shores caught up with him. "Mr. Everett," the dry old lawyer rasped, "I have some startling news. I've received a proposition from Geneva Records."

Vince glowered. "Don't mention that clip joint to me."

"Even if it involves three-quarters of a million capital gains?"

Vince whistled. "Mention it."

"They want to buy Laurel Records. In addition to the sale price, they want you under exclusive contract for recordings. For seven-and-a-half per cent of all the records you sell. No artist has ever received an offer so big."

"Man!" Vince breathed. And then: "What about Peggy?"

"I haven't discussed it with her."

"Good. Let *me* talk to her."

The night the final scene of the picture was shot, Vince threw another party. This one was on the set, and everybody was there. Everybody but Peggy—Peggy and, of course, Hunk, who'd needed a little more cutting down to size, in Vince's book. He'd ordered Hunk to take the Bassets for a long walk.

People were drifting away, calling back their thanks and good wishes, when Vince heard a tap of slim heels with a special sound. He looked up eagerly. Peggy was coming across the empty set.

"Where you been?" he asked. "Everybody's gone. Let me fix—"

"I missed a streetcar," she said wryly. "What did you want to talk to me about, Vince?" She might have been on some mountain peak, far away.

"Oh, yeah." His smiled faded. "It's about the record company—"

But before he could tell her, a voice boomed, "Mush, you coyotes! Who's buying the drinks?" And Hunk staggered from the shadows, drunk as a lord, dragging two exhausted dogs after him. Vince glared at him, and Hunk glared back. "You said exercise 'em! We covered eight miles and four saloons."

The sheer hate in Hunk's eyes would have prompted trouble, if Peggy had not said, quickly, "What about Laurel Records, Vince?"

"We got an offer for the label that's too good to turn down." He saw the look in her eyes and hurried on. "To sell out to Geneva. Seven hundred and fifty thousand dollars. That's two hundred twenty-five thousand in cold cash for you—*after* taxes."

"But Vince! I don't *want* to sell! I've got wonderful plans for our record company. Right now, it's my whole life. I—"

"I'm afraid you got no choice. I own—"

"I know. Sixty per cent." Her voice was dull, hopeless. "Dollars! Is that the beginning and end of the world for you? We started this thing together; we nursed it and brought it up. Maybe it's only a ledger page to you and Mr. Shores, but to me it's—" She was choked by an inarticulate sob of defeat. "Oh, go ahead and sell it! I don't care *what* you do!"

As the swift staccato of her fleeing steps faded, Hunk began to peel off his jacket. "It's not losin' the record company bothers her. Trampin' on me is one thing, sonny. Hurtin' a nice kid like Peggy is another."

Vince stared coldly back at him. "Don't get any ideas, Hunk."

"There comes a time when you gotta take a hand." Hunk spoke almost gently. "I'm just gonna beat hell outa you. On your feet, sonny!"

A big right fist lashed out and contacted with Vince's face, spinning him into a canvas wall. The set tottered. Bleeding, Vince got to his feet. But Hunk was after him.

Vince tried his best to avoid the blows without hitting

back. He'd done time for the last fight he'd let himself get into—for killing the man. And this was poor old Hunk.

"Fight, you yellow punk!" Hunk sobbed. Tears of rage were coursing down the older man's cheeks. He waded in savagely, hitting wildly. One of his fists plowed into Vince's throat and, into the ruined set. Vince went down again. When Vince did not rise, Hunk drew his contract from his pocket and slowly shredded it. The little snowstorm drifted down to a sound of ragged breathing.

Then, belatedly, Hunk took another look at the prone figure on the floor. Vince was clawing weakly at his throat —making the choked, gurgling sounds that were all he could utter. Hunk dropped to his knees by the boy for one horrified instant, and then was bolting for the stage door.

"Ambulance!" he was screaming. "Somebody get an ambulance! . . ."

The doctor at the hospital where Hunk and Peggy waited through tense hours, told them it was a close thing. The blow had bruised the larynx, causing it to swell and cut off the windpipe. A hole had been cut in the windpipe to make it possible for Vince to breathe. He would live. But it was likely he'd never sing again. That punch could have altered the whole construction of the voice box.

"We'll have to wait a few days for the swelling to go down," the doctor said. "Then—we'll see. You can visit him. But no talk."

In those long hours while he lay staring at a sterile ceiling, Vince couldn't check the whirl of his dreary thoughts. *Is this the way it ends? Back to the skip loader for Vince Everett? Without your voice, Vince, you're just another guy walkin' the street.*

Hunk came and sat beside him and mumbled heartbroken apologies. Vince reached out and patted the man's bent head with forgiveness, and Hunk was crying when he stumbled away. Then, soon, Peggy came.

"Hunk told me what happened in the fight," she whispered, tears in her eyes, too. "How you wouldn't hit him. Vince, I love you!"

When she bent to kiss him, his lips were gentle against hers, instead of savage. And there were tears—hers, or his.

The day the doctor made his final examination, he was blunt. The injury was healed; the surgery had been successful. But whether or not Vinces singing voice would sound as it had before could only be determined by trying it.

But what if it wasn't there? The terror froze him, holding him back from the test. The doctor said that if he didn't get hold of himself he might be a psychological mute, musically speaking. *But if it wasn't there—*

Peggy had come with him for this last examination. "Why don't you *try?*" she urged gently, pointing to a piano. "Now's a good time, Vince."

"But I—I got nobody to accompany me."

She opened the door to the waiting room, and all his outfit trooped in. They'd been standing by, he saw, to help if they could. Despite his terror, he couldn't bail out in front of them. He groped for Peggy's hand.

The music began. Low at first. But then—then Vince's old voice came soaring out over it, riding high, riding true.

Out in the waiting room where he sat listening, Hunk Houghton grinned down at the two mournful Basset hounds at his feet.

"Well, boys," he said huskily, "we're back in business!"

Adapted from the METRO-GOLDWYN-MAYER CINEMASCOPE
  Production
Copyright 1957 by LOEW'S, INC.
Directed by RICHARD THORPE
Produced by PANDRO S. BERMAN
Screenplay by GUY TROSPER
Adapted for SCREEN STORIES by JEAN FRANCIS WEBB

CAST

Danny Finnell	.... ELVIS PRESLEY	Mr. Finnell	.... DEAN JAGGER
Ronnie	.... CAROLYN JONES	Nina	.... LILIANE MONTEVECCHI
Nellie	.... DOLORES HART	Maxie Fields	.... WALTER MATTHAU

KING CREOLE

■ The days of Danny Finnell began at sun-up, when New Orleans' French Quarter just was stirring from its gaudy night—sailors lurching out of cheap dives, painted girls leering after them from iron lace balconies, gumbo and turtle vendors beginning to sing their wares up Royal Street.

This was the hour when Danny set out to do a day's work before school—sweeping out Maxie Fields' crummy night club. One man in a family had to hold a job; and in this one, it wasn't Pop Finnel. When Mom had died in the accident, three years ago. Pop really died too. All he cared about now was seeing Danny study for some professional degree.

Degree! What good had his own pharmacist's diploma done Pop? Mom gone, he'd let his drugstore slide downhill and out of their lives. The house had gone next. He couldn't even hang onto odd jobs. Food money, rent on their drab Royal Street rooms, these were up to Danny and his sister Mimi. But at least school was almost over. One more day until graduation. Then it would be full-time pay for Danny. No more peanuts! . . .

It began badly, that last day of school. Two surly drunks still sat in the Blue Shade when Danny showed for work. One of their girls Danny knew. She was slim and sensuous, was Ronnie. Maxie's personal property.

These customers were mean. When one of them insisted Danny sing, because the band had quit, Danny obliged. But then the drunk started slapping Ronnie around because she wanted to go home. Danny smashed a brace of bottles and, with jagged glass for a weapon, backed the girl outside.

Safe in the street, he sighed. "Guess I lose my job for this."

"They won't tell Maxie," Ronnie said drearily. "He loaned me for the evening. But a sock in the eye, that pleasure is for Maxie alone."

Ronnie insisted on dropping him off at school in a taxi. Kids raising the flag in the yard saw her kiss him in tipsy gratitude, before the car wheeled away. There were noisy jeers. On his way inside, Danny had to give one young hood named Leo a classic shiner.

So that was the end of graduation. His pious teacher, Mrs. Pearson, marched him into the principal's office to display his lipstick smears and report the fight. There'd be no diploma tomorrow for Danny Finnell.

On his grim walk home, he met Leo's big brother Shark and a few selected cronies with switchblades, laying for him in an alley. The battle wasn't pretty. But Danny—stung by rage and frustration—was a one-man army. He beat respect into the gang with slashing fists.

"You go pretty good," Shark panted admiringly when it was over. "And fast. You wanna hang with us? We got somethin' cookin' for tomorrow."

Danny shot him a contemptuous look and started backing off warily. Behind him, he heard Shark saying, "That's a good boy. He fights real dirty. . . ."

There wasn't much admiration waiting for him at home. Mimi was tearful, anticipating Pop's disappointment about the diploma. But Pop, when he turned up, already knew the story. The principal had sent for him and they'd had a talk. Things weren't hopeless. If Danny went to night school—

So Danny was going to night school and Pop was going to work. No son of a Finnell was going to consort all his life with Bourbon Street bums. There was a job open at the Regal Pharmacy. Pop would nail it, and *this* time—

Danny heard him out with bitter wisdom. Poor Pop. Poor, beat Pop. He remembered Shark's invitation, and smiled grimly.

The job the boys had cased was a five-and-dime on Charles Street. Shark had it figured. Word was out that Danny sang like a bird. So Danny was going to drift into this store, strumming a guitar. While folks listened—

Shoppers had the place well filled, next afternoon. As Danny ambled singing along the aisles, a strolling troubadour, people turned to smile at him in enjoyment. The trio sauntering in behind him—Shark, Sal, Dummy—split up unnoticed to work separate aisles. Watches, novelties, jewelry, all were scooped from the counters as if by magic.

The crowd clapped when his song ended. Danny made

for the soda counter casually, climbing a stool. A pretty
counter girl came to serve him.

"You sing nice," she said softly.

Danny studied her shy but appealing face. "Thanks."

"You were in on it, weren't you?" she said, just as softly.

His eyes widened in shock. Then he spotted the big mir-
rors behind her. If she'd been facing them, she could have
seen the whole caper. "G-gimme a-a soda." He felt numb.
"Any kind you pick." He watched her work it expertly.
Would she tell? "What's your name?"

"Nellie," she said.

"What time you get through work? Maybe I could
meet you—"

She hadn't any time to reply. A shrill shriek from one
of the salesgirls sounded the alarm. The merchandise had
been missed. There was a tumult in the aisles, as the
manager began tearing his hair.

"I have to go out that door at ten o'clock," Nellie said
quickly. "So if you're out front, I—I guess I can't help
but see you. . . ."

Pop had meant it. He came home that night with the
pharmacy job all set. Going to the Blue Shade, Danny had
news for Chico, the bartender.

"Better start looking for a new boy, Chico. My old man
got a job today. We made a deal. He goes to work, I go to
school nights."

Shark had come around to the Blue Shade to tell Danny
that a fence had paid a bundle for their haul, and that it
would be split in the alley at midnight. That was why he
was there when Maxie came in, accompanied by Ronnie in
a whistle-bait evening gown. Maxie's sharp eyes caught a
look between his girl and Danny, that made his thin lips
tighten. Even Shark's fawning greeting did nothing to
visibly soften the boss as he hustled Ronnie inside.

At his ringside table, Maxie sat smiling jovially. But his
hand held Ronnie's in a vise-like grip. "You know that kid!
Don't lie!"

"Maxie—stop it!" As he bent her fingers backward,
Ronnie went white with pain. "I heard him sing a song,
that's all—"

"That's *all*, huh?" Maxie lifted his head. "Hey, kid, cum-mere! This lady tells me you sing. It better be right. Sing for me—*right now!"*

Maxie was the boss. Taut with rage, Danny climbed onto the bandstand. The band did an intro. Eyes burning, Danny grabbed a mike and sang.

It was a hard, angry kind of song. He belted every line straight at Maxie. And after the first few bars, people listened. Not that Danny cared; he was too steamed up to be nervous. But Chico hollered: "Crazy!"

He hit his climax right on the button, and stalked from the stage without even a nod toward the applause. A good-looking man of about forty had been listening. He moved now, smiling, to block Danny's way.

"I'm Charlie Le Grand," he said. "Wanna stop being a bus boy?"

Danny flung a hard glance at Maxie. "I already stopped."

"I'd like to talk. I own the King Creole, down the street."

From behind them Maxie purred. "I was gonna offer the kid, myself."

"I beat you to it," said Charles Le Grand, not even nervous.

Danny couldn't care less. He wanted to get to Charles Street before they closed that five-and-dime. He didn't want a job singing. . . .

He was waiting as the lights dimmed. Pretty soon, Nellie appeared. He moved in beside her confidently.

"You're pretty sure of yourself," she breathed, looking up.

"Not always. I was real scared this afternoon. Where do we go?"

"I—I have to be home early. My mother—she's old-fashioned."

"How about *you?"* he asked boldly. "Some friends of mine are having a little party. We'll stop off for some laughs."

Afterward, he wasn't proud of it—the shabby hotel, the room where he took her on his flimsy pretext of a party. There was no one else there, of course. But when he made his first pass at her, Nellie neither fought nor co-operated. Instead, she just stood there with tears on her cheeks.

"I've never been in a hotel room before," she whispered, frightened. "But I want to see you again. Maybe this is the way. I don't know." She scrubbed at the tears.

"Get your coat on," Danny ordered. "The party's over." He left her in the hallway of her tenement.

The others were waiting at the alley. Shark had tried a split three ways, with only five bucks for Dummy because he couldn't squawk. Danny grabbed the roll and made an even division. His eyes sparked as he spoke to the grateful mute.

"He takes this back or lays hand on you, tell me."

Shark's face twisted. "I don't want you around, Danny."

"I'm not going to *be* around," Danny spat, and left them.

He was almost home when he passed the convertible parked in shadow by the curb. A husky voice called out, "Hey, schoolboy!" Turning, he saw Ronnie at the wheel. "You sure showed Maxie. You *really* sing."

Stirred by her, he bent closer. "What do you say we—"

"I'd like to, but Maxie'll be here any minute. Please go."

"Remember in the cab? You wouldn't take off until I kissed you."

She reached up quickly, pulled his face to hers, and kissed him deep and hard. When Danny straightened, his blood was pounding.

It pounded for a very different reason, next morning. Going around to wish his father luck on his first day at work, Danny overheard the shop's waspish manager chewing out Pop for nothing at all. The sound of his father's meek voice, back-tracking humbly, made Danny's skin crawl. He stole away, not letting Pop see him.

He went straight from the Regal to Le Grand's King Creole. It was a better place than the Blue Shade, but it didn't look prosperous. Charlie Le Grand sat balancing ledgers at an empty table.

"What does a singing job pay?" Danny demanded, without preamble.

"Eighty-five a week. If they like you, it gets to be more."

"I never sang professionally." Now came the doubts. "And Pop wants me to go back to school."

"Let me talk to Pop," Charlie said. "Invite me home to dinner. . . ."

The dinner try was as useless as Danny had anticipated. Pop paced the floor in anger. Charlie's arguments fell on deaf ears. In the end, with a wry smile to Mimi—whom he obviously found very attractive—Charlie gave up. Mimi

went downstairs to show him out. When Danny came bolting down, minutes later—stung by his own postscript battle
with their father—Charlie still was there on the steps holding Mimi's hand.

"Mind if I have a date tomorrow with your sister?" he
asked.

Danny's jaw squared. "Pop might. But *I'll* be at the club
tomorrow!"

He pushed on past them into the dark. A voice seemed
to lash him as he forged doggedly up the street—his own
voice, echoing things he'd yelled upstairs. *I don't want to
crawl. Pop, not like you crawl. They got you on the run
early. It's not going to happen to me! Eighty-five bucks a
week says I can be a performer, and I'm through fail-
ing!* . . .

The night he opened at King Creole, Mimi was there
with Charlie to cheer him up. But Pop, sternly disapproving, stayed away. Backstage, where Danny waited as nervous as a cat on hot bricks, the club's featured strip tease
queen, Nina, wished him luck.

"Handsome," she lisped. "I hope you bring business to
the place. People warm up a room—and in my line, I could
use that."

Just before zero hour, Charlie came back. "There are
only about fourteen people out there, Danny. But fourteen people can hate you as hard as a thousand. They're
expecting the best. Well—you're on!"

When Danny walked out into the spotlight a minute
later, he walked head up. He hit his first note as if he
owned it. And he built from there. Before he was halfway
through, the emptyish room had come alive. Nobody talked
or spilled drinks. They listened. He was solid. He was
in. . . .

Danny reached Charles Street that night before the five-
and-dime's lights blinked off. As Nellie came out, he fell
into step.

"You busy?" he asked. She shook her head. "Okay, we
got a date."

It was a very special place he took her. On the upper
deck of an excursion sidewheeler churning up the Mississippi, he sat beside her with gaze nailed savagely to the
passing shore. Nellie was breathless.

"Danny, you don't know how I've been hoping you'd come by. Fellows have come to the store before. But you— you came to *rob* the store. Yet—it's like everything just started with you."

He knew that she was rattled by her own boldness. His eyes never left the riverbank. "Look, Nellie, both of us did something that day we never did before. *I* never robbed a store. I guess there's a *last* time for everything, too." Abruptly, he pointed. "Look! See over there—that house?"

Perhaps to other eyes it might seem just another two-story house, in a nice neighborhood of houses, standing among others like it. But Danny's eyes held to it, fixed in worship, while the boat glided past.

"That used to be our house," he breathed. "Pa bought it when I was eight years old. We sure had happy times."

"There's nothing like owning your own house." Nellie was watching *him,* not the shore. "We've always rented."

Danny's jaw squared. "I'll buy that house back some day—or one just like it. And I'll keep it! No one'll take it away from me!"

Still she looked at him. "Danny, aren't you going to kiss me?"

"Nellie, don't. Don't keep saying *I love you.* I don't know what to answer. Love means getting married and having kids. I don't even know who I am yet. I've got to *be* somebody first, not like my old man!"

"You could still kiss me," she whispered.

He turned suddenly, and kissed her hard. But then he pushed her tenderly away. "Let it go at that, Nellie. For now, anyway. Just so it was *you* I wanted to show my house to, tonight. Just leave it at that. . . ."

Next morning, when he got up for the breakfast Mimi had fixed him, Pop had already gone to the drugstore. Mimi was radiant. Danny noticed how often the name of Charlie Le Grand came to her smiling lips.

"Did you see Pop?" he probed. "Did he—ask how it went last night?"

Her smile faded. "I told him they liked you. He said for you to—to wash your hands before you bring him his lunch."

Because he had to take that lunch over to the Regal, Danny

caught another of the scenes by which the vicious little manager contrived to humiliate his father. This time, he was making Pop scrub the floors—and never letting up on the ridicule for a minute. Spiritless as a sponge, Pop accepted the tongue lashing. Danny stole away, heartsick, leaving the sandwiches with a clerk.

He was plowing blindly past the corner when he realized that Shark had fallen into step beside him. Shark wore a fawning smile and spoke with new respect.

"Wowee, Danny boy, you got the whole street buzzin'! Already, they're saying you're the next somebody. Mr. Fields wants to see you, Danny."

Danny's lips curled. "I dont want to see him."

"He told me to bring you. You better come. Maxie's no guy to brush."

"If he wants to see me, there's three shows a night at the Creole."

Shark eyed him sharply. "That drugstore—that where your old man works? I was just thinkin': If *my* old man was gettin' knocked around, I'd sure take care of him if I could. You see Fields, Danny, and I'll try to come up with an angle. Do me a favor, I'll do your old man a favor."

Danny decided. "Where's Fields?"

"I'll take you to him. You and me can talk later. I'm on Maxie's payroll now. I'm one of his boys. That drugstore situation might just clear itself up"—and Shark snapped expressive fingers—"like *that! . . .*"

You got to Maxie's door by way of outside stairs rising from a private courtyard. When Danny knocked, it was Ronnie who answered. But Maxie sat waiting inside, among expensive paintings and rugs and antiques, like a slimy spider.

"Good news travels fast," he said, smiling. "I hear you're a smash at that joint. I'm always interested in any new attraction."

Curtly, he ordered Ronnie to serve them drinks. He loved humiliating her. Then: "Kid, I like to see people get ahead. And who knows, maybe some day we'll do business. You may be working for me again."

"I don't think so, Mr. Fields." Danny was sick for Ronnie's sake.

"Never can tell. I saw you first. And I was a little put

out when you quit to go with a crumb like Le Grand."

"Charlie's no crumb. He's pretty decent."

Maxie's smirk grew nasty. "Oh, yeah, I forgot about him and your sister. I don't like losing things, kid. Not even a bus boy. When I lose something, I want it back. Sooner or later, I get it. Show him out, honey. . . ."

Whatever grapevine brought Maxie his news must have been buzzing, that next week. Suddenly, there wasn't an empty table to be found at the King Creole. Women flocked in for every show, staring with silent hunger at the figure in the spotlight, keeping Charlie's cash register chiming. Nina, the strip girl, was the only one with a complaint. In an audience of women, who wanted to see *her* specialty? It was all Danny Finnell.

Danny came offstage after his early show to the usual applause, the night after he got a new message from Shark. Instead of heading for his dressing alcove, he belted into the telephone booth. Nobody answered at the number he dialed. Coming out again, he left word with Eddie the MC that he'd be back for the next show, and shoved outside into a night which stitched the gaudy neon lights together with needles of rain.

All the way to the Regal Drugstore, he was running. When he got to the corner, it was still a minute short of closing time. Near a parked car across the street, two figures waited—Shark and Sal, just as arranged.

"I tried to get you on the phone," Danny panted, nearing them. "I been thinking about it. Call it off. You owe me nothin'."

"You were all hot for it yesterday." Shark's face smirked. "It works out both ways. *We* get the money, you get even for your old man." Shark had been casing the Regal. He knew that each week on this night Mr. Primont, the sadistic manager, took deposits to the bank.

Danny's face darkened. "It's no good, Shark. The old man wouldn't—"

"He would if he could," Shark leered. "Look! He's ready to leave!"

The front lights of the drugstore had flickered off, leaving only a night glow from the office behind. A figure in fedora and raincoat came out into the rain, hunched against the weather, closing the door behind him. Shark breathed, "It's Primont! This is for your old man, Danny."

While Danny hesitated wretchedly, Shark and Sal began to stalk the plodding, muffled figure in the rain. He saw it all like a scene on a stage—the way they stopped him, asking for a match, the way Shark's sap came out from cover, the way the body crumbled in the rain. Snatching the money bag, Shark and Sal took to their heels. Danny remained rooted only for a moment longer. Then he, too, turned and ran.

He was breathing hard when he opened the backstage door at the King Creole. How long he had been plunging about out there in the wet, he couldn't have said. But he wouldn't be very late for his next show, and—

In the doorway, he paused sharply. Nellie was there. She sped forward, crying his name. "Danny! Where have you been?"

"Why? What's the matter?"

"Oh, Danny, it's your father! Mimi phoned from the hospital. He was taking some money to the bank, and some rotten thugs jumped him. He's in pretty bad shape, Danny. Charlie and Mimi are at the hospital now!"

Never, if he lived to be a hundred, would Danny forget the agony of those hours of waiting at the hospital. Mimi wept quietly in a corner, while Charlie tried to comfort her. Their own doctor examined Pop in the emergency ward and came back with a reoprt that chilled Dannys spine.

"He's alive, but there's been damage to the brain. He's going to need another operation immediately. A delicate one. Dr. Martin Cabot, he's the best—but expensive. A couple of thousand, maybe more."

They were staring at one another, stricken. trying to figure where they could possibly raise even a fraction of that amount, when the door opened. Dr. Martin Cabot, a brisk little man, bustled in, already preparing to operate.

"All right," he said as he came, "where is this man Finnell? You his boy?" He paused before Danny. "Maxie Fields must be very fond of you. Said you used to work for him and he wanted to help out. Let's go!"

It seemed forever that the doctor had Pop behind operating-room doors—but when they emerged again, Dr.

Cabot was smiling. "He made it."

Danny bowed his head and covered his face, as he listened.

"He'll be all right. Take a little time, but he's a real fighter."

Charlie cut in awkwardly. "Doc, about Maxie Fields—"

"Strange man. Coarse, vulgar, very powerful. I'll send him my bill."

"I'll pay back every cent!" Danny said slowly. "Every cent!"

Those next four weeks, while Pop was recuperating in the hospital, business at the King Creole grew to a crush. Crowds unable to get inside lined up in the street to wait for the next show. Danny Finnell was the pride of Bourbon Street, no doubt about it. And every week, most of his pay check went to Maxie. Drops in the bucket, but at least a start on repaying the staggering debt. If things got still better, so Charlie got his place out of hock and married Mimi and raised Danny's salary—

But none of that had happened yet, the night he found Shark waiting for him in the alley after the last show. He tried to brush past. But Shark had been waiting for a reason. "Mr. Fields would like to see you Danny."

"I don't want to see him."

"When Maxie tells me to bring somebody, I got to bring him. Here's the key to his apartment, Danny. Just walk up the stairs, understand? I'm remembering a rainy night and a guy carrying a bag of money. I hear your old man comes out of the hospital tomorrow. I'm real glad. Here's the key, Danny. You know the place. Just go right on in. . . ."

He shouldn't have been too surprised, when he opened Maxie's door, to find that Ronnie—in a clinging gown—was his greeting committee. When he demanded to see Maxie, she showed him Maxie—snoring on a bed in the next room, fully dressed but out cold. Danny stood there uncertainly.

"I guess he can't see me tonight."

"He didn't want to see you tonight. He wanted *me* to see you. He wants you to quit Le Grand and work for him. I'm supposed to—to befriend you," she said unhappily.

Danny shook his head, moving for the door. "Tell Maxie I wasn't in the mood. I'll be square with him in a few months. I won't owe him anything." He was ready to leave. "That's the way I want to keep it."

"I wish you wouldn't go," Ronnie said dully. "Shark's down below. He has orders to clock your entrance and exit. If you leave now, he'll punish me for having failed. I'm asking you to stay because I hate to be punished by Mr. Fields. He's not a very sensitive man."

Suddenly, she was sobbing. And suddenly his arms were around her, soothing her. The tears were real. They tore at him inside.

"Ronnie, what are you doing with this man? How'd you get into this?"

It did start as pity. But the warmth of her against him was a wild thing. He began to kiss her—faster, harder, until Ronnie herself broke free with a little strangled cry. "Go home, Danny, go home! If we keep on, I wouldn't know if it was because Maxie wanted you or because—"

Danny reached for her again. "Maxie has nothing to do with it."

"I wouldn't be too sure." The cold voice came from the bedroom door behind them. Maxie stood there, stone sober, grinning with cold glee. "Sorry to intrude, but let's not forget who's supposed to win. Me."

"I told you once before I'm not going to work for you," Danny rasped.

"Too bad. I was hoping it could be arranged on a—friendly basis." Cold eyes flicked Ronnie. "But it can be done the other way, too. Your old man's coming out of the hospital tomorrow, punk. Might not be so good for his health if he found out it was you who helped put him there."

"It was an accident." But Danny's heart had snagged on a beat.

"Was it? But you were in on it. You don't think he'd mind, tell him." Maxie picked up a sheet of blank paper from the writing desk. "Or I got an easier way. Just sign this. There's nothing on it, but don't worry—I'll fill it in later. Otherwise, I might fill Charlie's place with bombs. *Anything* can be made to look like an accident."

So now Danny knew how a man got into the clutches

of Maxie Fields. Anything Ronnie might have told him, he now knew for himself.

He'd never felt lower in his ilfe than on the night he told Charlie he was moving over to the Blue Shade because Maxie had made a better offer. He knew what Charlie and Mimi thought of his betrayal. And he felt so dirty that he called off the half-plan he and Nellie had made to go for a talk with Father Franklin about their getting married soon.

"Something's come up," he told Nellie, in the quiet gloom of Fountainbleau Park. "A lot's come up. I walked out on Charlie tonight, and—"

"That girl—Ronnie—does she have anything to do with it?"

"I don't know," Danny admitted, helpless before her grief. "Maybe. It's all—mixed up. I can't marry you until I'm sure."

One thing, though, wasn't mixed up at all. And that was Pop's reaction. Dummy, still gratefully loyal, caught up with Danny in the park and slipped him a note that sent him to Maxie's place on the double. *Your father is with Maxie,* the note read. And Danny's blood ran cold.

He never got the right of it until later—that Pop had gone to Maxie's place to thank him for the help with doctor bills, and to ask that he let Danny stay at the King Creole until Charlie was out of the red and could marry Mimi. That while they talked, Shark had burst in and Pop had recognized him and demanded that Maxie call the law.

But Danny didn't have to know all that, coming face to face with Pop while still a block short of Maxie's, seeing the dazed look in the old man's eyes—the look that turned to burning hate as he recogmized his son. One glance, and Danny knew: Pop had been told that his son was part of that attack!

As his father shouldered past him, he cried out, "Pop! I'm sorry—I tried to stop them! It was for *you,* Pop—"

The old man never turned around. Danny watched the stiff back merge into the crowd; then he turned and lunged on toward Maxie's place. The hate that blazed in him as he burst past that door was like a spew of lava.

"You told him!"

Maxie, who had been alone in the room with Ronnie, nodded with a grin. "Sure! He was running to the police about Shark."

Slowly, deliberately—cold hatred on his face—Danny began to prowl forward. Maxie lashed out with a foot, tripping him, clubbing him with a handy chair. But Danny shook his dazed head, staggered erect, and came on again. Maxie reached for his breast pocket.

From the bar, Ronnie caught up a Scotch bottle and smashed it as Danny once had done in *her* defense. Her voice was an arching rasp. "Stay away from him, Maxie!"

"You little tramp! I own you!"

"No, Maxie, you disgust me. You make my flesh crawl."

With a snarl, Maxie started for her. But Danny lunged forward, plowing a hard fist into Maxie's belly. Then he put everything he had into a left to the jaw. Maxie started to crumple, blood on his face.

"Run, Ronnie!" Danny gasped. "Get away—far away—and never come back!" His fist slammed again, like iron, on Maxie's chin.

Nobody beat up Maxie Fields! The truth of it ran after Danny—like pursuing feet—as he tried to make his way home to Royal Street, soon after he had stumbled down Maxie's front stairs. The goon squad was after him. The killer they called the Collector—and Shark, grinning evilly.

Like a hunted rat, Danny darted up one alley and down another. But the pursuing footfalls always gained. Over a fence, around a corner, into a cellar and out again—he never lost them. They were going to kill him.

Maxie must have alerted them while Danny was still on the stairs. But that didn't matter. All that mattered was that now, at the end of the chase, hey had him bottled up in a black cul-de-sac—and the Collector was coming at him from one direction, Shark from the other.

The sweat was clammy on his body as Danny flattened back to the wall as if he grew on it. From the street side, as Shark drew closer, Danny heard a soft jeer: "I knew it was your old man, that night. I knew it and I slugged him anyway. So come and get me, Danny!"

The Collector—who almost passed him in the blackness —reached him first. Like a cat, Danny jumped. The Collector went down like lead under his savage blow. Shark heard the sound and raced in, knife slashing. Danny ducked, took it in the shoulder, and felt flesh rip. But he reeled back, latched onto Shark's knife arm, and put everything he had into a desperate struggle to force the blade back— back—back. Suddenly Shark gave a strangled cry and slumped. The blade was in his heart. Danny reeled past the fallen body, out into the street, running, running, running.

The next thing he knew clearly was that he was pounding on the door of his own tenement, gasping his plea to be let inside. Pop's voice came back like a hinge creaking: "Go away!" Danny banged on the door again. But the thin line of light under it flicked off with grim finality.

The stairs going down seemed endless. He lurched and fell and pulled himself erect and lurched again. The damp wind searching an open street slapped his face. Must be outdoors again. Must be— The night spun.

A car cut in beside him. He heard a voice—Ronnie's voice, urgent.

"Danny, you've got to hide! They're all after you!"

"Where can I go? There's no place to go!"

He felt her arms supporting him, lifting him into the car. Weakly, he sank into the seat. The engine howled. Sagging, he saw—or half-saw—blurred headlights racing by, the arc of lights that meant a bridge, something like a boardwalk, Ronnie's face. And then blackness.

It was a shack. That was the first thing that registered, after he had opened his eyes. He was lying on a crude cot in a shack somewhere, and it was bright daylight. His cut shoulder had been bandaged.

When he got up and walked slowly outside, feeling better than he'd at first figured to feel, he found himself at a railing overhanging marsh grass and water. Down below him, a rowboat was tied up to a landing platform. Ronnie was lying on it, reading a book. She smiled and waved.

As he came down the wooden stairs to the platform, he was struck by the change in her. Gone were the penciled lips, the mascara, the rouge. This girl was windblown, young and fresh and clean.

"It's Sunday," she said. "You've been out of your head for two days."

"Maybe even longer." Danny glanced about. "Where are we?"

"Just somewhere to run to. I've kept it for years. Here I don't have to think about Maxie—or yesterday—or tomorrow. Why are you staring?"

He found it a miracle. "You look like a kid."

She moved toward him slowly. "I guess something happened that morning you rescued me. You had courage. I have so little, myself. I used to dream that when Maxie and I were through I'd meet you and we'd run away somewhere. Its never the way you dream it. But, Danny, do you think maybe—for a little while—you could make it be the way I dreamed?"

He spoke very softly. "It wouldn't be hard to love you."

"Then love me. Take a day out of your life and love me."

But she'd been right the first time. It's never the way you dream it. They still were reaching for each other, smiling, when they heard the car brake beyond the swamp lot where her shanty stood. Maxie was climbing out of it, past whomever he'd made drive him. Dummy, it looked like from a distance, as Danny scrambled for the stairs pulling Ronnie after him.

They made the top of the creaking flight and headed for the shack. They were almost there when Maxie's gun spat across the stillness. Ronnie went rigid. Then the wire that held her snapped. She crumpled to the ground. Dropping beside her, crying her name, Danny saw blood seep past her lips. He lifted his head in rage. Maxie was braced to shoot again.

Then Dummy—grateful, loyal Dummy—jumped Maxie from behind. The two crashed through the flimsy rail, still struggling for the gun. Down in the tall grass, a single shot barked angrily. After an eternity, Dummy came plodding up the stairway. Maxie never moved in the muck below.

Danny crouched over the girl in his arms, cradling her tenderly.

"It was a lovely day," she whispered, "for a little

while . . ." Like a child drifting off to sleep, she closed her eyes and died.

The signs were big outside the King Creole, announcing: *Return Engagement, Danny Finnell. Indefinite stay.* The crowds inside were bigger than ever. So were the smiles on Charlie's and Mimi's faces as they listened to the applause. Danny was home again. They welcomed him.

Afterward, as he came out the stage door, the gaudy din of Bourbon Street reached out as if to draw him to itself. Danny sucked deeply at his cigarette. Hesitantly, Nellie stepped out of the dark where she had waited for him.

He looked down quietly at her. His eyes were tired and there was an ache in them. But hope, too. "Not yet, Nellie," he said. "In a little while, maybe. But not yet."

"I'll wait," she said, understanding. "I have lots of time."

He moved on alone through the neon glare, heading toward Royal Street. The songs played by the pianos in the dives all might have been songs that Ronnie had sung. The tinny tunes were different, but the words were always the same. *"Take a day out of your life . . . and love me . . ."*

Because there was a mist in his eyes, he didn't recognize the figure coming toward him until they stood almost face to face. Then suddenly the pulse and excitement of the street seemed to sweep him forward. Because his father was smiling. Because his father's arms opened wide.

Adapted from the HAL WALLIS VISTAVISION Production
Released through PARAMOUNT PICTURES
Copyright 1958 by PARAMOUNT PICTURES, INC.
Directed by MICHAEL CURTIZ
Produced by HAL WILLIS
Screenplay by HERBERT BAKER and MICHAEL V. GAZZO
Based on the novel A STONE FOR DANNY FISHER
    by HAROLD ROBBINS
Adapted for SCREEN STORIES by JEAN FRANCIS WEBB

CAST

Glenn Tyler	ELVIS PRESLEY	Betty Lee	MILLIE PERKINS
Irene Sperry	HOPE LANGE	Davis	RAFER JOHNSON
Noreen	TUESDAY WELD	Phil Macy	JOHN IRELAND

WILD IN THE COUNTRY

■ It had surprised Glenn that his dead mother's relative had offered to assume his custody. Uncle Rolfe had never shown generosity before. And things had looked bad in court, with Pa spitefully claiming that Glenn's fight with his drunken elder brother had been assault instead of self-defense.

Still, beggars couldn't be choosers. So there he was. He slept on a cot in the stockroom of his uncle's home tonic plant, where he was to work. But he ate upstairs, with his uncle and Rolfe's daughter Nory.

Nory Braxton had a baby in her bedroom and a husband nobody knew, who was off someplace abroad for the Government. She always treated Glenn like dirt. But Uncle Rolfe was smirkingly cordial, making him at home.

"You got Braxton blood in you, boy," he said, that first night. "I'm going to see you get ahead.'

Maybe so. But being on parole to the law, and being obliged to report to some psychiatric case worker named Irene Sperry, wasn't going to be so pleasant. Impotently raging, Glenn spilled his hot resentment to Betty Lee Parsons; she was the only person he'd ever been able to tell things to since his mother had died. He'd even shown her some of the stuff he'd written in his spare time, trying to get down on paper the things that made him so angry. . . .

The first day Glenn was to report to Mrs. Sperry, Uncle Rolfe let him use the pickup truck to get out to her big, comfortable house on Jefferson Street. Mrs. Sperry's office was simple and pleasant, and she looked younger than she had that day in court.

"Before we start we should get one thing straight," she told him. "I'm not a policeman, Glenn. Just a volunteer worker Judge Parker appointed to help you, nothing more."

"Suppose I don't want help?" he asked, eying her sullenly. "If you think I'm nuts—"

"Keep pretending you're a slow-witted yokel, and I'll put you out," she interrupted him.

He felt he owed her an apology. "Ma'am," he said, "it's like I'm always walkin' with a full cup of anger, trying not to spill it."

"What do you want of life, Glenn?" she asked. "Money? Fame?"

"Money? My ma was enslaved to our farm, choppin' cotton while Pa and Hank was drunk. I'd have bought Ma away, had I the cash. Give her a house like this on a quiet street. She said I'd go to college—there's a laugh," he added bitterly.

"Did you want to go to college, Glenn?" the kind voice asked.

Glenn couldn't answer that. But at the end of the interview, he stood up slowly, and asked, "Can I come another time, ma'am? Monday, like?"

Waiting for Monday, Glenn wondered about what had been said. If there was a place for every man, maybe Mrs. Sperry might help him find his place. He pondered the question all week as he juggled shipment crates in his uncle's storeroom.

That Saturday, he had a date with Betty Lee, but it was past ten o'clock before he could call for her in the pickup truck. Uncle Rolfe had hedged him in with a talk about how lonely Nory was these days.

Glenn took Betty Lee out to a dance hall called High Tension Grove, but all the way there, they bickered about how late he had been. At the dance, Glenn spotted Cliff Macy, whose father was on the parole board. Glenn had a feud with Cliff, but he ignored his old enemy and danced with Betty Lee until the music stopped. He was buying a beer for Betty Lee when Arty Dace, Cliff's lackey, darted up.

"Betty Lee," Dace said, "Cliff wants you 'n Glenn to have a drink."

"Tell him we have a drink,' Glenn answered bleakly. As he and Betty Lee drifted outside into the cheerless picnic grove, Glenn recalled how Cliff had once lent him his car and then said he'd stolen it.

Then, Cliff staggered tipsily from the dance hall. He spoke with an exaggerated hillbilly accent, aping Glenn.

" 'Lo Betty Lee. How you all be, Glenn Tyler? I asked you both to have a drink."

Glenn spoke clearly. "You're as glazed as a ham; that's

the only reason I don't hit you. But don't think I've for-
gotten Christmas night!"

He'd have led Betty Lee back to the truck then, but
Cliff blocked their way. "I wish to continue my confidential
conversation with ol' Tyler, the car thief," his thick voice
taunted.

His face white, Glenn spun around. "You put a black
mark on me I didn't deserve," he snapped. "But take warning! Next time you fault me, it's your last livin' act! . . ."

The next time he talked to Irene Sperry, Glenn tried to
explain why he pitied Cliff Macy along with hating him.
She got him so interested in what he was saying that he
began telling her about how he tried to write things down.
The encouragement in her tone surprised him.

"Did you ever think of writing in any serious way,
Glenn?" she asked.

Suspicious of ridicule, he eyed her. "What makes you
ask it?"

"You turn a phrase a certain way. A metaphor. You
could write."

"When I'd mention in school how I'd like to write,
you'd think clowns came to town," he told her. "I liked
to die when I heard those giggles."

"Perhaps I can help," she said quietly. Looking at her,
his eyes discovered she was truly beautiful. "The thing that
happened out at High Tension Grove," she went on. "Write
that down, just as you told it to me. Try it."

It was a long week, and a very hot one. Late one night,
after he'd driven Uncle Rolfe to the bowling alley, Glenn
returned to find Nory sitting on the back steps with her
guitar and a bottle of her pa's "medicinal tonic."

"Didn't your ma have an old Mexican guitar?" she
murmured, strumming a sad tune. "Been a long time since
she give us both lessons."

Caught by the memory, he paused on his way inside.
"She was a sweet singer," he said. "Hank stepped on that
guitar—on purpose."

Nory giggled tipsily. "Pa's gonna catch us, one of these
nights. You and me, together in sin. That's his plan. So
you'll have to marry me."

Glenn was genuinely surprised. "What about your husband?"

"You *are* stupid," Nory declared. The baby wailed inside, but she didn't move. "I'm young!" She caught at his arm. "I want a good time! I wanta get out here!"

"Then *do* it, girl," Glenn urged. "Paint your toenails red and run away."

"It needs a man to go to hell with," she answered. "Hours of heaven that slide down into hell and we don't care. You're wild, just like me. Pa's got money stashed around. We'd take a slice and run."

"I got plans, Nory," Glenn said. "Mrs. Sperry thinks I—"

"I *want* you, Glenn!" she begged. "From the time I was only twelve!"

"Then why you been treating me like dirt all these years?" he asked.

"Who's the one who started it?" Nory challenged. "You never paid me no mind on picnics, or at school. You think I'm no good, don't you?"

In answer, Glenn moved closer to her. It might have gone further, if Dace and Cliff hadn't driven up just then. They were seeking a couple of bottles of tonic, because all the liquor stores were closed. Cliff made a couple of knowing remarks about Nory's baby; but he stood armed with a heavy tire spanner, and Nory's hand on his arm told Glenn to let them pass. Money and bottles changed hands. The car roared off. Hating it, Glenn glared after them.

The day he took his finished story to Irene Sperry, he was on pins and needles while she paced her office reading it. At last, she offered her opinion.

"Your grammar's atrocious, your construction nonexistent," she declared. "But those things can be taught. This story has what *can't* be taught—power, poetry, insight. It's all here, the raw material. The people are real."

"Seems to me like I get 'em all mixed up," Glenn said. "Sorry for 'em and want to smash 'em, all at once. Even real folks like Betty Lee. Nory, too. Proper folks'd say she's no damn good, but she never had her chance. Her ma ran out six years ago. Uncle Rolfe's took it out on Nory ever since. She skunked him just once. Got lost over the week end with a New York salesman who came through in a big car. That baby's father, ma'am, was a big green Cadillac. Seems I've got two girls—two.ways—beckoning."

"There might be a third way," Irene Sperry said. "What about what your mother wanted? College! You're no fool, Glenn. With your talent, you should have discipline— a formal education."

Disturbed, he studied her. "Never been near a college. Too much wrong with it—money for one."

"There are such things as scholarships," she went on. "Look, rewrite this story. Then let me show it to a friend upstate. This thing jumps off the page. It's a gamble. But you say you want to be a writer. Then *be* one."

"And supposing—supposing they start laughing at me again?" His dark brows lowered. *"Why are you trying to do this to me?"* he demanded. "Did the parole board tell you to take my life and twist it into something else?"

She looked as if he had struck her. Yet her voice remained calm. "I'm sorry. I have overstepped," she said. "But at least consider what I said. . . ."

Glenn considered a lot of things in the following days. He wondered what her dead husband had been like. Everyone knew Cliff Macy's father was in love with her. Did she return his love? What *was* Irene Sperry, anyway?

Still unsure of any answers, on Sunday, Glenn went out to the Parsons farm. He and Betty Lee were flying a kite together, and dreaming on the hilltop, when Mr. Parsons spied them kissing. Betty Lee's father ordered her indoors and told Glenn to get off the farm.

Betty Lee tried to catch up with Glenn as he dashed blindly across the fields. But what good was that? Parsons had desolated him with scorn, and Glenn knew he'd better not look for warmth there any more. Smart men kept free. He'd forget about Betty Lee! Forget Irene Sperry, too!

It wasn't longer than Uncle Rolfe's next poker night before Glenn and Nory got together the way she had wanted them to all along. Glenn hoisted the old typewriter he'd been aiming to fix back on top of her pa's safe. That stuff was over. This was good-bye to it.

By mid-July, stories started getting around town. They said Glenn Tyler was wilder than ever—carrying on a lot and drinking, and he and his cousin Nory drove around up in the hills at night. Betty Lee wept. Irene Sperry waited in vain for his return to their quiet talks.

Glenn knew that he was being whispered about. Maybe the parole board would find out. But that didn't stop him. He was still riding the crest of his bitter wave on the night that he and Nory drove up, raucous and drunk, before the darkened house on Jefferson Street.

"Mrs. Sperry!" he bellowed. "Hey, Mrs. *Sperry!*" He thought he saw a light flicker inside and then go out. He thought maybe she and her maid, Sarah, were at a window somewhere, watching. "I want my story back, Mrs. Sperry!" he called.

"Come on," Nory giggled. "You'll wake up the whole neighborhood!"

But he lurched across the lawn toward the door. In the dark, he tripped over a garden hose. This gave him an idea. *"I'll hose away the heat!"* he chuckled, and he turned on the water and sluiced her front porch. Before Nory could drag him back to the truck, he had gotten both of them dripping wet.

As the truck started and Glenn roared away in a cloud of drunken laughter, Irene stood motionless at her dark window and heard him go. She knew Sarah, grimly disapproving, thought she ought to report this wanton meanness to the police. But to Irene, it had sounded more like a cry for help. . . .

The following day, Irene turned up at the tonic plant where Glenn was loading trucks in the boiling sun. She set the manuscript at his feet, and said, "You wanted me to return your story, Glenn. Here it is."

Ashamed, he avoided her clear gaze. "You got a right, ma'am, to fault me for the other night," he declared. "But I don't wanna come see you any more."

"That's your right," she answered. "But I have a right to know why."

He clenched his jaws stubbornly. "Let's say I'm not worth it, ma'am."

"Surely, you realize you're gifted and—"

"Don't care to be gifted," he cut in. "A body gets knocked around when he's gifted different." He knew Nory was watching from the doorway. "My life's my own!" he exclaimed.

"We'd have no outstanding men—no doctors, artists, scholars—if we were all afraid to be different. No movers and shakers—those who shake the world out of its alligator sleep," Irene said as she turned away.

Afterward, Nory was loudly scornful and claimed it was plain that what Mrs. Sperry wanted of Glenn couldn't be done on any typewriter. The lewd suggestion enraged Glenn. He vaulted into the truck and revved it off up the alley like an echo of his own blind anger. . . .

Soon, it was Nory's birthday, and her father bought her a shiny new guitar. Perhaps repentant for having angered Glenn, Nory insisted that he accept her old one. Uncle Rolfe watched them and leered.

"Girls born in July," he said meaningfully, "they're home-lovin'."

It was the beginning of pressure, real pressure, for Glenn to ask Nory to marry him. Uncle Rolfe had damaged goods on his hands, but he was determined to get a husband for her and a father for her baby. Come the church fair for the organ fund, Uncle Rolfe bought both young people long strips of tickets to have a good time on.

Betty Lee was there, too, with some nice-looking neighbor. Glenn felt her sad eyes following him wherever he went. When somebody cut in on his dance with Nory, he joined Uncle Rolfe where he sat puffing a cigar.

Uncle Rolfe nodded to him. "Nory sure loves dancin'," he said. "Poor kid! I don't know how to break it to her. News today. Her husband's passed away." His eyes met Glenn's. "What's *your* plans, Glenn?"

"You're jumpin' like a cricket," Glenn hedged.

"No, I'm as continuous as beads on a string," his uncle replied. "If you and Nory came together, I'd make you a partner in my place. You know the business and—"

Glenn's voice was scornful. "How'd her husband die?"

"Funny, the telegram don't say. Hush-hush government stuff."

Glenn looked at him head on. "Don't box me in, Uncle Rolfe."

"Boy, you're *boxed* in, but not by me," his uncle declared. "You took Nory like a cheap postage stamp, got her drunk, and canceled her all over the place."

Glenn's blood pounded. "I didn't play post office all alone. You played postmaster. You had this idea in your mind all the time!"

"You're a ratty little liar!" his uncle exclaimed. "If the parole board finds out—"

Violently Glenn flung aside the clutching hand. Uncle Rolfe lost his balance and went crashing into a flimsy booth nearby, scattering all the prizes. Glenn bolted, but he could hear Rolfe shouting behind him, "Get that Tyler boy! He shoved and threw me down! Get Officer Polk!"

He drove around until late that night, then headed for the Parsons place and pitched pebbles at Betty Lee's window to awaken her. When she came outside in her thin robe, he waited bitterly to tell her what had happened.

"Had a fight with Uncle Rolfe," he said at last. "Broke my parole. Guess they'll say I stole his pickup truck, too. They'll take his word and put me in jail for a year or two. All I can see is to run away, get out of the state."

"What do you want me to do?" she asked simply. "I'm sorry for myself that I love you, Glenn. But I'm your woman for the rest of my born days. It won't stop. And you're unsettled and wild."

"I'll never housebreak," he admitted glumly. "I'm downright no account. But likely they're looking for me already. Can you scrape up twenty or thirty dollars to get me away? I'd never bother you again."

She looked into his eyes. "Don't you think it might be better to stay here and fight for your real born rights? Come in the house. We'll phone Mrs. Sperry for a starter. Come on! . . ."

Awakened, Irene told them to come directly to her place. By the time they got there, she had called Phil Macy, Cliff Macy's father. And Macy, as a favor to her, put the pressure on Rolfe Braxton not to prosecute. Macy knew about the bottles of tobacco juice Rolfe had sold to some widow as a cancer cure, and he had canceled checks and a witness to prove it. So, because Glenn had friends who went to bat for him, the incident was closed.

Glenn called at the Sperry place the next day. Disapproving, Sarah let him wait in the living room, which was lined with books and pictures. When Irene appeared, he held out an envelope.

"The story," he explained, "I wrote it over, like you asked."

"I'm very pleased," she said. And he was sure she meant it.

"My ma was good to me," Glenn remarked. "She'd see I was fed, had shoes. Now you're putting a clean shirt on my mind. Its scary. But I thank you, ma'am."

"What's scary about it, Glenn?"

"The Humpty-Dumpty side—the chance to fall with a splash," he answered. "But if you still want me to come here—I might surprise you yet. . . ."

Glenn wanted desperately to make Irene Sperry proud of him. He got a job at Mr. Dace's garage, and he got permission to use the office typewriter whenever things were slow. He was working there one rainy night when Nory drifted in, damp and abject. She gave him the old guitar he had left behind at his uncle's house.

"It's yours," she explained, in a lost voice. "You don't hold it against *me*, do you, Glenn? What Pa tried to do?"

"Of course not, Nory," he murmured. "I'm really learnin' to type and—"

"Don't I get to see you any more?" she broke in. Her voice held a painful yearning. "Glenn, I love you. Pa don't have to know. Can't we meet? I'd be your bounded slave. And I don't mean marriage. I'm not that good enough."

Her self-abasement angered him. "Don't talk like that," he snapped. "Don't let your pa beat your wings down. No, I can't meet you again. Go on home."

"All right, I'll go home." Obediently, she drifted back into the rain again. Hurt by his anger, she added, "You're mad. Gee, I wish you'd get mad in my arms."

Once a week, Irene went up to the State University for a course in psychology testing. When she invited Glenn to come along and see the place, he accepted—even though Betty Lee seemed doubtful that he'd ever want to write so badly, he'd put four years of study into preparing for it.

"This farm won't always be my father's," she reminded him one day. "And I'd like to stand beside you in a white dress. When would that be if you went to college?"

"If I became a real writer, where it might take me, I don't know." He felt nervous. "Some writers settle down with a woman. But some take off alone, like sailors out to sea. I got to find out which kind *I* am, or bust. . . ."

Irene's station wagon seemed a magic coach to Glenn, the day it wheeled him into the university quadrangle. She left him with all the riches of the library, while she looked up her old professor Joe Larsen, in his office. Larsen read the script she had brought him—Glenn's story. And when he was done with it, he nodded slowly.

"You've got some sort of real 'natural' on your hands, Irene," he commented. "Given time and seasoning, anything might develop. His contact with the paper is immediate. But don't go whole hog on this one, too. Your gifted husband—" He stopped and shook his head. "I'll try to work a scholarship for him," he promised.

Afterward, on the long drive home, Glenn and Irene sang gaily, because they both felt so good. But by dusk a storm came up. The mountain road twisted and turned, and Irene had trouble handling the car wheel in the pelting rain.

"Mountains in a storm! God's too angry and too close!" she said.

At last, after they had gone into a sickening and almost fatal skid, Glenn made her let him take the wheel. Rain continued to sluice down.

"Maybe we should somewhere until this lets up," Irene said.

A mile further on, they came to a motel called Spangler's Rest. The sly old man who signed them up quit his snide hints that they could save money by sharing a room, as soon as Glenn snarled a shocked challenge at him. The rain kept drumming on the cheap cabins.

Before she went to her own cabin, Irene borrowed one of the dog-eared old mysteries from a shelf in Glenn's shoddy quarters to read herself to sleep. One good-night kiss—hesitantly given by Glenn, only briefly accepted by Irene—was the limit of what passed between them that night at Spangler's Rest. But after that, whenever Glenn phoned the house on Jefferson Street, Irene had Sarah say she wasn't in.

Glenn couldn't guess how afraid she was, after that lone kiss—afraid of what might happen. She was so afraid that, a couple of days later, she went to Phil Macy's office to say she'd marry him as soon as he got the divorce he'd been talking of for months.

But Glenn had troubles of his own, those days. Uncle Rolfe stopped by the gas station and tried to pretend that Glenn had stolen the old guitar Nory had given him. Glenn's boss, Mr. Dace, didn't seem to buy that. But there was an odd, speculative gleam in his eye, nonetheless, as if he suspected something else—something sly and racy.

That night, Glenn went out to Jefferson Street in the garage runabout, and this time Irene did receive him. About to shower, she was clad in a light cotton robe. She led him into the living room.

"You're angry, aren't you?" she asked, watching his face sadly.

Glenn stared at her. "You break our appointments. You're never home. What did I *do?*" he demanded. "You take me up on a high mountain and show me the whole world. Next thing I know, I'm in the cellar. Does it make me a rat because I fell in love with you?'

"Glenn, stop!" she cried, deeply troubled. "It wasn't sup- posed to happen that way, for us to fall in love. I've been sorting my thoughts." She evaded his reaching hand. "No, don't touch me. This is only—"

"We fell in love," he broke in urgently. "You just said it yourself. So let's stick with *that!* What bugs you? That people might talk? The hell with people!"

"And the hell with my conscience, too?" she asked. "Listen to me! Love is a very brief word. It usually leads to something brief. I *had* something brief—marriage to a very gifted boy, so much like you. We damaged each other badly. Bruce committed suicide, and for several years—" Her voice snagged. "I'm more mature now," she went on. "But you're not. The other night—"

"Look," Glenn growled, rawly hurt. "I want to love you—all my life."

"It's not that simple," she explained. "This isn't rejection. I want to be your friend. But I can't do it with your arms around me. Doesn't what I said make sense?"

"You're the doctor—did it?" he asked. "I love you. I know I do."

Just then, Phil Macy strode into the room. As the prominent lawyer looked from one to the other, taking in Irene's garb and Glenn's tension, a sickness dawned in his eyes. He spoke to Irene. "A lover's quarrel, dear?"

"You know Glenn Tyler, Phil," Irene said.

"Yes! His uncle is spreading a story that you both spent Friday night at a motel. The story isn't true, is it?"

"Within limitations, yes," Irene replied quietly. And she tried to tell him exactly how it had been. But Glenn shouldered between them.

"Where did my uncle get that story from, Mr. Macy?"

"From my son," Macy said. "He's a specialist in motels, it seems. He was there, too. Today, Mrs. Sperry said she would marry me."

Glenn heard the words. His lips tightened. "Ma'am, I don't ever want to see you again," he said. "Mr. Macy, if I find your son around town—if he's shipped home in a box—don't say you weren't warned!"

He bolted from the house, ignoring Irene's pleading cry behind him. . . .

Uncle Rolfe was out bowling when Glenn let himself into the medicine plant, that night. But Nory was there, pale and eager as she saw him.

He took her in his arms and kissed her hard. "You all brag and no substance?" he asked. "You really want to shake this town for good? Get packed!"

Nory's breath caught. "You're not foolin' with me, are you?"

"Where's all this money your pa's supposed to have stashed away?"

Hastily, from a closet, she tugged out a metal box

filled with odd screws and bolts. "Bust this open. It's got a fake bottom," she told him. "I'll get ready!"

It didn't take her long. Glenn had broken open the box's bottom by the time she came back, and he was fingering the crisp bills hidden there.

"You're sure we should take the baby with us?" Nory asked. "We could leave—"

"We take!" Glenn declared. "He'd grow up a skunk with your pa."

The three of them were skimming through the night in the pickup truck before Nory let herself believe that what they were doing was real. "I'll never cry no more!" she exclaimed. "The wide blue yonder's ahead of us!"

"We better take back roads," Glenn said. "They'll be after us before long."

"Nope! Pa can't do a thing. That's all tax-dodge money we took. And I'd give my teeth to see his face when he reads the note I left him!" Nory said happily. She was too surprised to protest when Glenn wheeled into the parking lot at High Tenison Grove.

But Glenn knew what he was looking for. When he strode indoors, Cliff Macy and young Dace were there. With a single neat punch, Glenn sent the scared jackal sprawling. Then he turned to Cliff. The lawyer's son turned and bolted into the dark, running across the lot and under the electric towers. But, cornered in the picnic grove, he turned desperately.

"What point will you make by knocking me down, Tyler?" he asked.

"The point of a lifetime, friend!" Glenn rasped. He hit Cliff once; his long-time tormentor collapsed. Glenn swung back beside Nory in the truck, and started it rolling again up the lonely road.

They couldn't have been riding twenty minutes before Glenn heard a siren behind him and saw the red flash of police lights. He braked the truck.

"Look officer," he protested, as a state trooper appeared alongside. "Look, I was only doing thirty-five. The truck's monitored for that."

The trooper opened his door, and said, "I'm taking you in for manslaughter."

*   *   *

The town hall was crowded with leering onlookers for the coroner's inquest into Cliff Macy's death. Hating and silent, Glenn glared at a sea of faces around him. He recognized Irene, Nory and her pa, Dace and Betty Lee.

The coroner, Dr. Creston, got Dace's story on the record first; how Glenn Tyler had subjected both him and his friend Cliff to unprovoked assault, pursuing Cliff and then pounding him until he died. When Dace was finished, Irene Sperry was summoned to the stand. Snide, angry whispers followed her.

"This is an inquest, not a murder trial," the coroner said. But then the shrewd questions began: Had Tyler been at her home on the night in question? Had Mr. Phil Macy been present? Had Tyler uttered any kind of threat at that time against Mr. Macy's now-deceased son?

"I can't remember the exact words," Irene replied, looking wretched. "He was annoyed. He said something about fighting Cliff if he found him."

"Wasn't the remark that he'd send young Macy home in a box?" Dr. Creston probed.

As indignant mutters boiled from the crowd, Irene had to nod unwilling confirmation. "Mr. Tyler didn't mean it, though," she added quickly. "He had a reason to be angry. There was a slander being spread. A lie about us—"

"Some lie!" the crowd jeered, taunting and cynical.

"A lie!" Irene cried out, her cheeks aflame. "Glenn did nothing to be ashamed of. If anyone's to be blamed, it's me. It was my fault." She turned to Glenn. "I'm so sorry!" she said.

Dr. Creston continued gently. "Mrs. Sperry, we're merely trying to determine if a felony was committed."

"There *was* no felony!" Irene exclaimed. "You mustn't send him to jail, ruin his life! He had a reason to strike Cliff Macy. He was angry, so he struck him. But it wasn't his blow that killed the poor boy. Cliff had a bad heart. Ask his father!"

Creston turned to where a stone-faced Phil Macy sat. "Have you anything to say about this, sir? It's painful for you, but—"

Phil Macy stood up and stared at Irene. "There was nothing wrong with my son's heart," he declared. "He was in perfect health."

Crushed by the lie, Irene left the stand. She was followed by a storm of crude whispers as she walked stiffly from the hearing room. Other witnesses were called to testify: the bartender from High Tension Grove; parole officer Burdette; Glenn's minister; and finally Phil Macy, who swore that his son had never looked in better health than when he'd last seen him. Phil Macy could quote exactly what Glenn Tyler had threatened: *"If I find your son, if he's shipped home in a box, you were warned!"*

Macy was still on the stand when an attendant scuttled in and whispered to a trooper, who in turn whispered to Creston. People could see something was up. They began to shift in their seats, to mutter. Phil Macy was now conferring with the coroner. Macy's face went a sickly gray. Abruptly, he turned back to the witness chair.

"I want, God help me, to correct a statement of mine," he said. "I lied about Cliff's heart. It was very bad. I'd had him to specialists. It—it wasn't young Tyler's fault at all. I struck Cliff myself that night. Maybe that started it— who knows? *Anything* could have killed my boy!"

Suddenly, Glenn sensed disaster. "What's happened?" he demanded.

Grimly Creston leaned toward him and whispered the news. Irene Sperry had gone straight home from the hearing, shut herself into her garage, turned on her car motor and sat there until she'd died. Blindly, Glenn bolted from the hall and headed toward Jefferson Street.

"Let him go," Creston commanded as a trooper started after Glenn. "There's no case now."

When Glenn reached the familiar house, he stopped running. Two white-coated ambulance attendants were inside. There was nothing he could do. He sat down on the front steps, unaware of anything but his own despair, until Phil Macy paused beside him and touched his arm.

"Why did she do it, Mr. Macy?" Glenn rasped sickly. "Why?"

"Because," Macy answered, "she thought she'd destroyed you. She told me so."

Glenn looked up at the sky. "If I was that sun, I'd go down somewhere else today," he said, and he buried his face in his shaking hands. . . .

When the autumn term began, Glenn boarded his train for college. In his gear, was the magazine Irene had sent his manuscript to; it had been published beneath his printed name. In his sore heart, were memories of her.

Betty Lee came to see him off, to let him know she'd be waiting if he wanted to come back to her later. Phil Macy was at the station, too. Macy called, "Do us proud, boy. Irene said you would."

Then the train was moving, and Glenn was off on a new journey. Toward what, He couldn't know that yet. But whatever he found, maybe someday he'd know how to share it with another.

Adapted from the JERRY WALD CINEMASCOPE Production
Released through 20TH CENTURY-FOX
Copyright 1961 by 20TH CENTURY-FOX FILM CORP.
Directed by PHILIP DUNNE
Produced by JERRY WALD
Screenplay by CLIFFORD ODETS
Based on the novel WILD IN THE COUNTRY
    by J. R. SALAMANCA
Color by DELUXE
Adapted for SCREEN STORIES by JEAN FRANCIS WEBB

CAST

Chad Gates .... ELVIS PRESLEY   Fred Gates .... ROLAND WINTERS
Maile Duval .... JOAN BLACKMAN   Jack Kelman .... JOHN ARCHER
Sarah Lee Gates .... ANGELA LANSBURY
Abigail Prentace .... NANCY WALTERS

BLUE HAWAII

■ Chad Grant was home from the Army; yet he wasn't really quite home.

Maile Duval, the beautiful girl he left behind, met him at the Honolulu airport to drive him back to town. But the first glimpse she had of him was as he kissed the stewardess good-by. Having waited two long years for his return, Maile was furious by the time Chad caught up with her.

"My French blood tells me not to forgive you," Maile said. "But my Hawaiian blood tells me to," she added. "Welcome home!"

Maile had taken it for granted that they would go directly to his parents' house, but Chad startled her by saying, "Let's go to the beach. My folks don't expect me till next week."

"You mean you didn't tell your own family you were coming?" she asked.

He nodded. "That's right. I need some time to think— a week at the beach, alone with you." Before she could protest, he grinned and said, "Man, it's great to be back!"

Out at the beach shack, it seemed as though he'd never been away. He gazed at the thatched hut with tenderness.

"I used to think a lot about this place," he told Maile softly. "I was afraid it might change. But it's still beautiful."

Maile frowned. "You're not going to *stay* here."

"Why not?" he asked. "I've got a roof over my head, a cot, a stove." Chad took a deep breath. "All the time I was overseas, I thought about you and me—and the future. And every week, there was another letter from my folks, reminding me of my beautiful future in Dad's pineapple business. I knew I couldn't come back with the rest of my life laid out for me. Maile, if all of me's going to live—I've got to do it my own way, on my own!" he explained.

Maile understood. Even though Chad was all man when he took her in his arms, he still had a lot of growing up to do. Who could say he was wrong in this decision? So they abandoned themselves to enjoying that first day of his return.

As Chad and Maile were swimming together near the beach, four of Chad's pals arrived in their outrigger and welcomed him joyously. Wes Moto, Carl Tanami, Ernie

Gordon and Ito O'Hara were typical beach boys of the Islands, eager to celebrate in song and dance. But Maile lost the top of her bikini and couldn't come out of the surf to join them until Ito's mongrel dog swam out to her with a sweat shirt in his teeth. Then they all sang and laughed on the beach. These were the people to whom Chad had felt closest before entering the Army. These few, he really had missed. . . .

But Chad's peaceful interlude at the beach shack couldn't last forever. A few days later, his father appeared at the desk of the travel agency where Maile worked. After one glance at him, Maile knew why he had come.

"I'll come right to the point," Fred Grant said. "Is my son here?"

"Here?" she asked blandly, not wanting to betray Chad.

"I've heard that he's been home several days," Mr. Grant went on. "If that's true, you've seen him. I want you to talk with him, Maile. Chad's mother doesn't know; I want him home before she finds out. He does owe her some consideration. I'll leave it to you," he said, swiftly walking away. . . .

That afternoon, when Maile joined Chad at the beach cove, he greeted her with the news that they were going to an evening luau where his four friends would be entertaining.

"Can't," Maile said. "It's my grandmother's birthday."

"That's something to celebrate," he answered. "Am I invited?"

"Your father came by to see me," Maile said slowly. "He knows you're back. You have to go home sometime, Chad."

Chad had to agree. So that evening, instead of going to the luau, he drove his handsome white sports car, which Maile had been keeping for him, to Kaimuki, where his parents owned a beautiful house. It was almost dinnertime when Chad arrived. His parents were busy entertaining Mr. Gates' boss, Jack Kelman, who was visiting from California; so Ping Pong, the Chinese houseboy, was the first to see Chad. In a moment of excitement, Ping Pong drenched everyone present with a jubilantly waving garden hose as he announced Chad's arrival.

Mrs. Gates, a former Southern belle, flung herself at her

returning son ecstatically. "Chadwick! My boy! Oh, he looks so handsome in his uniform. Daddy, get the camera! Ping Pong, tell Cook we'll let her know when to start serving. We want to talk with our boy!"

After changing from his uniform to slacks and a bright shirt, Chad rejoined his parents and Mr. Kelman for cocktails. His mother was already planning a party to welcome him home—a party for their worthwhile friends, not those nasty beach bums she thought Chadwick had surely outgrown while he'd been away.

"We might as well have an understanding right off," Chad's mother told him. "You've come home to stay, and your life's going to be different. You'll associate with the finer element on this island, and take a responsible position in the Great Southern Hawaiian Fruit Company, and marry a nice girl of your own class and be a gentleman like your daddy."

"Do we have to discuss this now, Mother?" Chad asked quietly.

"Yes!" she insisted. "I don't want you wasting time with beach boys—or that native girl."

Chad stood up slowly. "I know what you expect of me. I've always known. I hoped that maybe after a hitch in the Army I could come back and do what you want. But now I know I can't. I've been back for five days, Mother," he went on. "I've been living at the beach shack and dreading the time I'd have to tell you that I am not going to work for the Great Southern Hawaiian Fruit Company."

"Home five days, and you didn't even call your mamma?" she wailed. As he started to stride from the room, she called, "Chadwick! You haven't had dinner!"

Chad's face was grim. "I'm not hungry now. Good night." He left the house.

Chad gunned the sports car's motor all the way to Haleiwa, where Maile was celebrating her grandmother's birthday. The warm, informal atmosphere of the celebration was like nothing he had ever known at home. He had taken with him a music box bought in Austria, and he presented it to the white-haired old lady with a courtly bow. She smiled wisely as she opened the package. "The light you kindle in my granddaughter's eyes is gift enough, Chad," she said. "Welcome home."

As they listened to the tinkling music box, Chad explained, "It's a European love song. But they're the same in any language."

"That's lovely, Chad," the old woman said.

He bent to kiss her withered cheek. "And so are you. . . ."

A day or so later, when he drove Maile out to their favorite hillside for a picnic, Chad tried to tell her how he felt.

"Boy, the difference between your family and mine!" he exclaimed. "I've never really felt about anything the way my folks do. If we're supposed to be what we make of ourselves—so far, I've goofed the job but good!"

"You did pretty well in the Army," she reminded him loyally.

"But that's over. If I'm going to make anything of myself, now is the time to get started," he declared. "I'm going to get a job, Maile—anything! Hawaii has a big future. I'm positive I can find something. But no red carpet to the pineapple plant, where everyone knows I'm the boss's son."

As he talked, excitement flowed through him. "I'm young, healthy, not too stupid." he said. "How about your business? The tourist industry is booming. I know every inch of these islands. I'd make a good tourist guide."

"You'd make a great one!" She beamed. "I'll put in a word—"

"I'll put in my own word," he cut in. "This mission is strictly solo, hear?"

"You're coming in loud and proud," she answered, her eyes shining. . . .

Mr. Chapman, who ran the tourist agency, seemed warm to Chad. But he was too vague a man to give any definite answer about a job. So Chad had to wait for his decision. But that evening, as Chad was dressing for the formal welcome-home party his mother was giving, Maile called to say that Chapman wanted him to start work immediately. An unexpected client had just shown up.

"It's a schoolteacher," Maile explained. "She wants to meet you tonight."

"I'll pick you up in ten minutes," Chad promised. And although his mother complained shrilly when he left the house, Chad went to meet his first client.

Maile accompanied him to the Hawaiian Village Hotel, where they were to meet the schoolteacher. Abigail Prentace was a shock to both of them. A smartly-groomed beauty in her late twenties, she was like no other teacher Chad could recall.

"I'm chaperoning four teen-age girls," she explained, studying him. "Frankly, I was expecting an older man."

Chad smiled. "I promise you I'll get a little older every day."

Miss Prentace was charmed. "What time do we start in the morning?"

"Nine o'clock," Chad suggested. "I'll meet you here."

"We'll be waiting," Miss Prentace said. "And thank you for coming by this evening."

Maile couldn't help squirming at the warm smile Chad exchanged with Miss Prentace. . . .

Chad's mother hadn't invited Maile to the party, but Chad took her there anyway. Mrs. Gates had condescendingly agreed to hire Chad's friends to provide music for her distinguished guests, but she'd firmly refused to have a native girl there.

When Maile arrived with Chad, his friends were doing their best to provide music that Mrs. Gates considered appropriate. The poor guys were really suffering as they played one waltz after another. But when they spotted the chill reception Chad's mother was giving Maile, they swung into a wild number to warm things up. Hurrying to join them, Chad sang the chorus. For once, the Gates house was rocking to the sound of youth.

The next morning, Chad was waiting in front of the Hawaiian Village when his five tourists emerged from the hotel. Miss Prentace was as attractive by day as she had seemed the night before. Her four charges were Patsy Simon, pleasant and chubby; Sandy Emerson, freckled and witty; Beverly Martin, dark and intellectual; and a sullen little blonde called Ellie Corbett.

Chad had brought an open touring car so they could see more of the country. His suggestion of starting the tour with the pineapple fields was agreeable to everyone but Ellie, who merely yawned in kittenish boredom. He took them on a scenic drive around Oahu, lecturing informally on the Island's customs and history, and pointing out spots of interest.

With deliberate insolence, Ellie switched on a transistor radio during Chad's lecture. Miss Prentace turned toward the back seat disapprovingly, and said, "That's quite rude, Ellie. Chad is talking."

But Chad began to sing. "We'll have lots of time for talk," he said. "Make it louder, *Duchess*."

By the time the car pulled up near a pineapple field, the girls were openly enchanted—all but Ellie, who hid a dawning interest with a sneer.

"This is one of our smaller fields," Chad told them, pointing.

"Small?" Sandy gasped. "It's bigger than Central Park in New York!"

"There are about seventeen thousand plants to each acre," Chad told them, leading the way into the field. He described the duties of the women picking the fruit and loading it onto conveyor belts to the waiting trucks. Then he took them to a little stand where they could sample fresh, cold slices of the fruit. The girls all ate eagerly—except Ellie, who had aloofly remained in the car.

Chad took a slice of pineapple over to Ellie and offered it to her. "I thought you might like a taste," he said.

"I don't," Ellie snapped.

"Are you always so bored?" he asked. "Or is it me?"

"Life is a bore," she answered. "I've had seventeen years of it. You're being paid to show us a good time, guide. When does it start?"

"The others seem to be enjoying themselves," he pointed out.

"Them?" she said scornfully. "It wasn't my idea to come over here with them. I've got two mothers and three fathers." For the first time, she smiled at him. "Just come up with some action, Mr. Guide," she said provocatively.

"What's your idea of action?" he asked calmly.

There was no mistaking her point as she purred, "What's yours?"

* * *

Ellie's disappointment withstanding, Chad's clients were so satisfied with their tour that, after two days, Miss Prentace informed Mr. Chapman they were extending their stay.

The second night, Chad took the girls to a *hukilau,* a native fishing party where everyone helps pull the nets of fish onto the beach. Flickering torches lit the water's edge, and dark figures deployed themselves along the net for the pull.

"This is like some fantasy land!" Miss Prentace breathed, admiring the scene. But Ellie Corbett, as usual, stood a little apart from the others and refused to be impressed.

At Ito's request, Chad wandered down the beach to hunt for firewood. Meanwhile, the girls were changing their clothes in a nearby shack, so that they, too, could wade out and help draw in the nets. Just as Chad came around a rocky outcropping, he heard Ellie's voice behind him.

"Want some help?" she asked, her eyes glowing.

Startled, he turned around and she pressed her lips to his. He drew back easily. "Congratulations, Duchess," he said. "Now go back with the others."

"Didn't you like it?" she whispered.

"Go back with the others and behave. I don't rob cradles."

With a taunting laugh, Ellie eeled out of her dress. She wore a brief bathing suit underneath. "Ever see anything like this in a cradle?" she asked.

"Come here," Chad ordered. And when she smilingly obeyed, he said, "Hold out your arms." He dumped his firewood into them, and said, "Now take that to O'Hara." Furious, she dropped the wood at his feet and flounced away.

Back on the beach, the *hukilau* crowd was gay and laughing. The nets came in full of leaping fish. And the fish fry that followed was a big success. The beach boys improvised a song in which Chad laughingly joined them. Later, he managed to steal a little time alone with Maile. . . .

The next morning, Mrs. Gates learned for the first time what Chad's new job was. She was shocked.

"Chadwick!" she exclaimed. "A common *employee?* When you could follow in your daddy's footsteps and wind up as a vice-president of Great Southern Hawaiian Fruit?"

"He just prefers to be a beach boy," Mr. Gates said.

"No, I don't," Chad protested. "But I *do* understand them. Not a care in the world—no worries about fruit ripening too soon, about the market, about labor problems. They live a happy life."

Chad's parents didn't understand what he meant, but Jack Kelman, who was still visiting, did. The head of the Hawaiian Fruit Company applauded Chad's comments, and even accepted Chad's invitation to join the group at a *luau* that night.

When Chad escorted Miss Prentace and her charges to the *luau* at The Polynesian, Jack Kelman went with them. Many other tourists attended the native feast, soaking up the Hawaiian atmosphere that the hotel was providing for them. Maile entertained the guests with an authentic hula dance. As they watched, Jack Kelman whispered to Chad, "And your mother doesn't know what you see in the girl! Boy!"

Abigail Prentace, who was close enough to overhear, raised her eyebrows.

When the dance was over and the feast began, Jack Kelman took the seat next to Miss Prentace. Maile sat with Chad. Further up the table, Ellie was pretending to a loud, red-necked tourist named Garvey that she was French. Though Garvey's wife was there, Ellie flirted outrageously.

While the roast pig was being carved, the visiting Mainlanders sampled poi, the natives' staple food; and like most newcomers, they thought it tasted like library paste. Rum drinks called Mai Tais were passed around, and after a little while, even Miss Prentace seemed a bit less proper. But Garvey was getting out of hand.

Chad saw what was building up between the big tourist and the provocative Ellie. He signaled the band to start playing. Then he asked Ellie for a dance and maneuvered her across the floor to his own empty seat beside Maile. Gently but firmly, he pushed Ellie into the seat and moved away. He dropped easily into the empty place beside Garvey.

"Dance with me, handsome," Mrs. Garvey giggled. "You wiggle like the natives."

"You dance with her, Mr. Garvey," Chad suggested amiably. "She's with you."

Garvey lurched to his feet. "I'm gonna dance with li'l Frenchy."

But before Garvey could stagger over to Ellie, Chad moved to stop him. "Excuse me, Mr. Garvey, but I think you should go home and sleep it off, sir."

"Get lost!" Garvey roared. "Or *you'll* be sleepin' it off!"

"Let's try to be gentlemen about this," Chad said, as Ellie watched in wide-eyed excitement.

Garvey threw the remains of his drink full in Chad's face. As Maile rushed to Chad's side to prevent a fight, the big tourist landed a glancing blow on Chad's head. Chad swung back, and the fight was on. Rooters for both contestants got into the battle themselves, swinging freely while the women screamed. In the distance, a police siren sounded.

Chad landed in the same jail cell with his four friends who had been playing at the *luau.* They harmonized sad, blues songs until the sun crept up. In the next cell, bawling at them to cork up their wailing, was Mr. Garvey, nursing a sore jaw and a swollen eye.

In the morning, Chad's father appeared at the police station to post bail, but he was extremely upset by the previous night's fracas.

"I went along with this tourist idea, because I thought it'd teach you some responsibility," he told Chad. "But after what's happened—"

His lecture was interrupted, however, by the sudden appearance of Chad's boss. Mr. Chapman was almost hysterical as he bustled into the police station, followed by Maile. After Chapman had fired Chad and threatened law suits all around, Maile quit her job with the travel agency. Defeated, Chad went home with his father.

Mrs. Gates rushed to embrace her returning son. "My baby!" she cried. "Home from the big house! Oh, Chadwick, I hope this doesn't get back home to Atlanta. A Gates in *jail!"*

"I'm sorry, Mother," Chad said. "But, honestly, it wasn't my fault."

"I know that, dear!" Mrs. Gates cooed. "It's your friends —mostly that Duval girl. She's the one to blame. She *was* there, wasn't she? And you got that job working in *her* tourist office."

Chad stiffened. "I won't listen to that kind of talk."

"Then listen to this," his father commanded. "You've tried it your way and made a mess of it. Now you'll try it our way. No more beach friends and no more harebrained jobs. If you remain in this house, you'll go along with it."

"Maybe the right thing to do is to get out of this house," Chad said slowly. He turned away and walked out. . . .

Chad found Maile and they headed to Waikiki together for a swim. After they had come out of the surf and settled down on the sand, Chad grinned at her. "This is the life!" he said. "How do you like being unemployed?"

"I don't," she answered simply.

"Well, how would you like being married?" he went on. Her dark eyes sought his. "Are you asking me?"

"Not until I know what the answer'll be. One more setback and I'll establish a record. First man ever to lose a home, a mother, a father, a job and a girl all in one day."

"Chad," she said, "don't quit! Bounce right back. There's so much you can do. Miss Prentace thought you were a good guide. She really blasted Mr. Chapman for firing you. And she canceled the rest of her tour."

"She's not taking the girls home, is she?" Chad asked.

"Unless she signs up with another guide service," Maile answered.

Chad suddenly jumped to his feet and gathered his gear. "Maile, you're a wonderful girl!" he exclaimed. "I'm going to bounce back, like you said."

"I'm glad I was able to help, Chad," Maile said, astonished. "But where are you going?"

"To see Miss Prentace," he said, with purpose behind his wide grin.

As Maile watched him leave, she said to herself, "Me and my big, fat brains! Miss Prentace!" she snorted jealously. . . .

Miss Prentace was amenable, even enthusiastic, about Chad's proposal—which was to take her party on a three-day visit to Kauai, loveliest of the outer islands in the

Hawaiian group. Chad telephoned Maile the good news.
He thought she sounded a trifle stiff as she agreed to book
their plane and hotel reservations, the job she had once
handled for Mr. Chapman; but with all he had to do
before the plane took off, Chad had very little time to
puzzle about the chill note in Maile's voice. Probably it
had only been his imagination, anyhow. By the time he
arrived in Kauai, he was deep into his new venture.

That first day, Chad took Miss Prentace and the girls
horseback riding over mountain trails that skirted water-
falls of breathtaking beauty. They got back to their hotel
barely in time to change for dinner. They were summoned
to the meal by a bronzed, young Polynesian who sounded
a blast on a conch shell. Other natives raced across the
hotel grounds to light torches among the trees.

"Their way of announcing chow's on," Chad said. "Im-
pressive, eh?"

After dinner, the weary travelers retired early. Equally
tired, Chad willingly went up to his own room. He was
already in his pajamas when there was an urgent knock at
his door. He hurried to answer it.

Ellie slid past the threshold, closing the door behind her.
She was wearing a filmy negligee, and smelled like a
perfume factory. Chad gaped at her. "This is off limits to
enlisted adolescents," he declared. "Back to your room!
Wow, that perfume! You better take a bath," he ordered.

But she sank alluringly to his bed. "I'm lonesome," she
murmured. "I want someone to talk to, and my roommates
are sleeping."

The jangle of his telephone interrupted her. Chad picked
up the receiver and heard the last voice he had expected to
—Maile's voice. She was right there in the hotel. She and
Jack Kelman had just flown over from Oahu on the late
plane. It seemed that neither of them had liked the idea
of having Chad chaperon Miss Prentace.

"Are you receiving visitors," Maile asked suggestively.

"I—I was just going to bed," Chad stammered. Catch-
ing the wicked leer on his uninvited guest's face, he
blushed. "Give me five minutes to dress," he told Maile,
"and I'll meet you in the bar." He hung up.

Ellie sighed seductively. "At least we have five minutes."

"I have five minutes. *Out!"* he commanded. "I've been in jail once on account of you."

Ellie smiled knowingly. "When you fought with Mr. Garvey at the party—I knew you cared."

"I wasn't fighting over you," Chad countered firmly. "You're a mixed-up kid who's too big for her britches. You're getting out of here."

"Wouldn't you rather hold me than Abigail?" she cooed.

"I'd like to hold you over a barbecue pit!" he retorted.

Then, to his horror, another knock sounded at his door.

This time, Chad's visitors were Patsy and Sandy. They had come looking for Ellie and had followed the trail of perfume down the hall. Ellie faced them furiously. Chad had to hold her back from physically attacking them.

"All of you go back to your room," he commanded. "I'll depend on Ellie to explain what happened and why you're here and—"

Incredibly, someone else was knocking. And this voice outside his door was cool and controlled.

"Abigail Prentace, Chad. May I see you?"

Frantically, he signaled his three young visitors to leave by way of the windows opening onto the hotel's back garden. When he opened his door, Miss Prentace came in looking lovelier and more elegant than ever.

"This is irregular, I know," she began, avoiding his gaze. "But—I was so restless I went out walking in the moonlight. It can be intoxicating."

"That's why I never touch the stuff," Chad gulped warily.

"I had to speak to someone—and now I don't quite know why." She was twisting a handkerchief nervously. "I hope you don't mind, but I just have to talk about this. Chad, I'm not as young as you might think I am; not old, but older than you. Not that that should make a difference," she added hastily.

"Oh!" A dreadful suspicion was dawning in him. "I mean, I guess not."

"I've been a schoolteacher for—well, never mind how long," she went on. "For at least six years, I've taken a vacation every summer alone, looking for—well, romance.

The first few years, I suppose I was frightened. I missed whatever chances there might have been. Later on, I was too selective. And still later, *men* were too selective. But I'll get quickly to my point. When Miss Thackery asked me to chaperon the girls on this trip, I accepted eagerly. I thought it would insulate me against the frustration. But instead, Chad—it's happened."

He was almost afraid to ask. "What's happened?"

"I've found romance," she said, and walked toward him. "Chad, you're a sensible person. Tell me the truth. Am I—" She broke off. The door which had been silent was being pounded upon again.

Sandy and Patsy were back. "Ellie's gone!" they announced. "In a jeep! She stole it, just now, and drove off like a maniac. She went—that way!"

"Crazy kid!" Chad grated. "I'll get a car and see if I can catch her."

Minutes later, he was roaring down the road in a hotel station wagon. Ellie had a good head start, and Chad kept looking from side to side for some sign of her. He slowed up at a dark side road and glimpsed the jeep. It was smashed against a tree, just a brief way past the turnoff. He braked in the side road and ran to the wreck, almost afraid to examine it.

But the car was empty. He saw one of Ellie's ridiculous shoes on the trail to the river bank and followed the path with long strides. He found her by the water's edge, dripping with water and sobbing. He called her name softly.

"Leave me alone!" she cried. "Don't touch me! I hate you!"

Gently, Chad draped his robe about her shaking shoulders.

"I—I tried to drown myself," she sobbed. "I can't even do *that* right. Nobody cares about me, whether I live or die—you, my mother, my father."

"Nobody *seems* to care," he said. "Maybe because you don't seem to care about yourself. Start liking yourself. Then others will, too."

"There's nothing to like," she declared.

"There's a lot to like, if you'll stop being something you're not."

"Then why does everybody hate me?" Ellie wailed. "Even you. You threw me out of your room. But you didn't throw Abigail out!"

So *that* was what had started this hysteria! Chad spoke sternly. "What you need, young lady, is a good old-fashioned spanking. Eleanor, I'm about to prove that someone cares enough about you to give you that."

"You wouldn't dare!" she exclaimed. But Chad already had her over his knees.

By breakfast time, a few hours later, the air had cleared considerably. Everyone, even Ellie, was in a bright mood for the day's riding. Everyone, except Maile. At breakfast, she scarcely spoke a word; and afterward, she stormed out of the dining room just as Jack Kelman appeared.

Chad was stunned at the way Abigail smiled when Jack took her hand.

"This is what I was trying to tell you last night, Chad," she explained.

The truth dawned on him shatteringly. "You mean *I* wasn't— You mean, it's Uncle Jack!" he cried. "Congratulations, both of you! That's great!"

"I've got *my* girl, fella," Kelman chuckled. "But from what I just saw of *yours*—She was headed for her bungalow, Number Four," he added helpfully.

Chad ran all the way to Maile's cabin, but when he burst in, she was already packing. She eyed him stonily, and said, "Go find Miss Prentace, Lover Boy!"

"Maile," he said desperately, "I can't even try to explain last night. But I love you and there's nothing between Miss Prentace and me. She and Uncle Jack—"

"You can do better than that!" Maile cut in sharply. "You must think I'm a fool!"

Disconsolate, Chad walked out, slamming the door behind him. But he had barely left the room, when Maile glanced out her window and happened to see Abigail Prentace strolling hand in hand across the garden with Jack Kelman. With a wild little sob, Maile raced from her bungalow to find Chad. . . .

Early that same evening, Chad's father arrived at the hotel in response to a summons from Kelman, who was, after all, the president of Great Southern Fruit. Chad was waiting to talk to his father

"You want me to work for Great Southern, Dad," he said. "I want to be in business for myself. But I've figured a way for me to do both. You have over three hundred salesmen scattered over the states," he went on, "and once a year, there's a sales meeting in Atlanta. Every salesman and your district managers all show up. Think how much *more* they'd all look forward to a trip to Hawaii."

"I think the boy's got something," Kelman said.

"Bring them over here," Chad suggested. "Let them see how we grow and process the fruit, and they'll go back to sell like they've never sold before. Give special incentive trips, a week's all-expense vacation in the Islands!"

Kelman nodded enthusiastically. "And we'll put you in charge."

"No," Chad said. "I'm going in business for myself— with Maile. I gave Great Southern this idea. I expect them to give us the tourist business."

"Gates and Duval Travel Service," Maile said, standing at his side. "Has a nice sound."

"Just—Gates of Hawaii," Chad said, drawing her to him. "*Gates* is plural, of course. And that, *wahine,* is a proposal."

Which was why Chad's mother, accompanied by the Duval family, flew over to Kauai on the next plane, to attend the wedding. And it was also why a great many Mainland employees of Great Southern Fruit will soon be basking under the sun of Hawaii.

Adapted from the HAL WALLIS VISTAVISION Production
Released through PARAMOUNT PICTURES
Copyright 1961 by PARAMOUNT PICTURES CORP.
Directed by NORMAN TAUROG
Produced by HAL WALLIS
Screenplay by HAL KANTER
Based on the story THE HAWAIIAN BEACH BOY
by ALLAN WEISS
Color by TECHNICOLOR
Adapted for SCREEN STORIES by JEAN FRANCIS WEBB

CAST

Toby Kwimper .... ELVIS PRESLEY   Alicia Claypoole .. JOANNA MOORE
Holly Jones .... ANNE HELM   Carmine .... JACK KRUSCHEN
Pop Kwimper ..... ARTHUR O'CONNELL
Nick ..... SIMON OAKLAND

FOLLOW THAT DREAM

■ H. Arthur King was feeling mighty set up about things. The new road was as smooth as glass, thanks to the competence of the State Supervisor of Highways—himself. The weather was behaving as Gulf Coast weather should, and everything was in order for the dedication ceremonies—with one exception.

At first, King couldn't believe it when he saw a family of squatters settled in on the filled land beside his new highway. But when he drove up for a closer look, there they were in all their squalid glory—a blight on the face of his public betterment project. There was even a line of laundry running from the family's jalopy to a recently-built lean-to.

The Kwimpers from Cranberry County, Arkansas, explained that they were there on a little vacation trip. The creaky-looking one was Pop Kwimper. The younger man was his son, Toby.

"Teddy and Eddy, here," Toby said, indicating the eight-year old twins, "they're sort of fourth cousins. When their folks died, we just took 'em in. They don't cost us much, on account we collect Aid for Dependent Children. That teen-ager, she's Holly Jones. Used to be our baby sitter. Then her folks got killed in an auto accident, so she kind of stayed on with us, too." He pointed to three-year-old Ariadne. "The little girl, she was orphaned just last year. Her name's—"

"All right," King snapped, "you're a self-appointed orphanage. Now, will you kindly get that mess loaded?" he said, gesturing at the family's belongings strewn about.

Toby started to comply, but Pop intervened, declaring, "He can't load nothing. He's on Total Disability for a bad back."

"What do *you* collect?" King asked him. "Unemployment Compensation?"

"Lately," said Toby, "he's been favoring Relief."

"All wards of the government, eh?" King grunted. "Well, in fifteen minutes, the Governor's going to drive along this road and dedicate it. And he's not going to be looking at any mess like this!"

King was wrong. The Governor certainly would see the mess, because he and his cavalcade were already coming down the highway. His car stopped near the desecrated area.

"What seems to be the trouble, King?" he asked.

"These people—we'll get rid of them right away," King stammered. He spotted a trooper. "Sergeant, arrest these people."

But Pop Kwimper ambled over to the official car. "If you appointed this man, Mr. Governor," he said, "you'd better put him straight. Man like you must know the law; and it's on the record, now, you was present at this violation of citizens' rights."

"Always happy to see justice done," boomed the Governor, glancing back at his constituents in the cars behind. "Are you a student of the law?" he asked Pop.

"Enough to know nobody can chase us, on account none of us is running," Pop answered. "We're homesteadin' from the end of the thoroughfare to the water's edge."

"Homesteaders, eh?" The Governor turned uncertainly to his aide. "Any public land can be homesteaded, can't it?"

"Yes, sir. If they put up a roof and stay on it for six months, they own it."

"Well, there's our roof," said Pop, pointing to the lean-to they'd put up.

Nodding, the Governor addressed King. "Respect private property at all times. That's the law. Justice has been rendered. Let's move along." The cavalcade started off again.

King was livid. "There are other laws," he reminded the Kwimpers. "One, for instance, provides that none of you receive any more pension benefits from your home state. You're residents here now, and I shall so advise the proper authorities." He got into his truck and raced away.

"Funny," Pop sighed after Mr. King had left. "I was just gettin' ready to give him back his land when he turned nasty. Now, I dunno what to do." He wandered off to think about it.

"Cross your fingers," Holly whispered to Toby, hoping Pop would decide to stay. Like Pop always said, girls were natural born nesters.

Toby didn't see anything wrong with that, but the Kwimpers already had a house in Cranberry County. Then Holly explained that she was a Jones and not a Kwimper, so the other house didn't really belong to her. If any other girl'd said that, Toby would've gotten real scared, because the girl might've had other notions that went with wanting a house—like wanting to get married. But seeing it was just Holly, he didn't get worked up about it.

Holly was nineteen and trying to make out like she was already a woman, but Toby knew better. Around real women, he had to rely on his education. Soon as one of them started pestering Toby, he had to close his eyes and do the multiplication table in his head. No need to do all that, though, when it was just Holly.

"Oh Toby," Holly said, "I want to stay so much."

"All right," he promised, feeling perfect safe. "I'll fix it."

"How?" she asked.

"Ain't you learned how to handle a contrary man like Pop?" Toby grinned. "Watch. Pop," he called, "we gotta get outta here."

"Who says?" Pop demanded.

"Holly and me, we don't believe you can get the best of a man as big a shakes as a highway supervisor," Toby explained.

Pop looked sort of riled for a minute. Then he said doggedly, "We're staying! We're homesteadin' and we ain't moving on till I say so." With that settled, he drove off to Gulf City to get some of the things they'd be needing. . . .

When Pop got back, he had a telegram from the government back home. "That fellow King didn't waste no time gettin' us cut off," he told Toby and Holly.

"We'll make do, Mr. Kwimper," Holly declared.

Toby went off to fish from the bridge that spanned the inlet near their beach. He was using a rod one of the twins had made. Just as he hooked into a whopper, a man drove up, and asked, "What have you got there? A tarpon?"

"Looks like," Toby said. "Too big to catch with the diaper pin I'm usin'. I'm trying to get rid of him jest as hard as he's trying to get rid of me."

"Trying to get rid of him?" The man scrambled out of his car, all excited. "I've been paying sixty-five bucks a day for charter boats and I never hooked one like that. I'd give twenty dollars to play him."

"You're welcome," Toby said, handing him the make-shift rod.

Well, the tarpon finally got away, of course. But the man, whose name was Endicott, didn't seem to mind. "Never had so much fun in my life," he told Toby. "Here's your twenty."

Toby shook his head in refusal. "All I done was lend you a public fish."

Suddenly, Holly stepped up. "Thank you, sir," she said, taking the money.

"I know what you was thinking," she told Toby, after Endicott had driven off. "Shame to take money from a crazy man, but we need it."

"You hear what that fella said about sixty-five dollars a day to fish?" Toby asked. "Funny, ain't it? There's fish right here for free, and free bait all around."

Holly looked thoughtful. If folks were loco enough to spend money just to fish, why not humor them? A half-hour later, she was in Gulf City buying up tackle and spreading the word around about the plentiful tarpon. In no time at all, the Kwimpers were in business.

"Ninety-two bucks in one day!" Pop exclaimed. "That's what comes of stickin' up fer yer rights, not runnin' away like a scalded dog."

"You're right, Pop," Toby said, winking at Holly. "I was wrong."

Yup, the fishing business had been going real good. As a result, the Kwimper place was fixed up nice as anything by now. The lean-to had a second room, plus a porch with a roof of webbed palm leaves. There was even a separate john room. "Can't nobody fret a family that's got its own private john," Pop always said.

But Holly still wasn't satisfied. According to her, they needed a dock.

"What for?" asked Toby.

"So we can tie up rowboats," she explained. She pointed

to the crowded bridge. "Right now, our customers are fishing from property that belongs to the State Highway. How long before that Mr. King puts a stop to it?"

"Be dammit, she's right," said Pop.

"I talked to some folks," Holly went on, "and it figures we could get used rowboats and build a dock for about two thousand dollars. And there's a good chance we can borrow money from a bank."

Pop looked dumfounded. "You mean they jest lend money for the askin'?" If that was how it was, he demanded, why all the shilly-shallying?

Accordingly, the next day, Toby paid a visit to the bank in Gulf City. . . .

At first, there was a little mix-up at the bank as to why Toby was there. When the teller asked him what he wanted, he simply answered, "Money!" And, the next thing he knew, somebody was yelling: "Holdup!"

Luckily for Toby, Mr. Endicott showed up just then. Seemed he was a vice-president there at the bank, and he identified Toby as a friend of his. Not that this made borrowing two thousand dollars quite as easy as Holly had made out. There was still the matter of something called security.

But, as Endicott pointed out to the rest of the bank people there was also something called honesty—like when a man refuses to take twenty dollars for a public fish. So they finally agreed to make what they called a "character loan."

"We do it now and then," Endicott explained to Toby, "but not enough for the good of our souls."

Weeks later, with two thousand dollars' worth of equipment installed, the Kwimper homestead had attracted so much attention that the local newspaper carried the story: BAY DEVELOPMENT OPEN TO HOMESTEADING. NEW ENTERPRISE TO CATER FOR FISHING PARTIES. "The exact status of this newly created development is a bit of a puzzle," the paper reported. "It cannot be restricted by municipal or county ordinances, as it lies outside their jurisdiction."

"That means the city and the county ain't got the say

on us," Pop explained, when he read the story. "That's how come we're gittin' neighbors," he added, indicating several parked trailers. "Folks can stand only so much government. Then they bust out fer any place where they ain't none."

As he was speaking, the biggest trailer the Kwimpers had ever seen pulled into the area, accompanied by two cars full of men.

"Kinda funny," said Toby, "all them fellers livin' in one trailer."

Pop shrugged. "No business of our'n," he declared.

But it was soon evident that the Kwimpers couldn't ignore their newest neighbors. By nightfall, the trailer was jumping with music, and with loud cries of: "Come on, Little Joe;" "Seven away" and stuff like that.

"Maybe we should pay 'em a call," Holly suggested. "I don't feel right, acting standoffish to neighbors."

So Toby agreed to accompany her on a visit to the trailer, but it wasn't easy, being friendly to the newcomers. As Toby and Holly approached the trailer, two men suddenly blocked their way in the darkness.

"Where do you think you're going, punk?" one man snarled, reaching for Toby. In the dark, his hand grabbed the hot pot of coffee Toby had been bringing them. The man let out a tremendous howl, and with that, the trailer door flew open, illuminating a third man, who rushed up, gun-in-hand.

"We're jest trying to be neighborly," Toby explained.

The man put away the gun. "You're from next door, huh? Come in and meet the boss," he said, ushering them into the trailer.

The man with the gun was named Carmine, and the boss was called Nick. Both of them looked like those characters Holly had seen in gangster movies, but Toby didn't reckon they could help that.

Anyhow, as it turned out, Nick and Carmine weren't going to be neighbors for good. They just happened to be stopping off there on their way to where they were going.

"Then you're not jest trying to get away from the government?" Toby asked innocently.

Nick gave him a sharp look. "What was that?"

"Toby thinks maybe you saw that piece in the paper," Holly put in quickly. "About there being no government out here."

"It says the state built the land," Toby added, "so the county's got no say about it."

"This on the level?" Nick looked real pleased. "Oh, baby! This is the sort of deal that comes once in a life-time."

"But what about after we file our claim?" Holly asked. "When we've lived here six months, we can claim the land. That'll make it part of the county."

Nick frowned. "That land claiming don't sound like a good idea."

"I bet it would if Pop explained it to you," said Toby.

Nick decided he'd better pay Pop a visit. But Toby could have told him he was wasting his time, offering Pop two thousand dollars for the land.

"We already got two thousand in it," Pop told Nick, "not counting our work."

"I'll make it five," said Nick.

When Pop didn't even answer, Toby explained, "We ain't fixin' to sell."

"I'm willin' to go a little higher," Nick said, "but don't push too hard."

"Don't you hear good?" Pop grumbled. "We ain't fixin' to sell, so there's no use talkin'."

"Well," Nick sighed. "I *tried* to do it nice."

In a short time, the lean-to had been replaced by a shack, and the place was really beginning to look like something. And all the while, the Kwimpers hadn't heard a peep out of Mr. King. But Toby knew that, sooner or later, King would be coming up with something.

Well, what he finally came up with was a ripsnorter: Miss Alicia Claypoole, State Welfare Supervisor.

At first glance—with her eyeglasses and her hair pulled back and all—Miss Claypoole looked sort of like a school-teacher. Only, as it turned out, she wasn't at all like any of the teachers Toby'd ever had.

He was willing to answer her questions all right—seeing

as how the Welfare Department was so interested in him,
but he couldn't see why they had to go into the woods for
her to ask them.

Besides, they were pretty silly questions, topped off by
a word-association test. In that scientific endeavor, Miss
Claypoole said a word and then Toby was supposed to say
the first word that popped into his head.

The first test word she gave him was: *"Hurt."*

"Ow!" Toby answered.

Miss Claypoole gave him a funny look, then continued:
"Help."

"Help," he answered.

"No, don't repeat the word," she said. "Just say what it
suggests."

"Nobody yells, 'Help!' " Toby explained. "They always
yell 'Help, help!' "

"I see," she said thoughtfully.

Well, things went along like that till she came to the
word *love*.

"Thirty," Toby answered promptly.

"You think love begins at thirty?" she asked him, bright-
ening.

"No, ma'am. Love is when you ain't got any points.
Like in tennis."

Miss Claypoole gave a little sigh. "Now, here's the last
word: *sex.*"

Toby knew the answer to that. "One times one is one.
One times two is two. One times—"

"What a fascinating answer!" Miss Claypoole pulled
off her glasses and loosened her hair. "Simple, primitive,
beautiful. What you just did was express the realization
that, with one person, sex is a sterile thing. But, as soon
as there are two, sex becomes productive."

The next thing Toby knew, Miss Claypoole was kissing
him. Looked like she aimed to keep on with it, too. Only,
just then Holly came rushing up.

"Toby, you've got to come home and collect bait," she
told him as she glared at Miss Claypoole. "Somebody
opened the bait box."

"Now, who would'a done a fool think like that?" Toby
murmured.

Miss Claypoole glared at Holly and said. "Holly and I know, *don't* we?"

Back at the homestead. Nick had decided to let things ride for the present—and they were riding high. Las Vegas on wheels! Games continued in the trailer every night from sundown till sunup. If their less sporty neighbors didn't like all the noise—well, it was a free country.

Too darned free, in the opinion of the other residents. There ought to be a law, they said. So they got together and elected Toby as sheriff of the community.

That was okay with Nick, just as long as Toby remembered to behave like a good little sheriff. But when Toby visited the trailer one night and suggested they shut the joint down at eleven, Nick saw they'd have to set him straight.

"You don't really want to be no sheriff, Toby," Nick told him. "Terrible things happen to sheriffs."

"Like what?" Toby asked.

Nick motioned to a couple of his henchmen. "Blackie, you and Al tell him."

"The full treatment?" Al asked.

"The full treatment," Nick said, leaving quickly. Violence gave him indigestion.

When Nick returned to pick up the pieces a while later, his two men were out cold.

"They were showing me how I shouldn't get hurt," Toby explained. "I sure wish they'd wake up, so I could apologize." With a regretful sigh, he strolled into the gambling room. At the sight of his badge, somebody hollered, "Raid!" and the panic was on. Three minutes later, the place was empty, and Toby went on his way.

Immediately, Nick picked up the phone. "Operator, get me long-distance."

"What are you doing?" asked Al, who was beginning to get his strength back.

"I'm calling for some people who really know their business," Nick said disgustedly. . . .

The four hoods Nick had hired drove in the following night.

"The joker ain't home," Nick told them. "Blackie saw him walking down the highway about twenty minutes ago. He's with a broad." He gave the men some money and they drove off along the highway.

"That's that," Nick said, ready to hit the sack. But Carmine had another idea.

"We're going fishing," he told Nick.

"You nuts?" Nick gasped.

Carmine pointed to the Kwimper place. "Rent a couple of fishing poles, and the old joker shows how to make with the bait. You like that for an alibi?"

Nick grinned. "I like it splendid."

As Toby and Holly ambled along the highway, a speeding car careened toward them, just missed and sped on.

"Darn fools!" Toby exclaimed. "They must be drunk."

"Maybe they were *trying* to run you down," Holly said.

"Now, jest 'cause they're drunk don't mean they're ornery."

Several yards ahead, the car had backed off the road in the process of turning around, and its rear wheels were spinning in the sand.

Toby pushed Holly toward the woods. "Honey, you run up there for a spell. I gotta teach them drunks a lesson."

A few minutes later, he came running back to Holly. "Man, are they ever drunk," he said. "One of 'em tried to shoot me. Must be on a hunting trip. The car's full of guns."

"They're coming after you," Holly murmured fearfully.

"I know. Guess I'll have to sober 'em up."

Dashing further into the woods, he picked up a log and tossed it into a nearby tree. Then, yelling, "Here I am, fellers," he ducked off in the opposite direction.

There was a series of gunshots and a lot of scrambling around, but Holly couldn't really tell what was happening, until one of the hunters cried, "He's got my gun!"

A moment later, she heard Toby yell, "Fellers, you're surrounded. Now, if you want to keep on making trouble, I give you one guess who's gonna be sorry."

"Look, Mac," one of them whined, "it was all a mistake. You quit and we'll quit, Mac."

"I ain't quittin' till I get them guns off you," Toby called back.

There were several dull thuds as the remaining guns were tossed away. Then Toby ordered, "Turn to your right and keep walkin'."

"Wait a minute, you're not gonna leave us in this jungle, are you?" one of the men called out.

"You gotta sober up somewhere," Toby answered. . . .

When Toby and Holly returned to the house, he spied somebody sneaking around the porch.

"Might be Mr. Kwimper," Holly said.

Toby shook his head and pointed to the bridge. "Pop's up there with Nick and Carmine."

While Holly waited, he went up to the porch for a look-see. When he came back, he was toting a package and a kerosene can. It was only Nick's man Blackie on the porch, he reported.

"What was he doing?" Holly asked.

"Dunno. He was carrying this stuff. Must belong to Nick," Toby reasoned.

"I'll drop them next door," Holly offered, and away she went. Toby joined the others on the bridge.

Nick and Carmine looked as if they didn't feel so well when they saw Toby. Then Holly appeared and told Nick about the package and the jug of kerosene.

"I took them back to your place," she said.

"You *what?*" Nick exploded.

"Right inside the door," she said. "You can find them easily."

"I can, huh?" Nick looked at his wrist watch. "Ten, nine, eight, seven . . ."

When he came to zero, there was a real explosion over at the trailer. Nick and Carmine made a dash for their car.

"I'm just as glad they're going'," said Pop. "Never did cotton to 'em."

Toby agreed. "Ain't nice to say, but I don't truly believe them fellers was honest."

Things were pretty peaceful for quite a spell after that. Then, one afternoon, Holly came high-tailing back from town in a fry.

"They took the kids!" she yelled. "I went to the school

to pick up the twins—I had Ariadne with me. They wouldn't let the twins go, and they picked up Ariadne, too."

"Who did?" Pop asked.

"A State Trooper. He said he was taking the kids to the Welfare Department."

"That means that Claypoole woman had somethin' to do with it," Pop said, and he was right. Before long, Miss Claypoole herself showed up, along with the highway fellow, King.

"The children are under State Welfare custody by court order of Judge Waterman," she said. "Judge Waterman respects my opinion and it is my opinion that you are not fit people to raise children."

Then King told them that the court hearing to decide custody was to be at nine the next morning. Unless, of course, all of a sudden they decided to go back to Arkansas and forget about homesteading.

"Jest like that, huh?" Pop sneered. "We're supposed to up and walk away from our property?"

King insisted it wasn't their property. "As a public servant, I must tell you again—this whole area was put in for the public's benefit."

"Be dammit, how come you think people is one thing and the public's another thing?" Pop stormed. You could see that Pop was getting ready for the court fight by practicing on King.

In court the next morning, Judge Waterman started out right nice. "Since this is a hearing and not a trial," he said, "let's keep it simple. Miss Claypoole, why don't you start off?"

"Your Honor," she began, "the Kwimper adults are immoral, defiant of authority, suspected of illicitly obtaining funds from government agencies, and they are also known to have associated with gangsters. As part of our proof that the Kwimpers are unfit to raise children, I will ask Mr. King to report his dealings with the family."

King described how the Kwimpers ruined his highway and deprived six million taxpayers of seeing an empty roadside. Then Miss Claypoole took over again.

"An unmarried girl," she said delicately, "lives with the

Kwimpers in a relationship I would not care to explore."

"Oh!" Holly gasped. "What a terrible thing to say."

"One final point," Miss Claypoole added, ignoring Holly. "As a qualified psychologist, I gave Toby Kwimper, a word-association test designed to reveal his basic motivations."

"What did the test reveal?" the Judge asked.

"Attitudes that shocked the entire Welfare Department. I submit a copy to the Court."

Judge Waterman studied the report like it was one of those books they don't let people read in Boston. Then he turned to Pop, and asked, "Well, what have you to say to all this?"

"Judge," Pop answered, "we'd like to hash this over for a while, if it's okay with you."

"By all means," the Judge consented.

Pop had been getting madder by the minute and it was clear that this wouldn't help any. So he figured he'd better let Toby do the speaking up for them. Toby stepped forward.

"I'll probably make a mess of things," he told the Judge, "but Holly and Pop got faith in me, so here goes. Now, Judge, would it be legal-like if first I was to answer things that was said again' me?"

The Judge nodded.

"About my back, then," Toby continued. "They told me at Fort Dix I strained my back in a judo lesson. I told the docs it warn't nothing, but they said I had to go on Total Disability. Well, I'm willin' to admit a doctor might know more'n me, so I been takin' the checks ever since."

Toby went on to explain about the gangsters, saying he certainly could prove the accusations were false. Then he added, "If I was the judge in charge of decidin' who should bring up three nice kids, I'd jest be wonderin' was Pop a good man and was Holly a good woman. You can ask the twins about Holly. I know they're jest kids, but kids know who they love, and who taught 'em everything they learnt. Yes sir," he concluded, "it were a lucky day for the Kwimpers when Pop took Holly Jones in."

Miss Claypoole gave an ugly snort and said. "I've already pointed out why he'd be prejudiced on that point, Your Honor."

"Don't like to say this, Jedge," Pop put in: "it ain't fittin' to speak again' a woman's good name. For the sake of the kids, though, I got to. *Hell got no fury like a woman scorned!*" he blurted, and then fell silent.

The Judge encouraged him to say more.

Pop braced himself. "That Miss Claypoole went after Toby like he came with green coupons," he declared. "Aleanin' on him and akissin' him, and when he paid her never-mind, she set out to give us what hell ain't got no fury like!"

The Judge turned to Toby. "Do you support what your father just said?"

"I'd ruther not answer that, Judge," Toby said.

"Briefly, then," the Judge persisted. "Did Miss Claypoole ever kiss you?"

"Yes," Toby admitted unhappily.

"Your Honor," Miss Claypoole cut in sharply. "May I remind you of my findings in this man's word-association test?"

"Got anything to say about that?" the Judge asked Toby.

"Yes, sir," Toby answered. "Could I say it in private?"

With the Judge's consent, Toby went up and whispered in his ear. Then the Judge told Miss Claypoole, "Counsel points out that his test has nothing to do with the case. It's his father who is the children's presumptive guardian."

"Then let his father take the test," Miss Claypoole declared. "I have one right here."

"A good idea. Please step up, Mr. Kwimper."

"Darn fool," Pop muttered as he passed Toby.

"Ready?" asked Miss Claypoole, when pads and pencils had been supplied. *"Court . . . child . . . moon . . . election . . . house.* Those will be sufficient, Your Honor."

"Then we'll proceed," the Judge said. He read off the first of the answers. *"Court . . . crime."*

"That," said Miss Claypoole, "is the simple-minded response of a criminal nature."

Judge Waterman gave her a funny look. Then he read: *"Child . . . labor."*

"Obvious. He thinks of children in terms of exploiting their labor."

"*Moon . . . shine,*" the Judge went on.

"An illegal liquor that is drunk by illiterate, irresponsible alcoholics."

"How about *Shine on Harvest Moon?*" the Judge inquired. "That's a song. What's it got to do with alcoholics?"

Miss Claypoole gave him a high-and-mighty smile. "I'm afraid you don't understand. Any qualified psycholo—"

"*You're* the one who doesn't understand," thundered the Judge. "Because those were not Kwimper's answers. *They were mine.* That was counsel's suggestion," he added.

In conclusion, Judge Waterman said, "This Court has had a remarkable experience today. It has had the privilege of listening to an honest man. It has heard the history of a little settlement that overcame hardships and every kind of legalistic and financial difficulty. It is gratifying to know that the spirit of the pioneer is still functioning today. *Case dismissed. . . .*"

It was as pretty an evening as a fellow could ask for Toby was sitting on the bridge, just sort of taking it all in, when Holly came over from the house. She was all decked out in a new dress and her hair was fixed some special way.

"Looks real nice," he told her. "Too bad there ain't anyone around to see yuh."

"Isn't it," Holly sighed. "Toby," she said, "what did that Claypoole woman do to make you kiss her?"

"Aw, Holly. *You* know," he muttered.

"No, I don't. Answer me."

"Well—she sort of run her hand over my forehead."

Holly started stroking his face. "Like this?"

"Not so much like you was ironing shirts. Softer—that's it."

"And then?"

"She had her hair loose."

Holly shook her hair and leaned over so he could run his hands through it. He had to admit it sure felt soft and tingly against his fingers. All of a sudden, Holly was kissing him. But just as suddenly, she pulled away.

"Toby!" she exclaimed. "You're doing that darned *times* table."

"That's right." He grinned. "But y'know somep'n? I never got to the twelveses so fast."

"Twelve times twelve is a hundred and forty-four," she murmured.

"I know, Holly," he said. "What frets me is what comes after the twelves."

"Me, Toby. *Me.*"

Darned if Holly wasn't right.

Adapted from the MIRISCH COMPANY PANAVISION
   Production
Released through UNITED ARTISTS CORP.
Directed by GORDON DOUGLAS
Produced by DAVID WEISBERT
Screen play by CHARLES LEDERER
Based on the novel PIONEER, GO HOME!
   by RICHARD POWELL
Color by DELUXE
Adapted for SCREEN STORIES by MARJORIE BAILEY

CAST

Walter Gulick ...... ELVIS PRESLEY   Rose Grogan .... JOAN BLACKMAN

Willy Grogan .... GIG YOUNG   Lew Nyack ... CHARLES BRONSON

Dolly Fletcher .... LOLA ALBRIGHT   Lieberman .... NED GLASS

KID GALAHAD

■ Cream Valley was a lovely little resort town in the Catskill Mountains. It had a few stores, a couple of small churches, a gasoline station, and a post office; but its main industry was the care and entertainment of vacationers at its two mountain hotels. It did have a third hotel, called Grogan's Gaelic Gardens, but the villagers were not inclined to brag of it. Compared to Shangri-La-Lieberman or Levine's Loch Lovely, it was a dump. Its signboard proclaimed it to be "The Cradle of Champions Since 1917," but the villagers knew Grogan's was just a training camp for a few punch-drunk meatballs and a cooling-off joint for hot Broadway racketeers.

At least, that was Grogan's reputation the day Kid Galahad arrived—dead broke and looking for a job after three years as a private in the Army motor pool. And he wasn't Kid Galahad then. Just plain Walter Gulick, whose only assets were a magic gift with a monkey wrench and an even more magic touch with a guitar. Still to be discovered were such hidden assets as a forged-steel jaw, a cast-iron rib cage, and a steam-hammer right.

Walter entered Grogan's by way of its Social Room. The overstuffed furniture was less stuffed than in its days of glory, but to Walter, it looked familiar and comfortable. Then, too, his first impression was considerably enriched when he saw the social director—a certain Dolly Fletcher, whose own upholstery had conspicuously suffered no deterioration.

"It's nice," said Walter, looking around with approval. "It's real nice here."

Dolly looked around, seeking the source of his approval. "Where?"

His gesture included the whole sagging Social Room. "Here."

"That's what I thought you said," she declared, still disbelieving her ears. She looked at him more closely. He was still in uniform, a crap game having separated him from his money and civilian clothes the same day he was separated from the Army. Her first thought was that he must have been shell-shocked. Her second thought was that his delusions had been induced by hunger.

"When's the last time you had a meal?" she asked.

"It's not really like that," he began.

"Don't apologize," she interrupted. "One thing about keeping chickens, you never run out of breakfast. Come on." And she led him into the kitchen.

The cook at Grogan's Gardens was a huge ex-pug who had discovered it was a lot easier to crack eggs than the jaws of his opponents. He ruled his ancient, wood stove like a fighter in the ring. His giant fists threatened instant disaster to any egg that dared splutter back when he fried it.

"Think you can find any food for the Army, Maynard?" Dolly asked, indicating Walter.

"Why? Things that tough at the Pentagon?" Maynard took a look at the starved expression on Walter's face, and decided they were. With a dainty gesture, he squashed a couple of eggs between thumb and forefinger, dropped them into a skillet.

Dolly started to sit down at the kitchen table, and Walter leaped to her assistance, pulling out a chair. Such gallantry so stunned her that she remained half seated in mid-air before collapsing with a jolt. "Well, *thank* you," she finally gasped. "I hate to say how long it's been since anyone did *that* for me."

"A captain I knew in the Army, he used to do it for his wife all the time," said Walter. "You got everything so nice and homey here, I was wondering if you was—" He hesitated.

"Mrs. Grogan?" she asked. "Well, not yet. I'm Mr. Grogan's fiancée." She had to struggle on that last word. "How do you happen to know Mr. Grogan?"

"I don't," said Walter, frankly admitting that he had dropped by in hope of finding a job. "Funny thing, though," he added, "almost all my life I've wanted to come here."

"Here? *Cream Valley?*" Once more, Dolly could scarcely believe her ears.

"I was born in Cream Valley, right here in this town," he explained.

"You're kidding. Nobody was ever born here," Dolly scoffed. "Only Rip Van Winkle."

"My mother and father are buried here," Walter said. "I was only fourteen months old when they passed away.

I grew up in Lowbridge, Kentucky, with an aunt. All the time I was workin' in the motor pool at Okinawa, never a day went by I didn't dream about openin' a shop of my own some place where I really belonged."

Dolly felt a wave of unfamiliar sympathy. It was one thing to feed a drifting bum, but what could she tell a dreamer who wanted to call Cream Valley home and was looking for a job at Grogan's. She couldn't bring herself to tell him that the joint was in hock up to its ears because Willy spent all his dough on horses.

They were interrupted by Willy himself, who was not happy. His credit at the local grocery store had been chopped off and his local bookie was threatening to turn him over to the New York mob for collection.

"What's with the soldier?" Willy growled when he saw Walter. "Who asked for a parade?"

Dolly stepped over to him quickly. "Not so loud, hon, *please*. He's looking for a job, that's all. He's some kind of an automobile specialist."

Willy looked anguished. "A what?"

"You heard me. All I'm asking is you brush the boy off lightly." She led Willy over to the table, where Walter was standing at polite attention. "Willy, this is Walter Gulick."

Willy managed a polite handshake. He felt his knuckles being crushed in Walter's responding grip. Surprised, he looked at the paw enclosing his hand, saw the massive wrist and the bulging forearm, and then looked up to take in the broad shoulders and the solid jaw. He didn't look any higher than that. In the fight racket, he knew better than to look for signs of intelligence.

"Only job open around here," he said, "is sparring partner for Zimmerman's tiger."

"Wait a minute," Dolly cut in hastily. "Mercy killings are not allowed—not even here."

In the ensuing argument between Dolly and Willy, Walter learned that a boxing promoter named Zimmerman had signed up a young pug who was so promisingly vicious that all his sparring partners had quit. Zimmerman was offering five dollars per round, but no one had ever lasted out the first round to collect.

"I've had experience," Walter said brightly, overcome at the thought of earning five dollars for each three minutes of work. "I did a lot of boxing in the Army, Mr. Grogan."

"Willy, you can't let him do a thing like this," Dolly protested.

"It's no skin off me," said Willy, as indeed it wasn't. "Talk to Zimmerman," he told Walter.

In spite of Dolly's pleas that he might as well fight a freight train, Walter went out to talk to Zimmerman. A half-hour later, he was in the outdoor ring of Grogan's Cradle of Champions, and he was not being cradled. Joie Shakes, the fighter, was all over him like a tent, giving him the beating of his life. Even Zimmerman was appalled. "Easy, Joie," he called. "Take your time in there."

Considering that three minutes of time would cost Zimmerman a full five dollars, his plea for mercy took Joie so much by surprise that he let his guard drop. Walter belted him one, and Joie was some hours in remembering what had happened.

"I'm sorry," Walter apologized. "I would never have hit him so hard, except—well, it was getting a little uncomfortable."

So Walter joined the motley collection of pugs and sparring partners at Grogan's training camp. When they all gathered in the Social Room that evening, Walter found that Joie was not a boy to hold a grudge. Joie offered his guitar to Walter with a magnanimous gesture. Walter hesitated, not sure of his standing with the curious crowd of battle-scarred pugs looking on.

Walter looked at Joie and saw no animosity in his face. He accepted the instrument, fumbled a couple of chords, and then got with it. By the time he got around to belting out the chorus, the joint was rocking. And when a bunch of pugs rock a joint, the plaster rocks, too.

"And he can sing, too?" Joie cried in genuine admiration at the conclusion of the number. Impulsively he flung an arm over Walter's shoulder; and from the applause of the other pugs, the homeless young soldier knew he had found a home of sorts. . . .

While the fighters were relaxing in the Social Room, Willy was doing anything but relaxing with a New York boxing racketeer named Otto Danzig. One of Otto's prize fighters had refused to throw a fight, and had been taken into a steam room to remedy his sudden puritanical streak. Unfortunately Willy had been in the steam room at the time of the beating and was being called to testify at a hearing by the District Attorney. Otto wanted to make sure Willy said the right things, though Willy insisted he hadn't been able to see through the steam.

"That's why," Otto said with suave menace, "Marvin and Ralphie"—he indicated two hulking morons behind his shoulder—"will be with you until September."

"Look, Otto," Willy protested. "I don't want these torpedoes hanging around my place. Do I make myself clear?"

"Let me put it this way," Otto said softly. "Rocky Virgil used to talk a lot like you."

Rocky being the pug who was now wandering around listening to birds who were not there, Willy got the message. He also got more bad news after Otto left. Hoping to borrow a couple of C-notes to restore credit with his bookie, Willy called his young sister in New York. For once, Rose Grogan seemed reluctant to part with her hard-earned money. While she didn't refuse him outright, she didn't promise to come through on schedule. Willy thought of the New York "collectors" his bookie would bring in. He closed his eyes and shuddered.

Still brooding about his fate. Willy wandered into the Social Room, later that night, just in time to see the kitchen door explode in an assortment of splinters. Through the debris came flying the figure of Ralphie, the torpedo. Ralphie landed on his back and lay peacefully still.

Walter stood apologetically in the shattered doorway. "It would never have happened, Mr. Grogan," he said. "Not if this feller knew how to behave himself with a lady."

Dolly pushed by Walter. "Thanks, Galahad," she said to him. To Willy she said, "I want to make one thing perfectly plain." And she began to sound off about having thugs around who tried to corner her in the kitchen.

The camp trainer, Lew Nyack, interrupted. "Explanations we can have later. Please get your Eagle Scout out of here before Ralphie wakes up and kills him," he said. He picked up a neat little pistol that had been jolted from Ralphie's shoulder holster; and at the sight of it, Dolly pushed Walter out of the room.

As they began the job of reviving Ralphie, Zimmerman suddenly asked, "Who's Galahad?"

"Galahad was a knight in a tin suit," said Lew. "A kind of hero with a halo, as I remember—very courteous to broads."

"He was also something of a square," Willy said sourly. "I can't state this as a positive fact, but he probably died very young."

Nevertheless, Willy had never seen a man more thoroughly knocked out than Ralphie. The more he studied the splintered door and shattered frame, the more he marveled at what one punch could do. He saw ready cash in Walter's explosive right arm. . . .

The next day, Willy got another jolt. His sister Rose arrived with her baggage and the alarming statement that she was there to reorganize the joint and put it on a paying basis.

"I had a talk with Mr. Provardis in cost accounting at the store," she told Willy. "Mr. Provardis said that for what you're charging for room and board, it's impossible not to make money." Rose looked at her brother accusingly and demanded to know where the profits had gone.

"Wait a minute," Willy began to yell.

"Don't shout at me. I'm your sister, and I own fifty per cent of this place." She smiled sweetly, and indicated he could carry her bags to a nice, quiet room. When he started to sputter, she added firmly, "It won't do you any good to shout."

Dolly came in, braking to an abrupt halt at the sight of Rose.

"Er—Dolly, this is my kid sister Rose," said the miserable Willy. "Dolly sort of helps out around here," he told Rose lamely. "She happened to—drop by this morning."

Dolly flushed at Willy's crude explanation. "It's nice to

have met you, Miss Grogan," she said and stalked out.

Willy hurried after her. "Look, Dolly," he pleaded, "she's only a baby, a protected baby."

"Come off it," Dolly scoffed. "If you're such a blue-nosed puritan about your sister, forget it."

"I didn't know she was coming up here, understand? I just wasn't prepared," Willy insisted.

"I know. You're not prepared for a lot of things," Dolly said, beginning to weep. "I'm just beginning to get the idea."

Left alone in the lobby, Rose did not remain idle. In a matter of moments, she was deep into Willy's ledgers, and already running into some curious deficits that did not seem related to the operation of a summer hotel. Suddenly, the door to the office burst open, and a dirt-covered figure rushed in.

It was Walter, and he came to a skidding stop at the sight of Rose. "I'm sorry," he gasped in open admiration. "I didn't mean to scare you."

"It's all right. I don't scare easily," said Rose. Her eyes widened. Under the layer of cobwebs and dirt, she suspected the presence of a handsome young man. "Are you a fighter?"

"I'm not sure," said Walter. "It seems like different people have different ideas about it. Do you belong around here? I mean, it's the first time I saw you around."

"I'm Willy's sister."

Walter's grin spread into a silly beam that covered his whole face.

"What's so funny?" asked Rose, not at all displeased.

"Nothing. It's just that—"

"Galahad! Hey, Galahad!" Lew Nyack called from outside.

"Who's Galahad?" asked Rose.

"Me," said Walter, rushing out as rapidly as he had entered.

In front of the hotel, Walter saw Zimmerman and his boy Joie Shakes seated in a stalled Cadillac.

"Zimmerman says it just died on him," Lew explained. "It's not ignition, and he don't need gas."

Walter raised the hood and tinkered a moment. The starter whirred; the motor caught and purred contentedly.

"What'd I tell you about the way this kid can tune a car?" Lew asked with satisfaction.

"So it's running," Zimmerman grunted. "Thank you."

"Thank you?" Lew said indignantly. "This kid can live on gasoline fumes? Pay him."

"It was nothing," Walter protested.

"The kid says it's nothing, then I'm satisfied it's nothing," said Zimmerman.

Walter poked Joie affectionately. "Good luck in your fight in Boston."

"I'll miss you, Galahad," Joie said sincerely as they drove off.

It can't be said that things settled down to dull routine after the departure of Zimmerman and Joie. Ralphie, for one, was not happy; and only Otto Danzig's warning that he wanted no fireworks kept Ralphie from exacting vengeance on the boy who had slammed him through the kitchen door.

Willy himself was unhappy trying to stall off Rose's questions about the mysterious deficits and trying to soothe Dolly's ruffled feelings. And Lew was unhappy about Walter. Set up with a few easy sparring partners, Walter acted more like a punching bag than a fighter. He also tended to bleed everytime he was hit. Walter required all of Lew's skill as a "cut man"—one versed in the instant repair of damaged fighters—to keep him in one piece.

Walter, on the other hand, was completely happy. In the old barn in back of the hotel, he had found an ancient Model T Ford, which he restored to perfect running condition. In the process, he made a good friend of old man Prohoska, owner of the Cream Valley garage and filling station. And he also made a good friend of Rose Grogan, who had suddenly developed a passionate interest in the restoration and care of old automobiles.

About his ring career, Walter was happily indifferent. The abuse he took and the blood he lost in the ring bothered him no more than mosquito bites, and he never got angry enough with his opponents to let fly with anything lethal. Yet, he made a handsome figure when he first stepped into the ring and threw off his dressing gown.

It was Walter's handsome appearance that gave Willy his only ray of hope after watching him box. He was convinced that Walter would never make a fighter but who would care about fighting ability if the handsome kid drew the female fans? With a few long-distance phone calls, Willy arranged Walter's first battle at the Capital Casino.

The Casino never drew a big gate, but the television rights were worth seven hundred and fifty dollars, or enough to get Willy off the hook with his bookie. For that amount, he signed up Walter without even asking who the opponent would be. And for the newspaper reporters, he invented the story of Kid Galahad, the U.S. Army's champion of the Pacific, with seventeen knockouts to his credit.

The Capital Casino was up in Albany, and for lack of any transportation, Willy drove there in the Model T, now painted a brilliant fire-engine red.

"Suppose somebody sees me in this thing?" Willy moaned to Lew.

Lew wasn't interested in Willy's embarrassment. He wanted to know who Walter was to fight.

"Some clown, that's all," Willy told him, evading the issue.

But he couldn't evade the big billboard outside the Casino. It announced a ten-round match between Kid Galahad, the sensational KO artist making his local debut, and Ezzard "Bobo" Bailey, the crowd-pleasing veteran from New York's East Side.

"How could you do a thing like that?" Lew demanded. "This kid never had a professional fight in his life. And Ezzard Bailey is no clown."

"It happens that I can use the money," Willy declared, but he wilted under Lew's accusing look.

Walter, or Kid Galahad, was not prepared for his reception when he stepped into the ring. This was not a crowd of his buddies rooting for him in a regimental match. This was a crowd of professional fight followers, and they didn't care who won as long as there was plenty of action and blood. A few women cheered ecstatically when he bared his chest; but the men booed at his pretty face, and somebody shouted, "Galahad, you bum! Ya better go home and get your shield."

Walter winced, and felt a sudden surge of annoyance. The bell rang and he felt a lot more: Bobo hit him with everything but the ring post. Walter looked to the referee for help, and was promptly floored by a right to the jaw. He was saved by the bell.

For the next four or five rounds, Walter felt a growing indignation. Bobo, the referee, and the crowd were not treating him with proper respect. At last, tired of the injustice of it all, he blasted Bobo with a right to the jaw. The punch was so loaded with power that it separated Bobo's hair from his hair oil. Bobo hung horizontally in the air for a moment and then crashed to the canvas in the same rigid condition.

To the local fans of Cream Valley, Kid Galahad was a hero. Garage owner Prohoska told him, "I seen fellers look worse than Bobo just from falling off a forty-foot ladder. It wasn't a bad fight, son."

And Constable Healy was even louder in his praise. "The greatest fight I ever saw on TV, kid," he said. "There was five different times I thought you was dead."

"You're very kind," said Walter. "I guess everybody enjoyed it more'n me."

The reaction of the television audience was even wilder. For once, the women viewers had found a handsome fighter with a virile right, and Kid Galahad's fan mail swamped the Albany station. After that, Willy had no trouble booking his tiger at ever-increasing fees. He even made enough money to settle the shortages in his own ledgers before Rose could learn that they'd been caused by bets on bad horses.

But if Willy was out of financial trouble, he was in deep trouble with Dolly. His ruthless exploitation of Kid Galahad sickened her. His reluctance to acknowledge her as his fiancée in front of Rose made her even sicker. And his spineless acceptance of Otto Danzig's revolting torpedoes in his hotel absolutely infuriated her. She finally

left him to return to her old job as hostess at Shangri-
La-Friedman. And just to make matters worse for Willy,
Rose was showing an interest in Kid Galahad that no respectable young sister of his should show in any prize
fighter.

What really rocked Willy was the day he overheard Rose
urging Walter to give up the fight game and go into the
garage business. His own sister was trying to turn his
breadwinning tiger against him! With righteous indignation, he ordered her never to have anything to do with
meatballs. But Rose was a grown woman now, and refused to be intimidated by Willy.

Willy's stake in Walter was saved by the Cream Valley
Chamber of Commerce, which asked to sponsor a Labor
Day prize fight between Kid Galahad and a popular New
York boxer. For the town's sake, Walter could not re-
fuse the bout, but he swore it would be his last.

"If I spill anybody's blood after Labor Day," he told
Willy, "it's gonna be my own. One reason is, I'm not that
much frightened by honest work."

"Shut up," growled Willy.

"You can't shut me up," Walter retorted. "Not until I
tell you what I think of the fight game. I think it stinks.
And when it's done for me what I want it to do, I'm getting out. I'm not marrying Rose because she's your sister,
Willy, but in spite of it!"

Willy's next bad news did not come until a week before
the Labor Day battle. Ralphie and Marvin, Otto's two
torpedoes, broke it to him.

"Galahad's opponent will be Sugarboy Romero," Marvin declared.

"How would you know that?" Willy asked, appalled at
the choice. "Jerry Bathgate's handling the arrangements
for the Chamber of Commerce."

"Jerry's had his instructions," Marvin said. "Jerry can't
blow his nose unless Otto gives him permission."

"I see," said Willy, feeling sick.

"No one's trying to hurt your boy, or kill a golden
goose," Marvin went on. "All Otto wants is a nice payday
for Sugarboy, and a chance to cover all the bets the local

sports want to make on Galahad. Makes sense, doesn't it?"

"I guess it does make sense for Otto," Willy said. "Where do I fit in?"

"You stupid or something?" Marvin sneered. "Horses won't pay off the way this thing will. Not only that, but Otto has adopted you. Like it or not, you're one of the family. It's that simple! . . ."

If Otto Danzig had left it that simple, things would have been all right. Sugarboy would have won easily, and he would have made a cleaning on the bets. But just to be on the safe side, Otto went one step too far. He tried to bribe Walter's trainer Lew Nyack, offering him five C-notes if he would forget his artistry as a "cut man." With Otto when he made his magnanimous offer was Ralphie and Marvin; and they had Lew all alone in his room.

"This is about it," said Otto. "Galahad's got a jaw like a curbstone, but he cuts and bleeds like anybody else. After three rounds with Romero, the referee will have to stop it —as long as you are not in his corner to patch him up."

"That's your insurance, Otto?"' Lew asked, wishing he were somewhere else.

"Let's say it's part of my business," Otto said smoothly. "Here's five hundred to help you get lost. There'll be somebody else in Galahad's corner. Somebody who'll know what to do."

It had been a long time since Lew had swung a fist in offense or defense. He was old, and tired, and flabby, but the fighting spirit was still there. He started for Otto.

Ralphie and Marvin grabbed him before he could reach Otto. Then slowly and methodically they broke all his fingers.

Willy found Lew an hour later. Lew was in a daze, but he was still articulate.

"Otto was here," said Lew, speaking through clenched teeth. "They busted my fingers, Willy, so I wouldn't be any help to Galahad."

"Otto?" Willy said softly.

Just then, Ralphie and Marvin reentered the room. "We're an old established firm that can't afford mistakes," Marvin said ominously.

"Who broke his hands?" Willy asked, still with the same soft voice.

"I was never a shy one, Willy," Ralphie admitted.

Willy, the worm, turned. "You hyena!" he screamed. "You shark-hearted, stinkin' no-good son-of-a—" He started swinging, flailing wildly at the two torpedoes. Gently, they held him off as though he were a flea, and gave him a few calming whacks in return.

At that point, Walter, attracted by the sounds of the altercation, broke in and entered the fray. By the time Walter finished, Ralphie and Marvin were stretched out unconscious. Willy staggered to his feet.

"It was a hell of a brawl while it lasted, Galahad," Willy said, shaking Walter's hand almost fraternally. "I'm kind of glad you came along."

Walter steadied his brother-in-law-to-be with anxious hands. "Feel all right, huh?" he asked in a worried tone.

Lew was more concerned about Walter than about Willy. "You sure you didn't break *your* hands?" he asked, gazing at the two rock-hard jaws Walter had just splintered. But Kid Galahad's fists were thoroughly intact, though Ralphie and Marvin were left sleeping peacefully on the floor. . . .

With the whole village of Cream Valley and all the summer guests at the hotels having bet their shirts on Kid Galahad, neither Willy nor Walter were in a position to call the crooked fight off. The night of the big battle arrived with Otto Danzig still sure of the outcome.

Drawn together by some mysterious impulse, Rose and Dolly found themselves sitting next to each other at ringside.

"I don't know why I came," Rose whispered tensely. "Do you? What good can we possibly do?"

"I don't know," Dolly replied with equal helplessness. "It's just that civilized people are supposed to bury their own dead."

On that helpful note, the bell rang for the first round and Kid Galahad gallantly sprang forward to meet the Mexican terror, Sugarboy Romero. Just as promptly he flew back, hit by Sugarboy's welcoming right. He leaned against the ring post, glad of its support, until the count of nine. Then he got up to be knocked down again.

Kid Galahad did not have a very good first round, most of the time being devoted to his lying on the mat while the referee counted to nine over him. By the end of the round, he could barely walk back to his corner under his own power.

While Walter was being pounded in the ring, Willy and Lew were in the dressing room. Lew's fingers were stiffly taped to wooden splints, but even so, Otto hadn't taken any chances. He'd sent another of his boys around to see that Kid Galahad got no help from his seconds.

"Otto sent me," said the man called Freddie. "To take loving care of your boy."

"That's nice. It's real nice, Freddie. Thanks," said Willy with his customary weakness. And while Freddie smiled with smug satisfaction, Willy picked up a three-legged stool and pacified him with a giant swing that nearly broke his arm and *did* break the stool. He and Lew got to ringside just in time to welcome their bleeding Galahad at the end of the first round.

Otto saw Willy and Lew from his seat in the audience. "What happened to Freddie?" he asked one of his henchman. "And you seen Marvin and Ralphie?"

"Come to think about it," said the henchman, straining at the unfamiliar effort of thinking, "no!"

Under Lew's expert instructions, Willy did an excellent repair job on Walter's cuts; and Walter was so encouraged by having friends in his corner that he stood up all during the second and third rounds. But at last, not even Willy could stand the punishment Walter was taking.

"Look, kid," he exclaimed as Walter sagged back against the corner post after the round, "you don't *have* to take this kind of beating. Win, lose or draw, they gotta pay you. You can still buy that lousy garage."

"What round is it?" Walter asked foggily.

"The sixth comin' up."

"I think he's gettin' tired," said Walter.

"I know," Willy said bitterly. "He's perfectly exhausted —like a machine gun."

But Walter rubbed his jaw and figured that the blows of the fifth round had lost a lot of steam over those of the first. At the rate the blows were losing their punch, he figured that by round ten he would be sailing home in a breeze. He wasn't going to outfight Sugarboy. He was just going to outlast him.

But when Walter learned from Lew that the whole fight had been framed in order to cash in on the bets, he got indignant again. Walter wasn't sore at Sugarboy Romero for being a better fighter, but as long as Sugarboy was a tool of Otto Danzig, he would have to take the consequences.

Kid Galahad thrust out his jaw in open invitation. Sugarboy could not resist. He swung a mighty right with such staggering impact that his arm went numb from wrist to shoulder. And while Sugarboy stood there with a paralyzed right arm, Kid Galahad set off the blast that blew Sugarboy so hard against the ropes that he bounced back into the center of the ring before touching the mat. The referee didn't even bother to count.

Assistant District Attorney Gerson had a few words with Willy before the victory celebration in Kid Galahad's dressing room.

"You will testify to what happened the other night?" Gerson asked.

"After what they did to Lew?" Willy drew himself up. "I'll sing for you like a bluebird."

Gerson nodded, satisfied. At his signal, a few of the D.A.'s boys moved in on Otto and his crew. When last seen the hoods did not look happy. Some of their misery could be attributed to having lost their money to the hicks of Cream Valley, but most of it could be summed up in a long sentence—like twenty years in prison for fight racketeering and extortion.

Willy plowed his way into the dressing room where Lew, splinted fingers and all, was doing a masterful job of making a grinning Walter presentable. He nudged up to Dolly.

"Hello, Dolly," he said, unsure of his reception.

But Dolly had heard of the fight Willy had put up against Otto's torpedoes, and she was all smiles and welcome. "Hello yourself," she said. "I heard what happened: and well, frankly, you clumsy clown, I couldn't help but feel proud."

"Like old times, isn't it?" he murmured, embracing her.

Dolly drew back, but not too far. "Not like old times, Willy. That's where you're wrong. I'll bet you three to one we're married before midnight." And she led him out.

Kid Galahad and Rose watched them go without saying a word. As a matter of fact, they themselves were so blissful that words were the last thing that would have occurred to either of them.

Adapted from the MIRISCH COMPANY Production
Released through UNITED ARTISTS CORP.
Directed by PHIL KARLSON
Produced by DAVID WEISBART
Screenplay by WILLIAM FAY
Based on a story by FRANCIS WALLACE
Color by DE LUXE
Adapted for SCREEN STORIES by GEORGE SCULLIN

CAST

Ross Carpenter .... ELVIS PRESLEY   Wesley Johnson .... JEREMY SLATE

Robin Ganter .... STELLA STEVENS   Chen Yung .... GUY LEE

Laurel Dodge .. LAUREL GOODWIN   Kin Yung .... BENSON FONG

GIRLS! GIRLS! GIRLS!

■ It was a tropical coast only a little less beautiful than paradise, and you wouldn't have thought anybody could have conjured up a worry under that brilliant sky. But trouble is no respecter of loveliness. Trouble, reflected Ross Carpenter, was the steadiest buddy he'd had for a long time.

He thought back to the day his father and he had finished building *West Wind,* the sleekest sailboat he'd ever seen. She was no sooner done than his father had died, and Ross had had to sell *West Wind.*

West Wind's new owner, a kindly Greek immigrant named Alexander Stavros, owned three other boats including a fishing vessel called *Kingfisher.* He let Ross live on *West Wind,* and Ross skippered *Kingfisher* for him whenever rich customers wanted to charter her for the day. What was most meaningful of all to Ross Carpenter, though, was the promise he'd had from Mr. Stavros that he could buy back *West Wind,* once he'd saved enough to offer a fair price. Only now there was more bad news. Papa Stavros had been told by the doctor that Mrs. Stavros would have to move to a dry climate—to Arizona.

"Doctors are all crazy; so is my husband," Mrs. Stavros told Ross. "Don't worry. We won't move away so fast."

"But if you're sick—" he began.

"Sick, sick," Mrs. Stavros said. "A woman isn't as young as she used to be, so everyone looks for a reason."

"It's serious," Mr. Stavros protested, but Mrs. Stavros shook her head.

"Don't listen to him! And if he tells you he has to sell the boats, also don't listen. You come to our anniversary party Wednesday night and forget all about this." She turned and waved to Chen Yung, Ross' first mate on the *Kingfisher.* "Chen, you come, too."

As she walked away, Ross and Papa Stavros exchanged a grave look. Ross pointed to *West Wind.* "This, too?" he asked.

Papa Stavros nodded unhappily, and turned to follow his wife away from the dock.

There was nothing more to be said, and Ross knew it. The Stavroses weren't rich; they needed the money from the sale of the boats in order to finance their move to

Arizona. Their dreams and his seemed to be ending together.

The night club where Robin Ganter worked was smoky,
but respectable. Robin was a curvy girl with a talent for
singing and a torch for Ross Carpenter. On this particular
night, however, she wasn't overjoyed when she saw Ross
at the bar.

"To what 'disaster' do I owe the pleasure of this visit?"
she asked.

"You know?" he asked, wondering how she'd already
heard the bad news.

"No," she sighed. "You come here when you want to
sing a little—or cry a little on my shoulder. Which is it
tonight?"

"I don't feel much like singing," he said. "The Stavroses
are moving to Arizona. They're reselling the fishing boats
—and the West Wind."

"Good," Robin said. "That's the only way you're going
to get it out of your system."

He was startled. "The hard way? Losing my pad and
my job all in one day?"

Gently, Robin answered, "Your father's gone, Ross,
and so is that time of your life. The worst thing that ever
happened to you is when Papa Stavros bought the boat
and let you live on it."

"I can always count on you to make that speech," Ross
said wearily.

"You can count on me, period," she said, making an
overture she'd made many times before.

"Here we go again," he protested, tired of explaining
his aversion to marriage.

"Do you want me to pretend I don't care?" she asked.

"No," he said. "But don't make it tougher than it is.
You don't have a bad time with me."

"I know," she said sardonically. "We're good for each
other."

"We are," he told her simply. "But we wouldn't be with
you working nights and me working days—coming home
to the vine-covered house."

There were tears in Robin's eyes, and Ross was apologizing when Sam, the club's manager, approached them.

"Ready for your number, Robin?" Sam asked.

"Let Sir Galahad take it," Robin snapped.

Seeing that Robin was in no mood to go on stage, Sam turned to Ross. "You sing, Ross," he urged. "Favor to me."

Ross nodded sympathetically and headed toward the bandstand. After Ross had finished a medley of songs, Sam told him. "Any time you want to make it permanent, let me know."

"I'm still a fisherman," Ross said, moving back to Robin.

Robin shoved a tray with a drink and a five-dollar bill on it across the bar toward him. She indicated a pretty blonde sitting at a table with a noisy drunk. "The swinger with the mink-look sent it over. You must smell of musk or something."

Ross picked up the tray and carried it to the blonde's table. "I don't work here," he said. "Thanks anyway."

The drunk man with her was insulted. "Whassa matter, not enough money for you? You sing lousy anyway!"

"Who's the intellectual?" Ross asked the blonde girl.

"A bad idea I had," she answered grimly. "A blind date." She rose to leave.

"He's blind all right," Ross said.

"Lissen, get your own dames," the drunk sneered, blocking the girl's attempt to leave.

Ross summoned help to remove the drunk from the premises; then he turned back to Robin. She was in no better humor than before.

"You're Sir Galahad, all right," she said, "to strangers!" And she stalked off.

Ross left the night club, and the blonde followed him out into the street to explain that she was sorry she'd made trouble for him. Her name was Laurel Dodge, she said, and she'd never seen the drunk man before in her life. "He said he was a friend of my father, and he wasn't," she explained. Then she switched the topic to Robin. "Who's the girl?"

"An old football buddy," he told her. "Where do you live?"

She smiled at him. "Down the road a piece. . . ."

Miss Laurel Dodge was a mysterious girl. They walked

through more streets than he'd ever seen before, and they didn't seem to be getting even remotely close to her house. Furthermore, she wouldn't tell him where she came from, though he was perfectly candid with her.

"I come from right here," he said. "I fish for a living, sing for laughs, and live on a boat. How about you?" But she ignored the question.

She finally indicated a ratty old hotel, known as the New Plaza. There were garbage cans on the sidewalk in front of it. "I live here," she said. "It's simple, and unpretentious, and just reeks of history."

He inhaled. "Well, anyhow, it reeks."

She wouldn't let him kiss her good night, but she did make a lunch date with him for the next day. They were to meet at a restaurant called The Grotto. She watched him walk out of the New Plaza lobby, and then she also left. She didn't live there, and she didn't want to. Miss Laurel Dodge was playing a game she didn't quite understand herself, but the next move had Ross Carpenter's name on it.

The next day, Ross had to show the Stavros boats to Wesley Johnson, a man he disliked at once. Johnson, a boat broker and operator, was being cagey. He wanted to go out in the *Kingfisher* before he made up his mind.

Ross gave quite a performance with the *Kingfisher* at sea—zooming up the side of a wave, porting hard into the trough, making wide sweeps, heeling over sharply.

Eventually, Johnson, who'd hung on poker-faced, spoke up. "Okay, you're Captain Blood. Can we go home now?"

"Why not?" Ross shrugged. Then he brought himself to ask what had been on his mind throughout the trip. "You going to buy the boats? These are three top boats."

"What's wrong with the fourth?"

"The sailboat? What would you do with that?" Ross asked.

"Make like a gentleman of the sea—if the Greek'll throw it in."

"It wouldn't look good on you," said Ross.

Johnson leered. "I have a girl. She'll teach me to sail. It's her second favorite sport. . . ."

After docking the *Kingfisher,* Ross got to The Grotto an hour and a half late. He saw that Laurel wasn't alone. She was sitting with a gray-haired old gentleman. Ross turned on his heels and left even as Laurel called out to him. He called back sourly: "Some other time, when you're not so busy. . . ."

When Laurel appeared at the dock the next day, Ross was mending the *West Wind's* sail, and Chen was helping. Ross greeted the girl bitterly. "Hello, Suzie Wong."

"You were very late," Laurel said. "I waited."

He snorted. "Long enough to pick up an aging gentleman."

"That was my father!" she said. "Why am I always explaining something to you?"

"Maybe it's something you do," he answered. "I checked the hotel. They never heard of you."

"You have to trust me on that one," she said, "because you like games as much as I do." Then she asked him to take her to dinner that night.

"All right," Ross agreed. "We'll eat at my boss' house."

"If you're broke—" she began, but he cut her off sharply.

"I'm not broke," he declared. "It's his anniversary. Besides, I'm curious to see what you can dig up *there!*"

She ignored the crack. "You're not one of those men who's dreary about money, are you?"

"Seven-thirty, here," he said. "You won't have to wander around hotel lobbies."

Laurel had no sooner started away than Robin appeared, just in time to get a good view of the other girl's retreating back. Robin glared at Ross. "I started out to apologize for last night."

"I accept it," he said.

"I withdraw it. I didn't know you had company," she declared. Always before, when he had drifted off with other girls, he had come back to her afterward. Was that what he was going to do this time, she asked in a shaking voice.

He answered her flatly, "I don't know."

"You're Sir Galahad, Don Juan and Casanova rolled into one," she stormed. "If it isn't the boat, it's girls. Girls! Girls! Girls!"

She ran off down the dock and Ross watched her for a few troubled moments. Then he went into his cabin and fetched out a jug of wine. There were times when a man just had to drink, and this was one of them.

At one point during the Stavroses anniversary party, while Chen was playing a folk song on his guitar and the guests were singing in Greek, Laurel leaned over to Ross. "This is really your family, isn't it?"

His tone was almost apologetic. "Well, sort of. When my Dad died, and I had to sell the boat to pay for— everything, Papa Stavros bought her. He didn't need her, and he paid a lot of money, so that's why I'm—"

"You don't have to explain," she interrupted gently. "I'm sorry they're leaving."

There were toasts to Mama and Papa Stavros, and more songs, and tears from everybody. It was a night to remember.

And the next day was also memorable for Ross Carpenter. He took Laurel out in the *West Wind*. The weather was perfect for sailing. "She's running fine," Ross said happily.

"It's good just to keep running sometimes, isn't it?" Laurel said.

"Yes," he agreed.

She touched his arm. "You can tell me what it is."

"We spent every spare minute working on this boat," Ross told her. "We measured and polished and sanded each board. The day we finished was the day he died." He looked away and tugged savagely at the sail. "I'm sorry," he muttered in self-reproach.

"Don't be," she said.

"Tell me what it is with you," he urged. But she shook her head.

Suddenly, a hard gust of wind hit the boat. Frowning, Ross tuned in his radio for the Coast Guard emergency weather information. *"Small craft warnings have been hoisted,"* the broadcast said. *"Vessels are advised to seek sheltered areas."*

"We'll go into Paradise Cove," Ross told Laurel. "Chen Yung's folks live there. . . ."

Chen Yung's father, a fisherman named Kin, came out of Paradise Cove in a fishing dory, pulled alongside the *West Wind,* waited for Ross to anchor her, and then took Ross and Laurel back to shore.

When they arrived at the Yung shack, Chen's mother greeted them. "Ross!" she exclaimed. "Robin!" And then, looking more closely, she corrected herself: "Not Robin."

"Definitely not," Laurel said.

Madam Yung indicated Ross. "You know this one long?"

"Forever," Laurel said. "Twenty-four hours."

"No harm done—yet," said Madam, and turned to Ross. "How's Chen?"

"Fine."

"Very fine son," Madam told Laurel. "Very scarce. Ross is adopted son. Also very scarce. Except when in trouble." She tossed a bag of pea pods to Ross and said, "Start." And then she slid a basket of shrimp to Laurel. "You are guest. You can clean shrimp."

But if cleaning shrimp was a chore, eating them with chopsticks was an even tougher one, Laurel discovered. Ross finally handed her a fork. After dinner, Madam Yung rose from the table and directed her husband toward the dishes.

"Use honorable detergent," she said, giving Kin a shove toward the kitchen.

Ross and Laurel headed for the porch to view the calm before the storm. The sky was threatening; the moon barely shone through a break in the clouds.

"I like your friends," Laurel said.

"They like you," he told her.

She was all innocence. "Do they like Robin, too?"

"You know how the Chinese are," he said, grinning. "Inscrutable. They don't show their feelings."

They weren't so inscrutable when it came to bedtime, however. Madame Yung had everything organized. Laurel was to sleep with her, and Ross was to bed down on the living-room couch. He sighed, "I must have gotten the wrong fortune cookie."

The storm finally broke in the middle of the night.

Laurel, huddled in a blanket, made her way out to the porch to watch, and found Ross gazing at the tossing sea. "Why is it you feel so much more alive in a storm?" she asked.

He put his arms around her. "I don't know. I guess because everything seems more intense, more real."

She put her hand over his. "This is real," she declared.

"Yes," he answered, but he said it doubtfully. There was still so much she wouldn't tell him, so much he didn't know. "You're not married, are you?" he blurted out.

She laughed, but the laugh had a sad sound. "Almost," she said.

"That's what you're running from?"

"Yes. Let's not talk any more."

"Do you still love him?" Ross persisted.

"He didn't love me," she said. "I was hurt. The whole thing was such a lie. That's why my father brought me here from Chicago. It's over with, but—I'm not all together yet."

"You're together enough for me," he said.

She held him off. "I couldn't stand being fooled again. It's me, and it's real, isn't it?"

A gust of rain showered them with spray as he kissed her, but neither of them felt the water at all. . . .

The trip back to the West Wind's home berth the next day was sunny and uneventful, but Papa Stavros met Ross and Laurel at the pier with unhappy news. "I sold the boats," he told them. "Johnson said take it or leave it. I need the money," he said apologetically.

"You don't have to explain to me," Ross said. "I'll start taking my gear off now."

Papa Stavros looked wretched. "No, no. Tonight, tomorrow—" His voice trailed off. Sadly, he walked away.

"Chen can take me in for a few days," Ross said, more to himself than to Laurel. "I'd better see Johnson right now."

"I live at One-thirty-six Bay Street, apartment three," Laurel said clearly. "And I'll be waiting."

He kissed her quickly and gratefully, and then he headed for Wesley Johnson's office.

Wesley Johnson, Tuna Fleet, Yacht Brokerage, Marine Insurance, the sign said, and Johnson's office included a chart table and a ship's bar. Mr. Johnson lived well, and he knew how to take advantage of people in trouble. He said he'd gladly sell Ross the *West Wind*—for ten thousand dollars.

"What did you pay Stavros?" Ross demanded.

"Six," Johnson answered.

"You're a thief!" Ross declared.

"I'm a businessman. You want to work for me, fishing tuna?"

Ross tried to swallow his loathing for the man. "If I work for you, will you sell the boat to me for so much a week?"

"Everything's for sale," Johnson said. "But I won't promise I won't sell her if I get a good offer."

They made a deal. Ross would work as fishing captain for Johnson and he'd get twenty-five per cent of the profits per trip. Chen Yung was to go along as part of the deal. And Ross was to continue living on *West Wind,* and maintaining it.

Johnson was almost admiring. "You remind me of me," he said, referring to Ross' bargaining powers.

After leaving Johnson's office, Ross went to the club with a proposition for Sam. He wanted to sing there nights "What can I earn?" he asked.

"Scale to start," Sam said. "More if you draw big."

"This has nothing to do with Robin," Ross said. "She stays."

"Of course," said Sam. And he propelled Ross toward the stage.

Ross sang a number, and got an ovation. But Robin didn't appreciate sharing the spotlight. And Laurel, who'd been waiting impatiently at her apartment for Ross to show up, appeared at the club just in time to see the confrontation between Robin and Ross. She wasn't close enough to hear them, but her view was perfect.

"Man, when you go, you go the whole route, don't you?" Robin was saying. "First you pull the rug out from under my feet, then you take the bread out of my mouth."

Patiently, he explained, "I'm singing for the money to buy the boat; so I'm doing two jobs at once, but it doesn't affect you. I—"

Sam interrupted them. "The other one was just here," he said. He pointed to the door. "She went thataway."

Ross hurriedly left the club and caught up with Laurel in the street. She was furious. "People don't stand me up. Not even once," she declared. "What are you doing with Robin, hedging your bets?"

"I'm working there," he answered evenly. "When I'm not working for Johnson, I'm here."

"When do you work at *us?*" she cried. "Split shift?"

"I need the money," he said. "I have to buy the boat."

"I never wanted anything that badly," she said.

"Who are you?" he asked, marveling. "What are you that lets you play it so cool?" And he strode away.

But later that night, he lay awake wondering the same thing. Wondering if he would ever understand women. . . .

The next day, Ross' wondering took a different turn. He began to wonder if he would ever make any money tuna fishing. His first trip for Johnson was disastrous. The crew had to turn back after the first, small haul, because the fishing net had gotten caught in the propeller. And when Ross returned, tired, cranky, and almost poorer than when he'd left, the first thing to greet his eyes was a big sign on the *West Wind* which said *For Sale.*

"How do you get to sell a boat if you don't let people know it's for sale?" Johnson asked bluntly, enjoying Ross' misery on every single count.

The only bright spot in Ross' day was that Laurel appeared at the dock to invite him to dinner at her apartment. But when he arrived there with a bottle of wine in hand, he found smoke pouring out of the oven and Laurel at a complete loss as to a course of action. Ross poured salt on the flames, and the fire went out. Then he discovered Laurel thought salad oil was something with which you lubricated squeaky doors. Resolutely, he escorted her out of the kitchen.

"You light the candles, dear," he told her, indicating the silver candelabra on the table set for two. "Take off your shoes and smoke your pipe and dinner will be ready in just a jiffy," he added, heading back into the kitchen.

Ross was a marvelous cook, and the dinner he served was festive. But Laurel still felt some tension between them. "It's the boat, isn't it?" she said, over coffee.

He nodded. "You think I'm a little dingy about this, don't you?"

"You can want a thing awfully bad for the right reason," she said. "But you ought to prepare yourself."

"If she's sold?" he asked. "Well, one good thing would come of it. I wouldn't work for Johnson any more."

Wesley Johnson was impressed by Miss Laurel Dodge. He was impressed by her lines, her *savoir-faire,* and the fact that she had ten thousand dollars with which to buy *West Wind.* He admired her check, but with reservations. "It's on a Chicago bank," he observed. "I'd like it certified."

"The boat can stay here," Laurel said tartly. "I'm not asking you to wrap it up for me. You're in the big time now, Mr. Johnson. Let's not be so shook up."

Laurel specified one condition. Johnson was not to tell anyone she'd bought *West Wind.* He agreed, and made one last pitch at selling himself to her along with the boat. "I'll have to show you how to sail her. I wouldn't want you to get your diamonds caught in the rigging or anything."

But Laurel acidly reminded him their deal was strictly business. . . .

Ross' second tuna trip for Wesley Johnson was a great deal more successful than his first had been. He calculated his earnings to be one hundred and three dollars. But Johnson declared he owed Ross only fifty-one dollars and fifty-nine cents for the haul. Infuriated, Ross swung a hard punch at Johnson almost knocking him down. He was ready to swing again, when his eye caught sight of the *West Wind,* and he noticed that the *For Sale* sign was gone.

Ross caught his breath. "Who bought it?"

"That's classified material, Skipper," said Johnson. Realizing the fight was all out of Ross, he turned his back, and indicated the fifty-one dollars he'd dropped. "Pick up your dough."

Ross never answered; he just brushed himself off and headed to see Laurel.

He took her out for coffee at an outdoor cafe. When Laurel didn't seem surprised by his news that the *West Wind* had been sold, he demanded to know why.

"I went down to look for you," she explained unconvincingly. "They were just taking the *For Sale* sign off."

"There's something out of focus about this," Ross said slowly. Laurel was so obviously lying, so terribly uncomfortable.

All of a sudden, she started to speak very fast. "Listen, Ross, the man I told you about, that wasn't the first time I've been fooled. With you—"

"With me, what?"

"With you, it's different. That's the point. It wasn't me before; it was my money."

"So that's the big secret," he said, "you're rich."

"Yes," she answered.

"Try to live with it," he said bitterly.

"Don't," she pleaded. "You don't know what it's like. You get to look at every man suspiciously; the more they think you're worth to them, the less you're worth to yourself. I had to get away."

"I'm glad I came here to tell you *my* problems," he said.

"I had to find someone who would love me for myself," Laurel went on. "I've been very lucky."

"We've both been lucky that way," he said quietly. "Your being rich doesn't change how I feel, but how I'll act. What about Johnson?"

She admitted everything. "I bought the *West Wind*, Ross."

He shook his head sadly. "When I was a kid—after my father died, I lived on what people gave me. Clothes that other kids had outgrown that didn't fit me. Toys that were broken and thrown out. I even got to think the food I ate was given me because someone had finished with it."

"I understand," she said.

"You can't," he snapped back. "You never will. A man has to *work* for what he wants.

"I have the right to do this for you," she said. "I love you."

He shook off her words. "I don't take handouts from anyone. I don't want to be kept." There was nothing she could do or say. Only stand and stare after him as he left her.

Robin was rehearsing with the band when Laurel came

into the club. Laurel waited until the song was over, and then approached her.

"I want you to know I'm sorry about the way things turned out," Laurel said.

"Boo hoo," Robin sneered.

"If it makes you feel any better, we had a fight."

Robin smiled. "Tough."

"Do you know where he is?"

"I ought to have you bounced out of here," Robin said.

"I have to find him," Laurel pleaded.

Robin couldn't hold back a sigh of sympathy. "He's always been like this. If he gets in a mood, he just disappears for a while."

"Where to?"

"Paradise Cove, I guess," said Robin. "That'll be home now that the Stavroses are gone." A thought struck her. "You know, I'm being too polite to you. I must be over the guy."

"How do I get to Paradise Cove?" Laurel asked.

"You'll have to hitch a ride," Robin said. "There's no regular boat."

"Thanks," said Laurel. "I bought the *West Wind* for him."

The other girl stared. "My condolences. That's a route you can't go with him. You can't give him things. *I* know."

There was no one available to sail Laurel to Paradise Cove on the *West Wind*. Johnson said he couldn't spare a man except himself and Laurel had to accept his offer. Once aboard the *West Wind*, however, Johnson threw an ignition switch which started an auxiliary motor. Laurel was flabbergasted.

"You didn't tell me there was an auxiliary," she protested. "I could have done *this* myself!"

Johnson only smiled. "You never asked. . . ."

It was Chen Yung, out on a tuna boat, who spotted the *West Wind* through binoculars. He saw Johnson stumble and fall on Laurel, and he misinterpreted the incident. Alarmed, he made his way to the bow of the tuna boat, and radioed Ross at Paradise Cove.

"I'm about four miles south of Paradise Cove," he told Ross. "We passed the *West Wind* just now. Laurel Dodge was on it. Over."

"Why not?" Ross came back. " She bought it. Over."

"Johnson's on the boat too," Chen reported. "It didn't look good."

"Thanks," Ross yelped, hanging up. He raced out toward the beach and called for Kin Yung to get his boat.

Out on the water, Ross caught sight of the sailboat and told Kim Yung to steer toward it. When the two boats were near enough, Ross leaped from Kin's boat onto the deck of the *West Wind*.

Johnson tried to stay calm. "Get off the white horse, Skipper, you've got it wrong."

But it was too late. Ross couldn't be stopped. After a brief scuffle, he stood over Johnson on the wet deck. "You're going to buy this boat back from her," he declared.

Johnson questioned Laurel. "Am I?"

"If he says so."

"I say so," Ross said.

Johnson waved a hand at Laurel. "For you, anything."

As Ross helped Laurel into Kin Yung's motorboat, Johnson rubbed his chin ruefully. "He still reminds me of me," he said to himself. . . .

Paradise Cove was throwing a party. The tables, heavy with food and wine, had been set up on the beach, but most of the fishermen wouldn't stop singing and dancing long enough to eat. Ross and Laurel were talking quietly together.

"You know," he said, "I'm the world's biggest jackass."

Laurel was silent.

"Say something," he urged.

She complied. "You're the world's biggest jackass— darling."

"I thought I had to have the boat to be happy," he said. "I don't. I'm over it. We'll build a new boat. Ours!"

"Is that a proposal?" she asked. "Or a proposition?"

He laughed. "Either you marry me, or live with me in sin."

"Couldn't I have a little of both?" Laurel said, as he kissed her.

Adapted from the HAL WALLIS Production
Released through PARAMOUNT PICTURES CORP.
Directed by NORMAN TAUROG
Produced by HAL WALLIS
Screenplay by EDWARD ANHALT and ALLAN WEISS
Based on the story by ALLAN WEISS
Color by TECHNICOLOR
Adapted for SCREEN STORIES by CHRIS KANE

CAST
Lucky Jackson ...... ELVIS PRESLEY   Mr. Martin .... WILLIAM DEMAREST
Rusty Martin .... ANN-MARGRET   Shorty Farnsworth .. NICKY BLAIR
Count Elmo Mancini .... CESARE DAÑOVA

VIVA LAS VEGAS

■ It was only a jalopy race on a dirt track in Southern California, but Lucky Jackson made it look good. In fact, Lucky finished up on three wheels to win it, a happenstance noted with interest by the Italian racing champion, Count Elmo Mancini.

Mancini was a rich man, a wordly man, an elegant man. He'd seen a lot of drivers in his day, but he had to admit he'd never seen anybody better than Lucky Jackson. He'd come out to the track three times to watch, and now he told himself, I'd better hire that man. I'd rather have him racing for me than against me.

That wasn't at all the way Mr. Thompson felt. Mr. Thompson owned the car Lucky'd been piloting. "You crazy or something?" he yelled at Lucky. "Bumper off! Wheel off! You might as well have smashed it altogether!" Shorty, Lucky's mechanic, sprang to his defense. "But he won for you, Mr. Thompson."

Thompson snorted. "And my car's a mess."

"Never mind the gripes, Thompson," Lucky said. "Pay up. And pay Shorty, too." Thompson handed some bills to Lucky and tossed Shorty's money on the ground.

"Here," he said. "You're fired."

"Just a minute, Jack," Lucky said to Thompson. "Hand it to him like a gentleman."

Thompson threw a punch. It hit—and knocked out—Count Elmo Mancini, who had approached from behind to talk to Lucky.

"You'll never drive for me again!" Thompson yelled.

"I'm not driving for anybody again," Lucky retorted. "Just driving for me!" he said, as he and Shorty stepped over Mancini's prone body and walked away.

Shorty appeared bewildered. "What did you have to tell him a fool thing like that for?" he asked. He pointed out that they still needed thirty-eight hundred dollars to buy the motor for the racing car Lucky had built. All they owned in the world was the trailer with their motorless racing car and the convertible that towed it. Plus the money Lucky had just won, and Shorty's life savings—some two hundred and fifty dollars and change. To Lucky, this seemed enough.

He got into the convertible and headed for Las Vegas, the one sure place where you could take a little money and run it up into a lot.

Waving good-by, Shorty looked nonplussed. Then he shrugged. Maybe, in the gambler's paradise of bright lights and naked girls, of one-armed bandits and card dealers with pinky rings, Lucky would get lucky.

Lucky did. He shot craps, ran up a bank roll, and wired Shorty to get the motor crated. He promised to meet Shorty in Los Angeles with the money for the engine before you could say seven come eleven.

But first Lucky towed his trailer and racing shell to the garage where the various drivers and mechanics were getting their equipment in shape for the Las Vegas Grand Prix. Lucky was assigned to the space right next to a gorgeous Ferrari. The Ferrari's owner turned out to be none other than Count Elmo Mancini. The Count asked Lucky to drive for him. "You mean you're not going to drive in the Grand Prix?" Lucky said.

"No," Mancini answered, "I mean I am going to win."

Lucky understood at once. Mancini wanted to use Lucky to block the other cars for him, so he could drive right through. "I'm not working for anybody," Lucky said, "and I never ride second to anybody. And one other little thing. I'm going to win."

Mancini shrugged and respectfully offered to show Lucky the secrets of his Ferrari. With like respect, Lucky accepted and thus it happened that both men were under the car, feet sticking out, when the beautiful girl with the long legs appeared.

She had to kick at their toes before they knew she was there, but once they'd had a glance at those legs, they oozed out from under the car to stare at the rest of the lady. She was really something, all blonde and tanned and looking for help. "I'd like you to check my motor," she said. "It whistles."

"I don't blame it," said Lucky.

He and the Count accompanied the girl to her car. Lucky fiddled around under its hood and disconnected a wire. Then he said. "Your motor's broke."

"It was running perfectly when I pulled up here," the girl insisted, "except for the whistle. Are you sure you're a mechanic?"

Lucky nodded and said the car would take two days to fix. But he added he'd be glad to drive the girl around meanwhile. Then he went into the garage to wash up, leaving behind him an astonished blonde and an equally astonished Mancini.

Mancini recovered fast. The next sound Lucky heard was a motor whistling, as the girl drove away. Lucky tore out of the garage. "You fixed it!" he accused Mancini. "And we don't even know her name!"

"What does it matter?" Mancini asked sweetly. "You are on your way to Los Angeles, and I must work on my car. Therefore, we have no time to search for a beautiful girl."

"Yeah," Lucky agreed. "Well, nice to have seen you."

That they were conning one another, neither knew until that night. The two liars caught up with each other at one of the biggest, glossiest hotels in Las Vegas, where both had come to scan the girls. Maybe they didn't have time to search for a beautiful girl, but they were doing it anyway.

Realizing that they were both engaged in the same mission—to find Miss Motor Whistle—they joined forces. They hit the chorus line of every big place in town, and then they started on the smaller spots. They gave a joint called The Swingers Lounge their patronage, but all they found there was a convention of Texans who were smashing up the place. Across the street from The Swingers Lounge, they found The Silver Slipper. A poster outside bore a picture of a stripper identified as Miss Susie LeBang, and, truth to tell, Miss Susie did resemble the girl at the garage.

Lucky and Mancini headed for Susie's dressing room, and Lucky greeted her enthusiastically. "I've found you," he began.

"Huh?" said Miss LeBang.

"Don't you remember, baby? When I fixed your motor?"

A man who looked like a gorilla came out from behind a rack of costumes. The gorilla was Susie's husband, and he was now threatening everyone with sudden death. Susie pulled off her blonde wig, revealing that she not only had black hair, but that she definitely wasn't the girl from the garage.

"Please, *signor,*" Mancini explained to Susie's husband,

pagne foamed out over his lap. Mancini, mopping himself off, complained at last. "This is too much. Where's my regular waiter?"

"You don't want me, Count?"

"No! Anybody but you!"

"Okay," Lucky said. As he left, he threw a few parting words at Rusty. "Go easy on that pop, baby. You got to be at your best when you lose that talent contest. . . ."

Rusty was at her best in the talent contest that night. She danced brilliantly, and Lucky didn't think he had a chance. But he played his guitar and sang and got the audience into his act. In the end, the master of ceremonies declared a tie and settled the whole thing by tossing a coin.

Rusty lost the toss. It was first prize to Lucky, second prize to Rusty. The two of them stood side by side on the stage, ignoring each other.

"For Miss Rusty Martin," the emcee announced, "a complete set of rust-proof patio furniture, *and* a barbecue, electrically controlled."

Trying to look pleased, Rusty thanked everybody. Then the emcee turned his attention to first prize, a huge, silver cup.

"This cup is yours, Mr. Jackson," he told Lucky, "for one year, when it will be handed on to our next year's winner. You also win a two weeks' honeymoon trip to Monaco, plus a free wedding at the charming Las Vegas chapel."

Frozen in disbelief, Lucky gaped. He wanted money. He had to have cash, and here he was stuck with this silly cup and this silly honeymoon. . . .

He was still in shock later that night, as he lingered beside the pool, along with Shorty, Rusty, her father and Mancini.

"If we don't get the motor by tomorrow noon, we're dead," Shorty said. Lucky glared at him, and walked away. Shorty hurried after him, explaining to the others, "He might shoot himself, if he had a gun."

Mr. Martin turned to the Count. "I don't suppose you'd consider backing the boy?"

"I'm sorry," Mancini said, "but why should I lessen my chance of winning?"

After saying good night to Mancini, Rusty steered her father into a private conference. "Now then!" she explained. "Why this sudden interest in racing?"

"Honey, I'm only interested in helping a young man's dream come true. Can't you give a little, my darling? You're young, too. Don't throw cold water on a man's dream."

Suddenly, Rusty wilted. "Please take me home," she said. "I'm tired."

The morning of the big race found Lucky in coveralls, down at the garage. He'd lost his hopes, his motor, his girl; but he couldn't stay away from the cars. He offered to help work on Mancini's Ferrari and Mancini was delighted to accept. Lucky was working under the car's hood when Mr. Martin and Rusty turned up, followed shortly thereafter by Shorty. Shorty was driving a truck with a crate on it.

"Lucky," he shouted triumphantly, "the motor! I got it! Take a look at the beauty!"

The miracle stunned Lucky. Trying to find a reason for it, he turned to Mancini. "You did this?"

Mancini shook his head. "Save your gratitude, *amico*. Why should *I* do it?"

Rusty also denied that she'd helped. "Do you think I'd have any part of this whole horrible thing?" she said.

"Gee, Lucky," Shorty said, "stop playing like a detective, and get to work!" It was already noon, and the race would begin at midnight.

As if by common consent, Lucky, Shorty, and Mr. Martin began to unfasten the motor. By four o'clock, the motor was in the car shell, but their job was far from done. They were still working madly as night came on.

Rusty, who'd left in a huff when she realized her father intended to help, now returned to the garage, all dainty in a summer dress. She carried a box of sandwiches and an electric coffee pot.

"I brought you some food," she said to her father. "If *he'll* allow you time enough to eat it."

Lucky waved a hand at the spread she was setting out. "Get that junk out of the way!"

"That junk is nourishment for my father," she said. "Do you really think you'll get *your* junk running by midnight?"

Lucky was too busy to get mad. "If you're here to talk," he said, "take yourself out. If you want to help, get into these." And he tossed her a large pair of coveralls.

She wasn't much help, to be sure. She didn't know a wrench from an icepick, and she kept connecting her percolator in place of Lucky's drill. When she attempted to hand over a grease gun, she covered her father with the black stuff, and then she got Shorty right in the face.

A few minutes before midnight, a voice over the track's loud-speaker boomed through the garage: *"Drivers, get your cars to starting positions."*

One by one, the cars were either rolled or driven past Lucky's car. Finally, Lucky jumped in and started his motor. The roar filled the garage, even as the voice over the loud-speaker announced, *"Car eleven is still missing an entry."*

Lucky fished in his back pocket and handed an envelope to Rusty. "Get this to the starter in the tower. Hurry!"

For a wonder, she took it and went. . . .

At the starting post of the race, the drivers waited anxiously. Some were in crouching positions, their eyes on their cars. Others sipped coffee out of paper cups and smoked nervously. The number four driver stood with two beautiful girls, one of his arms around each waist, and he was smiling. Count Elmo Mancini, icy-calm, watched the warning flares. He was all racing driver now, out to win.

The number six driver kept patting his wife, who studied his face with sick anxiety. She was holding two children, one four and one six, but she wasn't aware of the babies; she was in a private hell.

Rusty and Lucky were waiting beside Lucky's car, when Shorty tore up with news. Lucky's pal who owned the helicopter was willing to pilot Lucky's "crew" of mechanics in the copter. The crew would be composed of Shorty, Mr. Martin—and Rusty, if she were willing.

"Guys like the Italian champ got real fancy crews at every checkpoint, so we got to take to the air," Shorty explained. "We sure can't make it on foot."

"You know how I feel," Rusty told Lucky, "and you're still going to drive?"

"I have to," he said. "I made that car myself. Piece by piece. And I'm racing against a champ and his checkbook."

Rusty inclined her head toward the number six driver and his wife. "I don't want the look that's on that woman's face."

Gently, he pushed a strand of hair back from her forehead. "You already have the look that's on that woman's face," he said.

And then it was time for the race.

About everything that could happen in a race happened. One car clipped a rock while skidding off the course and a tire exploded. Another car smashed into a fence. But by the time the sun had risen, Mancini was in the lead, with Lucky right behind him.

Lucky gave it all he had, came alongside Mancini, then passed him. In passing, he forced Mancini off the road. The Ferrari bounced into a field and overturned. In his mirror, Lucky could see smoke rising from the Italian car. He spun around onto the field, jumped out and pulled Mancini free. Then he doused the fire with an extinguisher.

As Mancini opened his eyes and began to thank Lucky, the helicopter landed nearby and Lucky's crew hurried to the scene of the accident.

"Is he hurt?" Rusty asked.

Lucky shook his head.

"Then what are you standing here for?" she asked. "Get back in the race."

He couldn't believe his ears, but he vaulted into his car and was off.

"Come on!" Rusty shouted to her father and Shorty. "Call yourselves a crew? Get into the copter!"

Well, with backing like that, how could Lucky lose?

He got the checkered flag. Flying above him in the helicopter, his crew cheered. Shorty turned gratefully to Mr. Martin and said, "Boy, can he ever pay you back for buying the motor now."

Mr. Martin's finger to his lips was a warning which

came too late. Rusty had heard. "Father," she said, "if you think for one minute, I didn't know you paid for Lucky's motor——" And she started to laugh.

Now Shorty and Mr. Martin noticed that she'd discarded her greasy coveralls during the flight and was back in her pretty dress. "When I stand at Lucky's side," she said, "he's going to be proud of me."

He was, too. In the midst of fans and well-wishers, his hand reached for hers, and Shorty good-naturedly ribbed him about the free wedding and honeymoon he'd won.

"I think my father's lost a daughter and gained a champ," Rusty said adoringly, and again Lucky couldn't believe his ears.

"You mean that?" he asked.

She nodded.

To the world in general, he shouted the news. "She means it!"

Then he turned to the girl he loved. "What are we waiting for?" he said. "Let's go!"

Adapted from the CUMMINGS-SIDNEY PANAVISION Production
Presented by METRO-GOLDWYN-MAYER
Directed by GEORGE SIDNEY
Produced by JACK CUMMINGS and GEORGE SIDNEY
Screenplay by SALLY BENSON
Color by METROCOLOR
Adapted for SCREEN STORIES by CHRIS KANE

CAST

Charlie Rogers	ELVIS PRESLEY	Joe Lean	LEIF ERICKSON
Cathy Lean	JOAN FREEMAN	Harry Carver	PAT BUTTRAM
Madame Mijanou	SUE ANN LANGDON		
Maggie Morgan	BARBARA STANWYCK		

ROUSTABOUT

■ They called it Mother's Tea House, and maybe a nice old lady once served tea there, but that was before the hep set at State University got on the espresso coffee kick, with beer chasers. Currently, the teahouse was the "in" joint for the pampered sophisticates of fraternity and sorority row. And the big attraction at the joint, at least as far as the sorority sisters were concerned, was guitar-banging Charlie Main.

The proprietor gave Charlie a rousing introduction: "The young man whose clean-cut, boyish manner conceals the instincts of a Mau-Mau—Charlie Main!"

Charlie came onstage with a huge and gleaming guitar. The audience shouted for favorite numbers, but Charlie perversely chose to ignore them. With a crash of chords, he was off on his original composition—"The Poison Ivy League."

It was poison, all right. A bitter satire of the spoiled sophomores on fraternity row. The girls in the audience giggled and blushed; the boys seethed.

"Man, he's funny like a case of mumps," said one boy, Sam.

"I'll bet he never got farther than grammar school," said Sam's friend, Dick.

"That's right, scholar," the waitress, Marge, agreed, serving them beer.

"We going to let him get away with this?" Sam demanded.

"No," Dick answered. "But just cool it a minute."

Marge drifted away. She caught Charlie when he came offstage and told him what she'd overheard.

"It might mean trouble," she said, worried.

"So what else is new?" Charlie answered, uncaring.

"Why do you have to play tough, Charlie?" she asked, genuinely concerned. "Where does it get you?"

"If you don't play tough, you get squashed," said Charlie.

"I didn't have any folks, either," Marge said gently.

"What has that got to do with it?" His voice was hard.

"Everything." In the couple of weeks that he had been there, Marge had come to know a lot about this homeless Southern boy who had been knocking around the country, living on his wits and guitar.

"Save it," he said harshly. He started out, but his way to the side door was suddenly blocked by the fraternity boy Sam.

"Man, this is a crummy joint," Sam said with a calculated insolence. "There's more action in a zoo."

"From which side of the cage?" said Charlie, pushing by.

"What's that supposed to mean?" demanded the other boy, Dick.

"You figure it out, college boy. I'm going to get some air."

Charlie went out to the parking lot. Sam and Dick went back to their table for another friend, Craig. Marge went to the phone and dialed the police. She had seen things like this develop before.

Charlie was mounting his beautiful new motorcycle when the three students surrounded him.

"Made in Japan, huh?" said Dick, coming up on his left. "American cycles are not good enough for you?"

"You don't dig world trade?" Charlie answered easily. "After all the economics they tried to shove into you?"

"Turn around, buddy," said Sam, closing in on his right.

As Charlie turned, Sam released his punch to the jaw. Before the fist could land, Charlie broke Sam's arm with a chopping blow.

Dick and Craig charged simultaneously. Charlie met Dick with a stiff, two-fingered jab to the face that dropped him. He caught Craig's fist in his hand and heaved, throwing Craig to the ground.

"That's called karate," Charlie said calmly. "It comes with the Japanese bike. Want any more?"

A police car wailed to a stop in the parking lot. Charlie started to make a run for it, but the police stopped him. It was the college students who kept the town solvent, so it was Charlie who spent the night in jail. The chief let him out in the morning. And Charlie was glad to go.

The indisputable fact was that Charlie liked going almost as much as he liked singing. The two were inseperable. Stay in one place, and your songs got dull. Only in movement, in drifting from place to place, did he feel he could keep his songs dynamic.

On his motorcycle, tooling along at 60 mph, Charlie sang a folk song composed for his own ears alone. It was no satire, but a ballad of motion and emotion that might be closer to the real Charlie Main than he would care to admit.

The Midwest of State University was behind him, now. He swung his motorcycle around a jeep that was holding a wide course down the highway. Glancing at the occupants, he saw a beautiful girl sitting next to an unshaven man and a tough-looking dame. At the next opening in the traffic, he pulled alongside again. She was a beautiful girl, all right. And he could not fail to note that the ill-kempt driver was ill-tempered as well, because at that moment the jeep took a vicious swerve toward Charlie.

"Hey, stupid," shouted Charlie, recovering with expert ease, "this is a public road. Or didn't you know?"

"My aim must be getting bad," the driver retorted loudly. "I thought I hit you." And with that he made a swerve that drove Charlie off the far side of the road.

Charlie was agile enough to throw himself clear; but the motorcycle, his guitar, and his neatly bagged luggage were sadly scattered on the ground.

The jeep came to a stop and the girl rushed over to help him up. "Are you all right?" she asked, pleading for an answer.

Charlie looked around groggily. The jeep was parked on the opposite side of the road, and the unshaven brute behind the wheel was looking at him as though disappointed at the lack of physical damage.

"You hot-shot cycle riders think you own the world," the man shouted. "More of you oughta be run off the highway."

Charlie lurched toward the man. "All right, wise guy, you asked for it," he said.

But the woman in the jeep got out to detain him. "Take it easy," she soothed, putting a restraining hand on Charlie's chest. "I'm sorry for what happened. Joe just got carried away with himself."

"You'll have to carry him away when I get through with him," said Charlie.

"You won't get anywhere acting like a dead-end kid," the woman said. "You want to talk, we'll talk."

"There's nothing to talk about," Charlie said flatly. "You're going to pay for what you did to my bike, or I'm taking it out of this rat's fur."

"Get in," the woman said, pushing Charlie toward the back of the jeep. "We'll send somebody back for your bike. Some of my men and gear from the carny."

"The *what?*" Charlie asked.

"The carnival. I own it. We're setting up at the picnic grounds near here."

Charlie was dubious, but he looked at the beautiful girl again. "Okay," he said with sudden meekness. "So long as you don't try to pay me off in cotton candy. What about my guitar?"

"We'll buy you a new one. Now get in."

There didn't seem to be much choice. Either he went along with them and hoped to collect, or he'd be left stranded in the middle of the prairie with a wrecked machine. He collected his personal gear from the ruin, and climbed aboard. "I'm Charlie Main," he announced.

At least the girl was responsive enough to introduce herself as Cathy Lean, the woman was Maggie Moore, and the driver was, incredibly, her father, Joseph Lean. And with that, under the glowering hostility of Joe, the conversation ended.

At the fairgrounds, several trucks and trailers were ringed around the park, their brightly painted sides proclaiming them to be, somewhat inaccurately, the greatest carnival on earth. At least, they were the greatest carnival on that particular piece of earth at that particular time.

"This is a carnival?" Charlie asked, starring at the trucks.

"In a few hours, you won't believe what you see," said Cathy defensively.

"I hope I won't have to," Charlie answered.

But Maggie said, "You'll be around for a while. They're not very big with Japanese motorcycle parts around here."

Maggie proved to be right. The best the local garage could promise, after appraising the damage, was a week if it could get the parts flown in from Los Angeles.

"What do you do when you're not riding around on your bike?" Maggie asked.

"I sing," said Charlie. "The campus circuit."

"How about a job with the carny—just until the bike's fixed?" Maggie suggested. "I could use a good roustabout."

"Are you serious? Me work in a circus?"

"This isn't a circus. It's a carnival. On second thought, forget it," said Maggie, turning away. "You might be too soft for real work."

"Hey, wait a minute!" Charlie looked tempted. "What about Joe?"

"He won't bother you," she answered, "if you don't bother Cathy."

Charlie looked around and saw Cathy setting up kewpie dolls in a tent-like stand. "But that was the whole idea," he said with a grin.

Maggie shrugged. "That's your problem."

Charlie nodded. "Where do I sleep?"

"Now you're a roustabout," said Maggie, and led him over to a huge truck loaded with iron rods. The big guy at the truck was named Cody, and Cody needed all the help he could get in unloading the iron rods and bolting them together.

Charlie was exhausted and dripping with sweat, but rising from his own blistered hands, many hours later, was the gaunt skeleton of a ferris wheel.

Joe came up, and by now Charlie had learned from Cody that while Maggie was the owner and business manager, Joe was the boss on the lot.

"Go and help Estelle in the mitt camp," Joe told Charlie. "After that, report to me."

"Mitt camp?" Charlie asked blankly.

"The palmistry tent. *Go!*"

Charlie had no trouble locating the gaudy palmistry tent. "The Number One Boss Man sent me in here to give you a hand," he announced, as he entered.

Estelle, professionally known as Madame Mijanou, turned her dark eyes upon him. "Which hand would you like to give me? The left hand, being closest to the heart, reveals much about love."

"Forget the fortune, baby," Charlie said. "I get all I want to know out of rice cookies."

"But I can tell you what kind of woman will be attracted to you," she declared. And to prove she knew what she was saying, she kissed him.

Charlie heard a distinct noise outside the tent, and he drew back hurriedly. In strange territory he had learned it was best to be cautious. "What was that?" he asked.

"Probably my boy friend," Estelle said calmly. "He's a knife thrower."

Charlie shot out under the back side of the tent, scarcely touching the canvas.

Charlie was watching the fire-eater practice flame swallowing when he heard someone call, "Hey, you!" The voice was big, but when Charlie looked around, the speaker wasn't evident.

"Down here, stupid," the voice said.

Charlie looked down to discover an indignant midget.

"Joe's been looking for you," said the midget. "I'll show you where he is."

With the midget leading the way, they passed a group of house trailers and a portable booth that served as an outdoor shower. Two of the carnival girls were splashing in the booth. They were visible from the shoulders up and the knees down.

"Billy, don't you come any closer," shouted one girl to the midget. "You're so short you can see right under the panel."

Billy blushed; but Charlie was enjoying the situation immensely, until Cathy came up beside him.

"Is that on your work list?" she asked.

"Just getting to know the family," he said in self-defense.

"Joe's up near the grab joint," said Billy, glad to escape.

"What's a grab joint?" asked Charlie.

"Hot-dog stand," Cathy explained. "I'm going that way."

Cody was just getting ready to give the ferris wheel a test whirl when Cathy and Charlie went by. And Charlie, seeing this monument to his own blood and blisters, could not resist piloting the flight.

"Joe'll be mad," warned Cathy.

"He's mad at the world," said Charlie. "Come on, Cathy." And in spite of her protests, which were really not too strong, he helped her into a seat and snapped the safety bar in front of them.

"To the moon," he told Cody. "Twenty-seventh floor, please." The mechanical music box started to play and up they went.

When the wheel returned them to the platform, Joe was waiting there. "We open in three hours," he snarled at Cathy, "and you know better than this."

"Don't blame her," Charlie cut in. "I talked her into it."

Joe whirled on him. "Maggie owns the place, and she can hire tramps if she wants. But I'm going to tell you once, and I'm going to tell you flat! Stay away from my daughter."

As Cathy had predicted, by opening time that night, Charlie could scarcely believe what he saw. From out of the trucks had come a motordrome, a half-dozen rides in addition to the ferris wheel, several games of skill and luck, the candy stands and juice joints, and the big tent and bally stand for the girlie show. Blown by a big fan above the grab joint, the smell of franks, burgers, and onions wafted over the midway.

Everyone had a job to do at one joint or another. Only Charlie seemed to be at loose ends.

Cathy was working the cat rack. Throw a ball for one little thin dime, the tenth part of a dollar, knock the cat off the rack, and win your choice of a box of candy, a kewpie doll, a ukulele, a camera—or a score of other items called "flash" by the carnies. It looked easy.

"Let me take a crack at it," Charlie offered. "I've got a very persuasive way about me."

"So I've noticed," said Cathy, and because business was slow and there was nothing to lose, she let him take her place. "Good luck."

He started out loudly enough, but the jive talk that went big with the campus cats was not working on the rubes from the wide-open spaces. In desperation, Charlie clutched at the arm of a passing yokel. "Hey, I'm talking to you, daddio! Get over here and pitch some balls!"

Frostily, and with great disdain, the yokel detached Charlie's clutching arm. "Let go of me, or I'll call a cop," he said.

Charlie looked around thoughtfully, and his eyes lighted on the cheap ukulele that was part of the flash. Quickly he tuned it to his own needs. He crashed off a series of chords, and launched into his own contribution to the midway. . . .

Maggie, deep in her own troubles, was walking through the half-empty lot on her way to the office trailer when she saw the crowd gathered around the folk-singing cat rack. "Well, I'll be damned," she said.

Joe was waiting for her in the office. "Heard from the bank?" he asked bluntly.

"Stop worrying, Joe. We'll pay them eventually," she said wearily.

"Oh. Someone was here?"

"Yeah," she admitted. "Nielson." He'd been sympathetic, she explained, but his bank was pressing him, and he knew that Harry Carver was ready to pay the bank in full to get possession of the carnival at a forced-sale price.

"You used to tell me these things." There was a penitent, almost wistful note in Joe's voice. Shaved and sober, he looked like he could be a nice guy.

"You have enough to worry about," said Maggie. "We lost four men on our last move."

Joe's belligerence flared out of control. "Because of my pleasant personality?" he sneered. "They weren't much good anyway. And that bum you hired—"

"Come on, Joe. Not again," she pleaded. "He started singing in front of the cat rack and drew a big crowd. Maybe he can pull some of them into the big tent."

"You're making a big mistake," Joe said.

"Let me be the judge of that," she said curtly. Then she relented, as she had always done with Joe. "I'm making some coffee. Want some?" There could be something between them if Joe wasn't so all-fired protective about that motherless chick of his, or so Maggie reflected.

Maggie used the extra take from the cat rack to buy

Charlie a guitar the next day. It was rawly new, and covered with hard varnish and glitter. Not mellow at all like his old instrument, but in competition with the midway calliope, it would do.

Maggie herself was at the mike on the bally stand that night, making the pitch for the girlie show.

"Direct from the Place Pigalle in Paris," she exhorted the crowd. "Executing the most stimulating of dances—the Can-Can! A sheen of black lace, a flash of flesh, ladies and gentlemen, just as you would see it in Gay Paree! See it all inside for just fifty cents."

The canned music blared. Six girls pranced across the bally stand in a swirl of petticoats and flounced away with the promise of great things to come.

"And in addition, ladies and gentlemen," Maggie shouted, *"Charlie Main!"*

Charlie came on fast, batting out some crowd-stopping chords that didn't need the microphone. Then he was off and singing. It was as though he had thrown a loop around the midway and was pulling in the rope. In two minutes, he had the crowd packed around the bally stand, and Maggie was turning them toward the ticket stand.

"You like it?" shouted Charlie.

There was a responsive roar.

"Then come in and hear some more. Don't push. The show doesn't go on for thirty seconds."

It was the young crowd Charlie was pulling in, and the young ones were the spenders. The tempo picked up all over the lot, and it was a tempo set by a rollicking guitar beat. Maggie nodded in satisfaction. Get those wallets and pocketbooks pried open once, and the spending habit became contagious.

Maggie went up to Charlie after his first show. "I'm asking you to stay on with a contract," she said. "I'll pay you union scale."

"No," Charlie said firmly. "Next Friday is go-day."

"I'd pay you more if I could."

"It isn't only the money." Charlie gestured vaguely. "I don't buy the whole scene. I don't want to get involved."

That week, Charlie continued to pack the crowds in. Monday nights were always bad at a carnival. But that

Monday night was big. The word had spread over the week end, and the young crowds were pouring in from towns up to fifty miles away. Tuesday was bigger, and by Wednesday the joints were leaping. Even Harry Carver of Carver's Combined Shows drove across two states to see what the big attraction might be.

"Just a routine check on competition," he told Maggie.

"Who are you kidding?" snorted Maggie. "We're no competition for your show."

"You might be if you could hang onto a kid like this," he said, pointing to Charlie on the bally stand. "He's pulling in the teen-agers for you."

"Thanks. We'll hold onto him," Maggie said shortly.

"You better. He's the only sign of life I've seen around here. Carver's Combined Shows always has room for one more." He looked at her calculatingly. "Would you like an offer *before* you go under?"

"No."

"Sooner or later I get them all." Harry grinned. "See you at the morgue."

But to Harry's surprise, Charlie Main was not interested in Carver's Combined Shows, not even with an offer of three hundred a week for the season.

"If you get any second thoughts, here's my schedule for the next five weeks," said Carver, handing over his card. "You've got an open date."

"Thanks. I'll think about it," said Charlie, pocketing the card. Then he headed for Maggie's tent and signed a contract with her.

Thursday night, the air was cool, which made for brisk business. But it was rough on the girl who worked the water tank concession. After just an hour and some lucky shots that dropped her from her perch into the icy water, the regular girl came down with the sneezes.

It was bad for business. No red-blooded male wanted to dunk a girl when he felt sorry for her. In desperation, Joe sent Cathy up on the perch and took over the tank joint himself. There was a gimmick under the counter he could work with his foot; when that was on, you'd have

to hit the target with the force of a cannon ball to trip
the perch.

Joe hadn't counted on coming across a human cannon.
When the man appeared, his fat and giggling girl friend
Hazel was already loaded down with the flash he had
won with his pitching arm. And when he let fly at the
tank target, Cathy went down with a splash that nearly
drowned her. She climbed back gamely. Crash!—the man
was on target again.

"Freddie boy, you kill me!" squealed Hazel. "You
oughta be with the Yankees."

Her squeals and the constant splashes drew a big, admiring crowd, and Freddie was in his element.

"Anybody bet she drowns before I get tired?" he bellowed and homed in another one.

"You're good, mister," said Joe, trying to give him the
brush. "Now how about giving somebody else a chance?"

Freddie pulled out a fat wallet and laid it on the counter. "I don't quit until I miss," he roared, grabbing up
another ball. Joe trod with all his weight on the gimmick,
and this time the thing worked. The ball bounced off the
target, but Cathy remained on her perch.

"Well, that's the end of the winning streak," said Joe.
"Now, who's next?"

"That ball hit, mister," said Freddie, outraged.

"Not hard enough," said Joe.

"I say it did!" Freddie declared.

Charlie saw the trouble from the bally stand, and moved
in quickly. But Freddie saw Charlie coming, and felled
him with a fist that landed like a mallet. Charlie went
down, and almost out. By the time Cathy had led him
groggily out of the way, two deputies from the sheriff's
office had the situation under control. But Joe was in
deeper trouble.

"Where's my wallet?" Freddie was shouting. "They
stole it!"

A search of the tank joint turned up nothing.

"You want to swear out a complaint?" demanded a
deputy.

"He sure does," said Hazel.

"You're it," the deputy said to Joe; and Joe, knowing

any protest would only hurt the carnival, submitted meekly to arrest.

"You stay here, Cathy," he said as he was led away. "They can't prove anything."

After the carnival was closed for the night, Cathy went off with Maggie to see what they could do about bailing Joe out. It wasn't easy to do in a strange town, especially with the carnies having a reputation for jumping bail.

Charlie wandered around the empty lot. He was drawn back to the scene of the trouble. He distinctly remembered seeing the wallet on the counter just before that mallet-like fist had slammed down on him. He peered under the counter. Nothing there. But then, below a crack in the plywood flooring, he saw it. With a sigh of relief, he drew out the wallet.

"Finders-keepers?" It was Estelle, standing nearby.

"What do you think?" he asked.

"I think you are hung up between splitting it with me, and getting a good mark from Cathy for springing Joe."

"Nothing like seeing the best in everyone," said Charlie, starting for Cathy's trailer.

"You louse," said Estelle.

He really went to the trailer to give Cathy the wallet, but the subject never came up. Suddenly they were a boy and a girl in love, and they were kissing.

"You better go, Charlie," she gasped. "Please."

"Because it was good?" he asked.

"Because it isn't right for me. I'm not a one-night stand."

Charlie stepped back, his face taut. Those were his words, "a one-night stand," no permanent attachments.

"I'm sorry, Charlie," said Cathy, responding to the hurt in his eyes. "I like you, too, but you're just passing through." And before he could say anything, she pushed him through the door and closed it.

Charlie climbed into the carnival jeep parked outside Maggie's office, the wallet thick in his back pocket. He took it out and looked at it. Hell, he had no love for Joe, and certainly Joe had no love for him. Let him spend the night in the cooler. It might sober him up. He climbed out and went to his bunk in the roustabouts' trailer. He'd get Joe cleared the first thing in the morning.

But the next morning the garage man brought Charlie's rebuilt motorcycle to the lot, and Charlie had to try it out. The roar of its motor brought out Ernie and Gus, the two demons of the carnival's motordrome. With one comment leading to another, Charlie decided to prove he could ride the vertical wall of their drome as well as they could.

It was nearly suicide. The centrifugal force that held the motorcycle glued to the vertical walls of the drome drained the blood from his head. By the time he'd circled the walls a few times, he'd had it. As he descended, he lost control of the bike. Luck kept him from falling beneath the slicing spokes of the back wheel as he fell. The wallet and everything else in his pockets were strewn everywhere.

Maggie and Cathy, who'd been about to start for the sheriff's office, had heard the wild roar of the upended motorcycle. They rushed into the drome. Cathy flew to Charlie just as Ernie reached the motor to cut it off.

"Charlie," she gasped.

"I'm okay," he said, some blood returning to his head. "I'm feeling better every minute." And he let his head drop back into her lap.

But Maggie had spotted the wallet and was looking accusingly at Charlie.

Charlie looked back evenly. "It belongs to the guy who got in the beef with Joe," he admitted. "I found it under the floor. I was on my way downtown to turn it in."

"That's what he told me," Ernie put in.

Charlie was glad, now, that he had made no secret of his finding the wallet. But Cathy and Maggie were far from satisfied with the story.

"Charlie," Cathy exclaimed in shocked disbelief, "you let Joe sit in jail all this time?"

"What difference does it make?" All of Charlie's resentment of the abuse he had taken from Joe returned. "It gave him a few more hours to dry out."

"Last night he was in jail, and you could have gotten

him out." Cathy's eyes were wide and stricken. "And all you could think of was to make a silly pass at me." She fled, her hand muffling her sobs.

"You're a cruel boy, Charlie," Maggie said slowly. "You must have been hurt pretty badly."

Charlie gathered up his possessions. "You don't stay where you're not wanted," he said.

"Do you think she'd get this upset if you weren't wanted?" Maggie asked. She tried to make him understand that in the carnival world one carny was loyal to another, regardless of personal differences. To a kicked-around loner, this was too much to understand.

"I'll get my gear," said Charlie.

The lead outfit of Carver's Combined Shows was big, gaudy, noisy, and profitable. Charlie liked the money and he liked the crowds. He liked being a success.

"Don't let it go to your head," Carver warned him. "I've seen performing seals draw that much applause."

"Try one out there next show," said Charlie.

"I'd like to," grinned Carver. "You pay them in fish."

They understood each other, Charlie and Carver. Two loners, each out for himself. And only occasionally did Charlie wonder why he worried about how Maggie was getting along. . . .

Maggie was not getting along at all. Joe had been cleared, all right, with the return of the wallet. But the newspaper stories of the carnival fracas had been big, and there was no news value in the follow-up story of a rube recovering his lost wallet. The carnival moved under a wet blanket from week to week until even Maggie, bally-hooing the black lace and pink flesh of the girlie show, sounded as though she were auctioneering a church rummage sale. Nielson had to return with a court order.

"You can't convince them we're worth more alive than dead?" Maggie asked helplessly.

As far as Nielson could see, without any attraction to bring in the teen-agers, they were already more dead than alive. "I'm sorry, Mrs. Moore. I wish I could help. I'm told that you were getting them for a while with that young singer."

Maggie had no answer to that.

Estelle tried to find some answers for Cathy in her crystal ball.

"Knock it off, Estelle," Cathy said curtly. "You know I don't believe in that stuff."

"Who does?" Estelle said. "I know how you felt about Charlie, and I know how he felt about you," she went on. "That's why I couldn't get to first base. Get him back —for the show," she urged. "There hasn't been a spending teen-ager near this place since he left."

"He wouldn't—even if I begged him."

"Oh, he will," Estelle said. "If you run over to Carver's and give him the business, he'll come back."

"No," Cathy said.

"You got a family to support, kid." Estelle saw Cathy weakening and bore down. "Your dad, and Maggie, and the show. And I don't want to be back in some tearoom reading coffee grounds. Think it over. But think fast. We're drowning."

Harry Carver spotted Cathy roving down his crowded midway, and he moved back to warn Charlie. "They're in trouble," was his accurate explanation. "She's here to try to get you back there."

For some reason, Charlie was glad. "Everyone isn't as big a crook as you are, Harry," he said.

"Everyone tries," said Harry.

And Cathy did try, but she was too honest to bring it off. Suddenly, she burst into tears. "Listen, Charlie," she confessed, "the only reason I came over was to try to get you to come back to the show, no matter what I had to do. Only I just don't have the guts. I wish I did. It probably wouldn't have worked anyway. We're losers, and you know it."

"Cathy—" Why couldn't he say what he wanted to say? He who was supposed to be so fast with the ad-lib? Everytime he had something really important to say, he somehow couldn't think of the words. He watched Cathy move away, a small, disconsolate figure, and he could only knot his fists in frustrated silence.

But at the end of the midnight show he knew what he had to do. So did Carver. "I know exactly what's going through your head," said Carver. "The answer is no."

"It'll kill Maggie to give up," said Charlie.

"Who you kidding?" snorted Carver. "You're not worried about Maggie. It's Cathy. And what's your problem? If you want the girl, all you have to say is 'Cathy I love you,' like the grownups do. You don't have to prove you're a knight in shining armor."

"You're a carny—a rich one, but a carny," said Charlie. "You should understand."

"I do. I even feel a little bit guilty about it. But I've learned how to feel guilty in comfort. That," said Carver, "is how I got to be a *rich* carny."

"I'm going there, Harry." Charlie's voice was firm.

"One small detail. I'll sue you and take half your salary. Remember our deal."

Charlie took out his well-stuffed wallet. "You've paid me a thousand and fifty. Here's fifty. I'll owe you the rest."

Carver saw the other money stuffed away in there, but what the hell, he could afford to lose once in a while. He waved as the motorcycle roared, and Charlie was away into the night.

It was a dead carnival he reached shortly after sunup. The sheriff was in possession, and Nielson was arranging for the final disposition of the rolling stock. An auction, a bid from Carver to cover the bank's investment, and the chances were good that in another week or so the employees, minus Maggie and Joe, would be back to work as a unit of Carver's Combined Shows.

Small wonder that Joe's mood was more ugly than usual when Charlie wheeled into the lot.

"What the hell do you want?" snarled Joe. "Get out of here."

Charlie was not awed. "Listen, Joe, I'm not here to save face for you. But I can't let Maggie go down the drain without trying to help."

"I said get out." And then Joe made the mistake of throwing a punch.

It was one of those wide-open punches that any good karate man could have turned into a broken arm, but Charlie elected to fight Joe's way. It became a brutal slugfest with sledge-hammer blows unglossed by skill or science. When Joe went down for the last time, it was for the long count.

Charlie wasn't in much better shape, but he was on his feet when Maggie and Cathy rushed out from the trailer. And he had a wallet that could speak more clearly than he could.

"You can send the vultures home," he said when his eyes could focus on Nielson. "There's a thousand dollars. Will that hold them until I can prove I can make this outfit pay off?"

"I think so," said Nielson.

But Maggie, like Carver, was not convinced that Charlie had come back for the altruistic purpose of saving her tough hide. She forced the issue. "Say it straight," she commanded.

"Okay, okay," stammered Charlie. "I came back because I wanted to. Because you were stuck and I thought I could help."

"And?" Maggie asked relentlessly.

"And because I love Cathy," Charlie exploded.

There. It was out. All the tender words he had been unable to voice had angrily burst from him in front of a crowd of carnies.

"You don't have to yell at her," Maggie reproved him happily. "If you use the energy you spend trying to be a louse—"

"Stop picking on him," said Cathy, recovering her composure.

Charlie, because he didn't know what else to say, roared, "Let's get going. We got work to do."

Joe nodded. "Let's get this show moving," he said, starting down the midway.

Cathy, Maggie and Charlie followed.

"Hey, Joe," shouted Charlie. "Wait for us."

Adapted from the HAL WALLIS TECHNISCOPE Production
Released by PARAMOUNT PICTURES
Directed by JOHN RICH

Produced by HAL WALLIS
Screenplay by ANTHONY LAWRENCE and ALLAN WEISS
Story by ALLAN WEISS
Color by TECHNICOLOR
Adapted for SCREEN STORIES by GEORGE SCULLIN

CAST

Johnny Tyronne .... ELVIS PRESLEY   Prince Drana .... MICHAEL ANSARA
Aishah .... FRAN JEFFRIES   Zacha .... JAY NOVELLO
Princess Shalimar ...... MARY ANN MOBLEY
King Toranshad .... PHILIP REED

HARUM SCARUM

■ It was a good will tour that had brought Johnny Tyronne to the Near Eastern country of Babelstan, and the State Department was delighted with the way things were going. At the première of Johnny's latest movie, *Burning Sands,* the people lined up to meet the American star as though they were teen-agers meeting Elvis Presley.

The American Ambassador introduced Johnny to the important guests, including the President of Babelstan and his wife. Prince Dragna, from the nearby country of Lunarkand, was there, too. With him was a gorgeous girl called Aishah, who fixed Johnny with hot eyes. "Mr. Tyronne," she said, referring to a scene in *Burning Sands,* "is it true that you *actually* killed that tiger with one blow of your bare hand?"

Embarrassed Johnny answered modestly. "Yes, but it wasn't in the script. That chain actually broke, and I had to keep us from getting all clawed up."

Prince Dragna said he'd like Johnny to be the guest of his brother, King Toranshah, in Lunarkand.

The American Ambassador beamed. "Johnny, this is a tremendous honor," he said. "Do you realize you are the first American His Majesty, King Toranshah, has ever invited into his kingdom?"

The ravishing Aishah urged Johnny to accept. "When you cross the Mountains of the Moon into our country, you will be stepping back 2,000 years, and you will find the pageantry and beauty almost unbelievable."

"How can I refuse?" Johnny said.

"A limousine will be at your hotel at eight in the morning," Prince Dragna said, bowing low. . . .

Later, looking back, Johnny could never quite remember all the events of that next day. It began with an airplane ride to Bar Esalaam, and a trip on horseback through the Mountains of the Moon. Then the travelers stopped to have supper beside a campfire on a grassy bank near a river. Afterward, Prince Dragna excused himself and went into his tent, leaving Aishah and Johnny alone. Aishah poured wine into a goblet for Johnny and sat very close to him as they stayed there drinking. His head suddenly began to spin, and he passed out cold.

He never saw the hooded men with no eyebrows, and

mysterious symbols tattooed on their foreheads. He never even felt their hands as they bound him and carried him away. . . .

Amid the pink and white roofs of the city of Taj, sat the Royal Palace of King Toranshah. The King and his beautiful daughter, Princess Shalimar, were playing chess when Prince Dragna and Aishah hurried in. The King was surprised by this visit from his brother. "Did you tire so soon of the pleasures of the modern world?" he asked.

"I would have come bearing a surprise for you both," Dragna said. "I met Johnny Tyronne, the American cinema star, in Babelstan, and was bringing him to be our guest here at the Palace. But our camp was attacked, and our guest was abducted, which is the reason I rode with all speed to warn you. For the attackers were the Assassins! And they may soon be approaching the city!"

The King and the Princess paled. The Assassins were a notorious group of evildoers whose very existence threatened the peace of Lunarkand. Prince Dragna continued, his voice oozing concern. "We must make every effort to find Mr. Tyronne for fear of international complications. And we must tighten the security of the Palace, and send Shalimar to the Summer Palace in the mountains where she will be safe."

It was agreed that, for the sake of protocol, the King would remain in the city, under guard, until the Fast of Ramadan ended, in four days' time. Then he would join Shalimar at the Summer Palace.

Shalimar bowed her head in submission. An Eastern Princess did as she was told.

When Johnny Tyronne woke up, he thought he was still asleep. There was a beautiful, half-clad maiden massaging his temples, and another one playing a lute. He was lying on some cushions beside a fountain. One of the maidens said the place was called the Garden of Paradise, but Johnny couldn't recall getting there.

His memory wasn't even jogged by the appearance of four huge, black-robed, eyebrowless creatures with tattoos on their foreheads. One of the men held a gun on Johnny and said, "We're taking you to Sinan, Lord of the Assassins."

It sounded like a joke, until he was ushered into a torture chamber, where the walls were hung with chains and whips. Astonishingly, the beautiful Aishah sat on a golden throne in the room.

"My Master, Sinan, Lord of the Assassins, wishes to know if Johnny Tyronne really carries death in each bare hand," she said.

Grimly, Johnny stared at her. "So you told your Master about my killing the tiger! You mix quite a nightcap!" he commented.

But he had no more time to reflect on the perfidy of women. A gong sounded and Sinan, the great, bald Lord of the Assassins, moved into the room, looking like a huge vulture.

At first, Sinan's tone was silky. "I need your skilled hands," he told Johnny, "to eliminate a person of great importance."

Johnny gasped. "You don't understand. I use Karate strictly for defense, not for killing off people I don't like."

Sinan's patience was short. He ordered his men to persuade Johnny with their whips.

When Johnny regained consciousness, he was back in the garden, with a slave girl oiling his whiplashed back. A raggedy-looking man was trying to lift his wallet, but Johnny grabbed it back.

Caught, the man explained himself. "My name is Zacha, a member in good standing of the Honorable Guild of Marketplace Thieves. You are a stranger in a strange land with none to advise and protect you. You need me, O Noble Client."

Johnny gave him a bill out of the wallet and asked him for information about airports and American Embassies. Lunarkand had neither.

"You forget, Noble Client," Zacha said, "this kingdom has been isolated from the rest of the world for 2,000 years."

After thanking the girl who'd been anointing him, Johnny sat up and began questioning Zacha. What was a thief doing in this place anyway?

"I perform various services for Sinan, for which he pays me very handsomely," Zacha answered.

"Then what do you want from me?" Johnny demanded.

Zacha sent the slave girl out to prepare a scented bath before he answered. Then he spoke confidentially. "It is dangerous to talk before witnesses, O Noble Client."

Johnny studied his new "employee." "Would the subject of my escape offend your sense of loyalty to Sinan?"

"Not if your generosity outweighs my horrible fear of having my throat cut by Sinan."

"Get me out of this," Johnny said flatly, "and I'll pay you $10,000."

Zacha agreed that they would escape when darkness fell.

The escape came off very well after a certain amount of hiding in lily ponds, and using Karate chops, and ducking bullets, and scaling trees. In full flight, Zacha and Johnny got separated, but they had foreseen that and knew where to meet later. Johnny ran until he came to a great, high wall. He vaulted it and landed right in a little pool on the other side.

He didn't know it, but he'd invaded the garden of the Summer Palace, and the sanctuary of Princess Shalimar, who was staring at him as he climbed out of the pool.

"Don't scream," he begged. "I'm in enough trouble already. I'm Johnny Tyronne, an American. I was kidnapped and brought to that fortress back up the hill."

Shalimar was puzzled. "But the Sheik El Hussein dwells in the fortress—a kindly old man who would harm no one."

"Does he have a house guest named Sinan?" Johnny asked.

Shalimar's breath caught. "Sinan—the Assassins—here? I must go to Taj at once and warn—warn my Master!"

"I'm to meet my friend at the Pool of Omar," Johnny said, remembering Zacha's final instructions. Shalimar offered to provide horses for Johnny and his friend. She agreed to lead him to the Pool of Omar. Then they would all ride back to Taj together. . . .

The Pool of Omar was a lovely spot. As they waited there for Zacha, Johnny found himself very much drawn to his charming guide who told him she was a slave girl named Yanee. He sang her a love song, and he asked if he might buy her from her Master. She said perhaps, but first her Master would want to know why Sinan had kidnapped Johnny.

"He brought me here to assassinate someone of great importance," Johnny said. "On account of my hands. There's a science known as Karate, where a man's bare hands become the deadliest weapons."

Now Shalimar was frightened. Sinan was her father's enemy, and, he'd brought this stranger here to kill her father. As Johnny turned away to demonstrate a Karate thrust and break a piece of slate in half, Shalimar sprang to her white horse and galloped off, leading the other two horses.

As soon as she had gone, Zacha crept out of the nearby bushes. When Johnny turned around, he was doubly astonished—by Yanee's sudden departure and by Zacha's sneaky appearance.

Zacha decided they would make their way through the mountains to the market place in Taj, where they would join up with a small troupe of entertainers. Disguised as members of the troupe, they could travel to Bar Esalaam when the Feast of Bairam began and the performers left Taj. It cost Johnny a thousand dinars to convince the musicians to take him on, but Zacha assured him it was a bargain. . . .

Shalimar rode like the wind back to Taj, flew into the palace and interrupted her father and her uncle at their chess game.

"The old fortress of the Sheik El Hussein has been taken over by Lord Sinan and his Assassins, Father," she cried.

The King stood up and addressed his Captain of the Guard. "Take a group and raid the old fortress. Any Assassins you find are to be exterminated!" The Captain left at once.

"The young American was imprisoned there," Shalimar went on. "He escaped and climbed our palace wall. He told me Sinan kidnapped him to assassinate some important personage!"

Dragna lifted pious eyes to heaven. "And to think that

by inviting Mr. Tyronne here I played right into the hands of Sinan!" he said.

The troupe Johnny and Zacha joined in the market place was composed of three young dancing girls—their names were Amethyst, Sapphire and Emerald—and a drummer boy named Julna. The most important member, though, was a midget called Baba. While his confederates performed, he eased through the crowd stealing purses from the unwary onlookers.

On the day that Johnny and Zacha joined the performers. Baba was caught stealing from a scar-faced Bedouin, and a mad pursuit ensued. A whole group of Bedouins chased Baba and the dancers, who fled with Zacha and Julna. Johnny, too, was in danger of being carved up by a Bedouin dagger, when suddenly two little children came to his rescue with slingshots. Finally, they all outran their pursuers and arrived, breathless, at the ruined gates of what had once been a palace.

Zacha went to a crumbling wall of mosaic tile and pressed the eye in what appeared to be a tail feather of a peacock. A section of the wall opened.

"Enter the Palace of Jackals, O Most Valuable Client," Zacha invited.

Once inside the crumbling sanctuary, Johnny thanked the children for helping him. The little girl's name was Sari and her brother's name was Yussef. Johnny offered to take them home to their mother, but they said they had none. An avalanche had killed both their parents, and now Sapphire, Emerald and Amethyst took care of them.

"Here in the Palace of Jackals," Zacha told Johnny, "you will be safe until it is time to go through the Southwest Pass to Bar Esalaam."

"Where we will grab a plane for Istanbul," Johnny said prayerfully. Then he told Zacha he had another errand for him. He wanted Zacha to find the beautiful slave girl Yanee, whose Master dwelt in Taj.

"Your wish is my command until payday, O Most Valuable Client," Zacha said, and hurried away. . . .

That night, in the Palace of Jackals, Johnny and the troupe amused themselves with dancing and singing.

Zacha still hadn't returned by the time they went to sleep.

Sometime later, Johnny awoke to find the visitor Zacha had brought. She was kissing him. But it wasn't Yanee. It was Aishah.

"Our most trusted spy tracked you down," she told Johnny.

Johnny glared at Zacha. "Working both sides of the street, pal? It figures."

Aishah wasted no time. She indicated little Sari, Yussef, and the three sleeping girls. "Are they all orphans? Yet, even for orphans, life can be sweet. Such a pity—"

"What are you trying to tell me?" Johnny demanded.

"Only that, unless you obey the orders of my Master, and kill with your Karate-skilled hands, the lives of these orphans will be forfeited."

Even as she spoke, a group of black-robed Assassins, led by Mokar, Sinan's chief lieutenant, moved into the palace room, brandishing their whips.

Awakened, little Sari screamed, and the other young people looked toward Johnny in terror. He had no choice. Their lives depended on him.

"Who do I have to kill?" Johnny asked.

"King Toranshah," Aishah said. "Ruler of Lunarkand!"

In the Royal Palace, the King and Princess Shalimar prepared for a feast in the great hall after sunset, when the Fast of Ramadan ended and the Feast of Bairam began. But they were interrupted by Prince Dragna, who brought news that the guards had returned from their raid on the fortress and had found Sinan and the Assassins gone!

"The Assassins may even now be within the city walls," Dragna said. "If I am late for the feast tonight, it will be because I am making sure of your safety. . . ."

Aishah had arranged for Johnny and the performers to entertain at the Feast of Bairam at the Royal Palace. The rest was up to him. Once Johnny had assassinated King Toranshah, he and his band would go free. Sari and Yussef would be held at the Palace of Jackals until then.

King Toranshah suspected nothing unusual about the troupe. Johnny strummed a lute, Zacha and Julna beat the drums, and the three girls danced. Johnny noticed that the

King was surrounded by six guards, and that handmaidens tasted his wine and sampled his food before he ate or drank. Johnny also noted that Prince Dragna was not there. Beginning to sing he edged closer to the throne.

It was during Johnny's song that the Princess Shalimar came running in. She had not attended the celebration. Upstairs in her room, she'd heard the music and recognized Johnny's voice. She hurried to warn her father.

"Father, he's here to kill you!" she shrieked, throwing herself between the King and Johnny.

Johnny was confounded at the sight of Shalimar. His slave girl a Princess? "All I want is to talk to your father," he began, but a guard hit him over the head, and he dropped solidly to the floor.

Prince Dragna ran in then, praising Allah that the King was safe, and issuing orders to the guards. "Throw this carrion and his confederates into the Citadel."

The jailbreak was spectacular. It couldn't have been done, however, without the midget Baba, whose presence with the troupe had been overlooked. He scampered in and out of the palace rooms—hiding in statues, stealing ropes, and braining guards—until he finally made his way into the troupe's cell.

Johnny threw the silken rope Baba gave him over a parapet and helped the girls and Julna climb down. Then he sent Zacha after them.

"You still want that $10,000?" Johnny asked Zacha. "Then get back to the Palace of Jackals fast and protect Sari and Yussef," he ordered, "because I'm going after King Toranshah!"

Then, with Baba's help and using the same silken rope, Johnny swung, like Tarzan, across the parapet and into the arched recess in the Tower of Royal Chambers.

Once again, Johnny interrupted the Princess Shalimar in her own quarters. This time, he slid down the rope right into the small bathing pool in her room, with Baba clinging to his neck. This time, though, Shalimar's father was with her. When the King saw the invader, he snatched up a dagger.

"Wait!" Johnny implored him. "All I ask is five minutes to explain."

"You were sent here to assassinate me," said the King. "There is nothing to discuss."

"I wasn't going to assassinate you," Johnny cried. "I'm in love with your daughter, so how could I assassinate you!"

King Toranshah sighed. "I'm willing to listen."

Still hanging onto the edge of the pool, Johnny began to explain. "We're in deep trouble, sir. You, because someone in this palace has hired Sinan to have you assassinated. Me because if I refuse to harm you, my own throat will be cut, along with the throats of two little orphans in the Palace of Jackals. But I've got an idea how we can flush into the open the man or woman who hired Sinan and his Assassins to murder you."

The King smiled. "Then it seems we do have matters to discuss, Mr. Tyronne. Pray forgive me for leaving you in the pool." He turned to Shalimar. "My dear, a towel for Mr. Tyronne, and one for his small assistant."

Late that night Prince Dragna was roused from sleep by a frenzied guard. "King Toranshah is missing!" cried the guard. "The bed ripped by dagger thrusts, and heavily bloodstained!" He showed Dragna a bloody sheet and handed him the Royal Ring found with it. "We greatly fear for His Majesty's life, Your Highness."

Prince Dragna closed his eyes. "My poor, dear brother." He took the ring from the guard and stared at it.

"The assassin must be the young American," the guard declared, "for he has escaped from the Citadel."

"Then don't just stand there," Dragna raged. "Find my brother's assassin. Kill him on sight!"

After the guard had gone, Dragna slipped the jade ring with the Great Lion Seal of Lunarkand onto his own finger. . . .

Dressed as beggars, Johnny, Baba, the King and Shalimar hurried to the Palace of Jackals and let themselves in through the secret wall. They hid in the shadows of the great columns which surrounded the throne room, and they stood there silently observing. Zacha, Julna and the three dancers had returned there as Johnny had told them to.

Zacha was being whipped by Sinan's men, though he

swore over and over that the American had killed the King. Aishah watched calmly. "It is possible," she said at last to Sinan, "that, for once, Zacha is telling the truth, My Lord?"

Sinan stared contemptuously at the groveling Zacha and said, "The client who is paying for my services will prove or disprove your babbling." He motioned to Mokar, his chief aide. "Bring my client here."

Mokar bowed and left the palace. He was back a few moments later with a hooded stranger.

Behind the columns, Johnny and King Toranshah strained to recognize the newcomer.

"I see you already wear the Royal Seal," Sinan said.

Prince Dragna dropped his hood, and tossed two leather purses at Sinan's feet. "It is my pleasure to conclude our bargain with the payment of these fifty thousand gold dinars," he said.

In their hiding place, the King and Princess Shalimar gasped.

"So now," Sinan was saying, "Your Majesty is free to let Bakir Oil Company open those vast oil deposits in the Valley of the Moon. The yearly returns will put millions in my coffers."

"In your coffers!" shouted Dragna. "Your participation has ended. I am the King now, and you have been paid generously for your services."

Sinan's smile was cold. "True, you are the King. However, I am taking over the kingdom, and you will remain in the Palace as the puppet ruler."

Four Assassins bound Dragna. "You will immediately order the entire Royal Guard out of the city to the Summer Palace," Sinan continued. "When the time comes, they will be attacked and destroyed." Sinan turned to Aishah. "My most beautiful one," he said, "comfort His Majesty in his defeat—and watch him closely!"

Dragna was hauled away, and Aishah followed him. Then Sinan turned his attention to the frightened group of performers. "These spawn of the gutter have eyes," he said. "They have ears and tongues to babble in the market place! Destroy them!" he told his Assassins.

It was time for Johnny to move. He leaped from behind

a column, bounded up the steps to the throne, and threw a death grip around Sinan's neck. "Call off your goons, fast, or I'll break your neck!"

In agony, Sinan barked at his men. "Drop your weapons! Drop them!"

The Assassins dropped their daggers, their whips, and their ropes. The King and Shalimar came out of the shadows, and soon Sinan and all his helpers were tied and gagged. But, with the Royal Guard out of the city, Johnny and the King still had to face a huge problem. The Assassin forces were arriving from all over the Kingdom to take over Taj.

"Seems we only have two choices, Your Majesty," Johnny said. "Either we try to escape to Bar Esalaam and bring help to retake the city—or try to join the Royal Guard at the Summer Palace."

But Zacha, recovered from his whipping, now volunteered a third choice. He felt the Assassins could be beaten right there in Taj. "It would seem that all that lies between us and victory is lack of manpower," he said. And he could supply the manpower—for payment. Half the royal treasury was his price.

King Toranshah agreed. He had nothing left to bargain with.

Johnny, Zacha and the King entered the Street of Jackals leading an old, two-wheeled cart, drawn by a burro. In the back of the cart was a rolled-up Persian rug. Inside the rolled-up rug was Sinan, bound and gagged. Sitting on top of the rug were Shalimar, Emerald, Amethyst, Sapphire and Baba. As the procession moved through the street, Zacha called out the cries of a jackal. From the coffeehouses, the balconies, the alleys, the bushes, the rooftops, came Zacha's friends—all the thieves of the city—in answer to his cries. They carried slingshots, bows and arrows, clubs, and rakes. They congregated at the fountain in the town square, where Johnny was binding Sinan to a post, and they waited for their orders.

"Spread out over the market place, and attack small groups of Assassins as they arrive!" Johnny directed. "We must not allow them to assemble in force! Now move out!"

Then he told the girls to run for cover and stay hidden. The battle was on. . . .

It was a marvelous fight. The Assassins were hit with everything from watermelons to Karate chops. Sinan was accidentally killed by one of his own men, and the battle was soon over. The foes were tied up, and the streets were silent.

Suddenly, Shalimar realized that the King was missing. "Johnny, where is my father?" she gasped.

"He insisted on going to the palace after Prince Dragna," Johnny explained.

Led by Johnny and Shalimar, the whole crowd of victorious battlers hurried across the square and up the hill to the Palace.

But there was nothing to worry about. The King had vanquished Dragna in a sword duel. Their hands tied, both Dragna and Aishah sat in front of a chessboard, looking sour.

"I could not kill my own brother, Johnny," King Toranshah explained, "but I am sending him into exile—with his favorite chess player."

Johnny grinned. "Just be a nice King, and don't exile them to the U.S.A. . . ."

As it turned out, Dragna and Aishah were almost the only natives of Lunarkand who *didn't* end up in the United States.

The poster advertising Johnny's next show said: *The Galaxy Hotel, Las Vegas, presents Johnny Tyronne and his Harem of Dancing Jewels from the Near East*. Sapphire, Emerald, Amethyst and little Sari were all there.

The loveliest jewel of all, however, was Princess Shalimar, sitting at a ringside table, studying her huge diamond engagement ring, and her wedding ring, too, and occasionally stroking her brand-new mink coat, while her father smiled from his chair beside her.

An Eastern Princess had found a Western Prince, and nobody could tell Shalimar or Johnny that the twain never met.

Adapted from the METRO-GOLDWYN-MAYER
PANAVISION Presentation
Directed by GENE NELSON
Produced by SAM KATZMAN
Screenplay by GERALD DRAYSON ADAMS
In METROCOLOR
Adapted for SCREEN STORIES by CHRIS KANE

CAST

Jesse Wade	ELVIS PRESLEY	Sheriff Ramsey	JAMES ALMANZAR
Tracey	INA BALIN	Sara Ramsey	BARBARA WERLE
Vince	VICTOR FRENCH	Billy Roy	SOLOMON STURGES

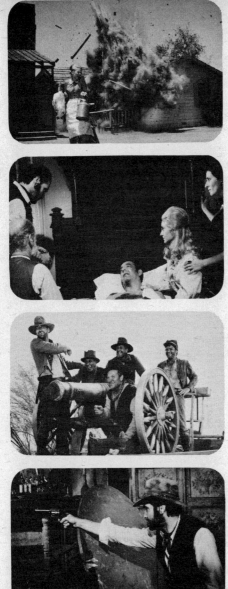

■ The man who stood over him, grinning like a wolf, was the same man who had held the redhot poker to his neck the night before. Vince Hackett, boss gunslinger.

It had taken all Jess Wade's guts to keep silent while the iron seared his flesh. The wound still burned, these hours later, with dawn spilling into the canyon. Here the gang—Heff, Gabe, Lige, Gunner, Mody, stupid Billy Roy—had herded him like a steer for branding. And here Jess still lay, arms trussed, ankles rope-hobbled.

"Wound looks better." Vince loomed in the early light. "Looks real good, Jess."

It had taken a smart ruse to trap him. They'd sent a message from Tracy Winters to the gold vein Jess had been prospecting, with meager results, through this past year since he'd broken from the gang to go straight. And when he'd ridden in to Montelmo in response to her supposed summons, they'd been lying ready to ambush him.

But they hadn't gunned him down. Instead, they'd outflanked him and taken him here to this remote place. All that long ride, Jess had been wondering why. Now he knew.

The answer lay lashed on a mule-drawn wagon, covered by a tarpaulin. It was a cannon; a Napoleonic twelve-pounder, its bronze barrel completely plated in pure gold. Its mount and its wheels were encased in solid silver. Jess knew at once it had been stolen.

"And you're going to melt it down."

"You been away from me too long, charro," Vince had leered back. "I never think short, always long. This gun isn't just gold and silver. It's what they call the Victory Gun. It fired the last shot against Maximilian to free all Mexico. It's a shrine."

"How far ahead of the Federales are you?" Jess had grated.

And Vince had roared.

"Not us, Jess. You. They're after *you!* And I wanted to make sure you were still in the neighborhood. Remember Norm? They shot him in the neck while we were getting away. I buried him in the desert. But I let out it wasn't him at all, it was you.

"They got reward posters out on you, north and south

of the border. *Wanted, Jesse Wade, American, six-foot-two, dark hair, fair complexion, only identifiable member of the thieves who stole the Victory Gun from Chapultepec Palace on July eight last. This man can be identified by a severe wound across his neck. . . .*"

So while they held him down and branded him, Jess didn't have to wonder why. He had outraged Vince Hackett by quitting his gang; and by winning his girl, Tracy. This was the revenge. They had made him a marked man, a price on his head and nowhere to hide.

Staring down on him now, with sunrise at the canyon rim, Vince was relishing it. The rest of the outfit had ridden out hours ago, rolling the cannon and taking along Jess's unsaddled horse with them. But Vince had remained, to stand guard and gloat.

"So you see who they're after, Jess? You!"

Covering Jess with his gun, he knife-slashed the rope binding the prisoner's arms.

"Tend to your hobble later, boy. After I'm gone. I leave you grub. You're free to run, Jess. Anywhere the Mexican Federales or the United States Cavalry can't hunt you."

It was three nights later when Jess rode cautiously into the border hamlet called Rio Seco. By then, he was forking a big, freshly-gentled bay horse; a beauty.

A safe while after Vince had ridden out after the others and left him, Jess had worked loose his hobble and picked up the saddle they had dumped—to start off afoot across the desert. He'd come on the wild horseherd in another canyon, a dead-end, well after merely setting one blistered foot before another had become a torture.

But desperation had lent him the strength to cut out the spirited bay from among the others; and skill had steadied his hand during the roping and breaking.

Lamps glowed behind Rio Seco's windows as he passed. He headed direct to the Sheriff's office. There was no Wanted poster tacked up by the door as he eased it open. At the desk, oiling a gun, veteran Sheriff Dan Ramsey looked up in silence.

"Hi, Dan!" Jess said it tentatively, not knowing what to expect.

But Ramsey beamed. "Jess! I'm glad. Or—am I? If what I've read is true—?"

"No need to read, Dan." Jess reached up to loosen his neckerchief. "Look."

Ramsey's glance flicked the ugly scar. "You rode with Vince when I told you not to. You did everything I told you not to. But you never lied to me. Is the story true?"

"No. This thing on my neck—it was put there."

Without asking, Ramsey knew it would be Hackett's work. He drew Wanted posters from a desk drawer, glanced at them, thrust them back. "I showed one of these to *her*. Wanted to know if she believed it. She thinks maybe yes, Jess."

"The important thing is, you don't." But that wasn't the important thing really.

From the Sheriff's office Jess headed direct for the Town House, Rio Seco's sole saloon. Inconspicuous as a shadow, he eased in by a side door. The kitchen help—three Mexicans, a man, a woman, a girl—all froze at sight of him. He passed them and eased open the door to a big main room. Noise and music blasted him. Business was booming.

Jess shut the door, turned back, and in silence climbed crude stairs mounting from the kitchen. Before a door in the upstairs hall, he paused to use a key he had with him.

By Rio Seco standards, the bedroom was luxurious. A lamp was burning and lit him across to the big rolltop desk. He began going through its drawers with frantic haste.

What he sought was not there. He turned to the marble-topped wash stand, probing behind its commode. Nothing. He grabbed for a music box on a table, and music tinkled as he searched its innards. Still nothing.

"It's been a year," said the voice behind him. He whirled, to find her standing in the alcove—Tracy Winter, lovely and feline in the sheer, sheer robe she wore.

Jess stared at her, breath sucked in. "Where is it?"

"Right where you left it—like me. I wondered how long it'd be before you came."

The eyes fixed on his said she hated him as much as she loved him. He moved toward her slowly. When he kissed her, his hands ran over her ripe body as if its thin garment did not exist. But in the very instant of submitting, she pushed him away.

"You're still with Vince, aren't you? You were going to try to go straight."

He had never stopped looking at her. "The poster! Dan Ramsey showed you?"

"He wanted to know if I thought you could do a thing like that. He—didn't."

"But you thought so, Tracy? You believed I did?"

"Stealing a Mexican national shrine! It sounds like your idea—Vince couldn't think it up. The Victory Gun would be worth a fortune to any of those bandits down there trying to take over the government. Get them bidding against one another and—"

"You don't believe I sweated it out by myself for a year?"

"I believe it's Vince again. And you're worse than Vince ever was. At least he never made himself out to be anything but a crook and a killer."

Hard-eyed, she walked across to the lamp and lifted it and drew from under its base the gun he had left with her. From behind a wall mirror she jerked down a holster and a gun belt. "Here they are. How did you steal a cannon without a gun?"

"Whatever I told you, you wouldn't believe it."

"The poster said a severe wound across the neck." She came to him, reaching for his neckerchief. Jess let her look. She gasped. "You need something on that!"

"The wound can wait. I figure after three days fighting that mule wagon across the desert, Billy Roy's going to head for the nearest liquor and the nearest woman. *Here.*"

"My place? This town doesn't need any part of that Hackett bunch!"

"Just go about your normal business. Nothing'll happen, Tracy. Trust me."

"*Trust* you?" As she stared back at him, savoring the irony of that, Tracy was slipping into the gown she would wear downstairs to greet her evening's customers.

"Go down as usual from the balcony. Mingle. I'll come out from the kitchen."

As she turned to go, Jess spoke again behind her. "Tracy? There was a time when you'd kiss me. Just leaving me for an hour or so, you'd kiss me."

"That was when I thought the sickness was leaving you. But it's come back. Strong."

Billy Roy Hackett shouldered through the saloon's batwing front doors not ten minutes later. Harvey the bartender saw him coming and anxiously signaled his boss.

As Tracy moved forward, a hush fell over the end of the room nearest the entrance. She paused to face the new arrival calmly, disdainfully.

"None of the Hackett bunch is allowed in my place, Billy Roy. Get out."

He had swooped up whiskey off the bar. He swigged deep, grinning. "You're the most beautiful woman I ever wasn't allowed to look at. You can forget Jess Wade, Miss Tracy. You can even forget my brother Vince. I'll make you forget 'em!"

He broke it off as, across Tracy's shoulder, he saw Jess striding quietly toward them. Eyes narrowed viciously, he watched Jess approach until they stood face to face.

Jess spoke. "Outside. Billy Roy. No fracas. You and I just leave."

"Maybe I got something to say about who leaves and not." Billy Roy scowled sourly.

"Don't be stupid, Billy Roy. Don't grab for your gun. Just walk."

At this moment, Sheriff Dan Ramsey walked past the batwing doors. Tracy had sent one of her dancing girls, little Marcie, to summon him as soon as she heard from Jess that a Hackett brother might be coming in. Ramsey carried his newly oiled shotgun.

"Everybody against me 'cause I'm a Hackett?" Billy Roy's grin had faded. "All right, Jess, I do like you say. I just walk out." And he began to inch along the bar.

But as he reached the spot where Tracy stood, he grabbed her suddenly and whirled her around to act as a shield. He was twisting her arm up behind her cruelly.

"All right; Mr. Big Jess Wade, what do you do now?"

"Throw down your gun, Billy Roy." Ramsey blocked the exit. "Let Miss Tracy go."

Billy Roy spun like a snake striking. He fired once, twice, and Dan Ramsey was blown backward clear through the swinging doors. By then Jess was onto the gunman, shoving Tracy aside and slamming his own weapon across the base of Billy Roy's skull.

The younger Hackett went down like a poled ox, unconscious. Grabbing the fallen man by his collar, Jess dragged him out into the street. But on the saloon steps he dropped his burden, to kneel at Ramsey's side and study his wound.

A knot of curious, alarmed townsfolk gathered quickly, some spilling from inside the saloon. Glancing up, Jess saw the bartender Harvey hovering frightenedly.

"Get Dan home to his wife, Harvey. Get Opie Keech there quick." He watched them make a start; then headed across the street toward the Sheriff's office, dragging a revived and struggling Billy Roy in his wake.

Four leading townsmen trailed along as Jess opened the single barred cell with Ramsey's keys and thrust Vince's brother inside. They would have detained him with questions. But Jess pushed past them impatiently, headed now for the Ramsey home.

The Sheriff lay on his bed, perhaps dying, with his wife Sarah hovering anguishedly nearby and Opie Keech—the town's barber and medic-of-a-sort—trying to force whiskey into his patient before probing for two bullets. He read Jess's unspoken query.

"How can I tell how Dan is? He's got a pulse, that's all."

Tracy, who also had followed the wounded man home, caught Jess's searching glance about the room and knew what he sought. Wordlessly, she collected Dan's guitar from a closet. Standing at the bed's foot, Jess began to strum a ballad he and Dan had harmonized often together. Weakly, the Sheriff's lips began to move to the tune.

When it was over, Jess poured a shot of the whiskey Ramsey had been refusing and held it to his mouth. The older man swallowed like an obedient child.

"You sing no better than when we were fishing the river, Jess," he whispered.

"You sing better," countered Jess. "Tonight I couldn't hear you."

Now Opie, seeing the whiskey taking effect moved in to probe a second time.

But Ramsey still had something to say. "Jess? I spent twelve years getting this town safe to live in. You got to keep it that way for me till I get on my feet."

"Me?" Jess shook his head. "Dan, I'm no lawman."

"You are now. I hereby swear you in as my deputy. Badge, Sarah? All right, Opie, dig."

Dan lay unconscious but breathing evenly when Jess returned to the Sheriff's office. In his cell Billy Roy was singing insolently. The four men waited for news of Ramsey.

"He's no better," Jess said woodenly, "than I'd be after taking two .45 slugs."

"If Ramsey dies," grated Joslyn, livery-stable owner, "we hang *him* fast."

Billy Roy laughed uproariously. "Fixing to hang Vince Hackett's little brother? Hear that, Vince? They don't know what you're going to do, do they?"

Jess Wade, at least, had a fairly good idea what Vince might do. Grimly, he strode to the rifle rack and unlocked it with Ramsey's keys. He tossed a rifle to each of the four startled townsmen. "Protect your livery stable, Mr. Joslyn. Your bank, Mr. Carter. Your general store, Mr. Selby, and Mr. Tilford—your hotel."

"Anything happens to me," jeered Billy Roy, "Vince'll pick this town to pieces!"

But Jess, the deputy's badge bright on his vest, was facing the others. "Gentlemen, you better get some sleep. I want you in this office at sunup, with those rifles."

Up in the rocky hills where Vince's riders had made camp, guarding their stolen cannon, it was daybreak before Billy Roy's failure to return from town became worrisome. Some of the gang protested that Billy Roy was only going to get them caught if they waited for him longer; but Vince saddled up for Rio Seco with his chief aide, Gunner. Back in the war days of '65, Gunner had handled artillery for the Union Army.

On their way, the elder Hackett spotted a platoon of

Mexican cavalry far off among the hills. Reining in, he watched them through binoculars. They were searching.

"Well?" grunted Gunner. "Riding slow. Won't make town for half an hour."

"No reason to hurry. Probably twenty patrols like that are out." Vince spurred forward again. "We'll fetch Billy Roy at the saloon, sober him up, and watch 'em."

Morning business had begun in town. Homeward bound from the store, Tracy spotted Jess in Opie's barber chair and marched into the shop to confront him.

"You're making it very easy for Vince Hackett to ride into this town, Jess."

It was an accusation. Jess went blank-eyed. "All in how you look at it."

"Can I ask why you're leaving your prisoner unguarded? *I'd* have men on the roofs."

His grin was cold. He merely shrugged. Tracy flounced from the shop—and halted in astonishment. Each atop his own place of business, each bearing a rifle, Selby and Tilford and Carter and Joslyn stood on sentinel duty. Chagrined, yet still not sure how far she dared believe in Jess Wade, Tracy went on her way. And back in the shop, his trim and shave completed, Jess was signalling Opie to open up a locked closet in one corner. Huddled inside, handcuffed, was Billy Roy Hackett. Jess shoved the prisoner ahead of him across the street and back into the single jail cell.

Not many minutes later, two riders from the hills moved slowly up the street. They were well aware of the guns trained on them, and were careful how they rode. But Vince was smiling thinly. He had left certain instructions with the boys remaining in camp.

Tracy's was the first face he saw as he entered the saloon. Once, years ago, before she had fallen in love with Jess Wade, Tracy Winter had been Vince's girl. A longing for her still lit his eyes as they fixed on her, and his voice was soft.

"Good to see you again, Tracy. Wish you could still say that to me."

There was no welcome in her look. "Billy Roy started with that same line last night. Ended up claiming he could

make me forget Jesse Wade *and* you. Have you and Jess the
cannon?"

Vince's jaw set. "When's the last time you saw Jess,
Tracy?" He waited until it became obvious she would not
answer. "Billy Roy sleeping it off up in your room?"

"He'd never be allowed in my room. He's in jail. He
shot Dan Ramsey. Dan may die."

"Self-defense?" Vince's hard expression changed only as
Tracy shook her head. For an instant, then, pain twisted it.
A viewer might read the story of the pain his kid brother's
brainless bullying had brought to Vince. But he stiffened.
"Witnesses?"

"Me," said Tracy without hesitation. "And everybody
in here. No excuse for it."

Vince swallowed that and turned on his heel and
shoved out through the doors.

Jess was waiting as his one-time saddle companion entered the Sheriff's office.

"That what you're looking for, Vince?" He jerked his
head toward the cell. Back of the bars, dull eyes lighting
with pleasure, Billy Roy came up off his cot.

"I want him loose," Vince said, almost tonelessly.

"You *want?* I tell you what you *get.* That cannon back
in Mexico where it belongs. You in a Mexican court, telling how you stole it and framed me and fixed my neck."

"Make him open the door, Vince!" bleated Billy Roy.
"Get these irons off me!"

Vince did not even glance toward his brother. "You
got two hours to let Billy Roy go, Jess. If he isn't walking
free down the street by then, I'm going to let that cannon
loose. I'll wipe this town off the face of the earth."

"You're not leaving here," Jess countered. "Step outside
with me."

While Billy Roy still jabbered, the other two stepped
out into the street together. Jess indicated the armed men
on the rooftops. But Vince threw back his head and
laughed.

"You forget how I operate, Jess? Think I'd come in here
naked as a jaybird? He pulled a fob watch from his
pocket and glanced at it. "Just about time now."

He had no sooner spoken than a brace of rifle shots
cracked from the bleak hills up behind the town. Joslyn,
caught in the hip, spun and dropped his gun. Tilford tottered and plunged from his roof perch. The other two
sentinels dove flat.

"I want him out, Jess." Vince did not raise his voice.
"Right now."

Jess's reply came even softer. "He stays."

"And what about them?" Vince gestured up the sun-
baked street. Just cantering into view came the Mexican
patrol, led by its Lieutenant. They reined in by the water-
ing trough, weary, dusted with desert alkali, to let their
horses drink.

"They're coming to ask about a man with a new shot-
mark on his neck, Jess."

Jess stepped back through the open door, drew his .45
and leveled it calmly at a suddenly shrinking Roy. "You
just make sure he doesn't, Vince."

"I'll get rid of them. After I do, you got two hours to
let Billy Roy free."

Watching narrowly from a window, Jess saw Vince
amble up to the Lieutenant and engage him in conversation. He seemed from his gestures to be describing a
wagon with a tarp-covered cannon on it. The Lieutenant
straightened eagerly. Vince seemed to be agreeing to lead
the patrol to their quarry, after a haggle about the posted
reward. The Lieutenant barked an order. His men snapped
to attention and remounted.

Having regained his own horse from the saloon's hitch-
rail, Vince led the platoon out of town at a trot. Every
eye in Rio Seco was watching them go. Nobody much
noticed Gunner emerging from the general store with
three heavy sacks, which he piled onto his pinto. Nobody
watched him start walking for the hills, leading the animal carelessly.

But it was not to be much later that they all remembered how he had gone.

For a man of Vince Hackett's guile and cold-bloodedness,
disposal of the Mexican platoon was no great problem. He
led them straight to the river. By then, Gunner was back

at the camp and giving the others orders for hauling the
cannon to a high rise. Two of the riders, Gabe and Lige,
were emptying the sacks Gunner had fetched from town.
Each contained fifty sticks of dynamite, caps, fuses, powder in kegs.

The platoon never had a chance. Vince led it to a
shallow spot where the river could be forded, and himself
was first to ride across. As the soldiers moved to follow,
the cannon on the hilltop opened up on their unpro-
tected backs. They were blown from their saddles like
chaff in a wind. For awhile, as their dying screams faded,
the river was tinged red. But it all was over in a matter
of minutes. Vince began to whistle a snatch of tune as he
cantered back to rejoin his smirking followers.

And back in town Jess had crossed to the Ramsey
house to check on Dan.

"I've come to ask a favor," he told the bandaged
Sheriff on the bed. "Give me permission to let Billy Roy
go loose, Dan."

"That's admitting you're guilty as accused. You're one
of them."

"Let me set Billy Roy loose. Or else Vince will blow up
your whole town. He's got that cannon out there in the
hills. There won't be much Rio Seco left."

"Can't give in to them." Ramsey spoke weakly but
definitely. "Let a handful of filth scare us—nothing left.
Hold the prisoner, Jess. That's an order."

After a long moment, Jess nodded grimly. "I'll hold him,
Dan."

But as he left, Sarah Ramsey stepped outside with him.
"Jess! Do you want to kill Dan? He can't be moved. If
all it takes is to let that animal out of jail—"

"I do what Dan says, Mrs. Ramsey," Jess interrupted
softly.

"Don't be a fool! My husband made this town safe!
Don't listen to him now! He's hurt, he's out of his head—"
But with a sad, compassionate look, Jess was walking
away.

Up in the hills back of town, Vince had complimented
Gunner on his pinpoint shooting. As they stood alongside
the golden cannon, the elder Hackett was smiling tightly.

"All of a sudden we've got a timetable, Gunner. Two hours until Billy Roy's let loose. Get the cannon moved in a quarter-mile from town. Get started!"

Mules and men toiled and sweated under the noonday sun, carrying out Vince's crisp command. The Victory Gun had been hauled and pushed and prodded into position before the sun began to cast longer shadows. And one less rider saw it set there. Lige had fallen under the wagon's wheels and been crushed to death in the process.

In the Sheriff's office, Billy Roy jeered cockily from inside his cell.

"Well, Mr. Wade, you're silent as a cricket with its throat cut. Waiting for those Federales to come back and get you? Or waiting for Vince?"

Jess, pacing the office, had reached a sudden decision. "Your brother'll come in." He took Ramsey's keys and unlocked the back door to the office. Then he crossed back to the front window. Sure enough, Vince could be seen loping alone into the single street.

"*Deputy* Wade!" guffawed Billy Roy. "You couldn't make breaking away from my brother stick, could you? Here you are back with him again. And Vince is still calling the shots."

Jess stepped out into the street to confront the rider just reining in there. From her saloon, Tracy was watching. So was virtually every other eye in town that had seen Vince approach. Still mounted, Vince chuckled. "Less than an hour now, Jess. I thought maybe you could hand him over to me, we could ride out, there'd be no trouble."

"Get off your horse," Jess commanded tersely. "Walk toward me. And if you make a move when you do it, Vince—that's all I ask, make a move."

Vince laughed and flung up his hands in a mock gesture of surrender and slid from his horse. As he walked toward Ramsey's young deputy, he still was laughing.

"You know me, Jess. No violence. I don't approve of violence."

At some distance in the hills, a sudden explosion sounded. This was followed by an ominous hissing sound. And then, with terrifying abruptness, the belfry of the

town's little wooden church disintegrated and collapsed
into a billow of flames. Debris showered the street. The
heavy bell crashed to earth with an ominous clanging like a
requiem.

Suddenly the street was filled with frightened citizens,
all converging on the Sheriff's office. And over their
heads, following a second explosion in the hills, came once
more that ominous hissing as if a nest of serpents had been
let loose.

This time, a huge crater was blown from the dead center of the street. The concussion knocked several running
people flat. Others dove for whatever cover they could
find. The invisible artillery roared yet again. This time,
the Ramsey house was hit and caved in upon itself like a
structure made of tissuepaper. Sarah had been in the street,
and whirled in dismay. But she could not even have recognized the awful extent of the disaster before the walls collapsed, crushing her husband to death as they fell.

Jess, too, had seen it happen. He began to race for the
smoking ruin. But as he neared it, a woman like a wild-
cat sprang to face him. Sarah was screaming hysterically.

"You killed him, Jess Wade! You killed Dan sure as if
you'd put that gun to his head! I told you to let that animal
go. I begged you! But to save your own skin, you killed
Dan!" Past him, into the office, she sped. From Dan's
desk drawer she yanked out a handful of the suppressed
posters and began to hurl them hysterically into the crowd.

"See this? A Wanted poster! This man is wanted by the
Mexican government! He stole the cannon that's firing on
us! That killed my husband! That will kill all of you! It
says he can be identified by the wound on his neck! He's
one of them! Make him let that prisoner loose—force him
to—while youre still alive to do it!"

And Vince spoke: "It's very easy to get that gun out
there to stop firing. Just let my brother go and no more
trouble." The crowd heard him. Their shouts began.

*"Let him go, Wade. . . ." "We want no more vio-
lence . . ." "Our homes, our families . . ." "It's our roots
that are here in this town. Wade, not yours. Keeping Billy
Roy for the circuit judge tears up our roots, not
yours. . . ." "Turn him over to his brother!"*

"Quiet!" Jess had to shout to dominate the hubbub. "All

of you, quiet!" A drawn gun was in his hand as he backed to the office door. "First man who wants to come in and release the prisoner—just step up."

"That cannon's going to blow this town apart," Vince countered contemptuously.

A girl who was Selby's clerk at the general store screamed. "He can do it! I sold his man enough dynamite to blow up three towns like Rio Seco! I'm only a clerk, not God. How was *I* to know he wasn't a prospector?"

And from inside, from the cell, came cackling laughter. "What now, Mr. Wade? You aim to let that cannon bust their town down, or don't you?"

Vince suddenly swung up into his saddle. "Stick with it, Jess! I'm overdue out of here. I can get killed like anybody else, if you don't let Billy Roy go."

As he spurred off up the street, scattering onlookers, Tracy stepped up to Jess. "You've done all you can do, Jess. Let Billy Roy go."

"I'm keeping him here," answered Jess, back tight to the door. "Clear the street, all of you. That cannon's due to hit a few times more."

They scattered, muttering, but he knew they'd be coming back to enforce their demand once that Victory Gun let them hear a little more of its persuading. Tracy was the last of them to turn away, and before she did so she touched his sleeve.

"I apologize. I was wrong. You're what you said you'd be, Jess."

"Don't count on it," Jess said between set teeth. "Get off the street, Tracy."

He watched her until she had entered the saloon. The street lay empty now. The very silence hanging now above the distant hills seemed ominous. He went inside.

In the cell Billy Roy was capering, gleefully. His elation grew as he saw Jess take down the cell keys from the wall peg where they hung. Oblivious, Jess crossed to the street door and locked it. Then he swung back to the cell door and unlocked that.

"Come out!" he grated. But something in his tone made Billy Roy shrink back.

Uneasily, the prisoner emerged. "Finally seen the light,

eh, Mr. Wade? Going to take these handcuffs off and let me go back to my brother?"

Jess disdained to reply. Instead, he thrust a startled Billy Roy out the back door and into the alley, just as the ominous mutter of townsfolk re-emerging and beginning to close in on the front of the office asserted itself. They were coming to set the younger Hackett free, to give Vince what he demanded, to save their town.

They were so intent upon their business of breaking into the jail that they never saw the two riders galloping now for the hills. But far short of the rise on which the cannon stood, Jess reined them in and forced a still-handcuffed Billy Roy from his saddle. Slamming him down the steep side of a gully to the bottom, he stood with drawn gun tight at the gasping bully's throat. From far above, the cannon roared again.

Rio Seco shook to another virulent explosion. Milling about the jail, a baffled crowd had been babbling that the empty cell proved Jess Wade was indeed still one of the Hackett mob. But this new assault said eloquently that Billy Roy had not been returned to his brother. And Tracy, glaring at her fellow citizens, spoke out for all.

"I guess this makes it plain Wade didn't turn Billy Roy over. Somebody's got to ride up there and tell Vince his brother's no longer in this town. Harvey, get the buckboard. Drive me up there to the hills. I'll find them!"

The sun was sinking now, and twilight purpled desert and hills. The hour Vince had set for wiping Rio Seco clean off the map had arrived. Jess jabbed his gun.

"All right, Billy Roy, now you yell. Let Vince know you're here, right below him."

Jabbering with terror at the gun-muzzle's jab, Billy Roy obliged with a wailing shout. In the same instant, pressure at his throat relaxed. Jess had vanished in the dark. And from overhead Vince was calling down, demanding his location.

"I'm down here in the gully, Vince. Watch out for Wade! He's up behind them rocks!"

Vince was thinking fast. He gestured his two men, Mody and Heff, to circle the rocky eminence directly opposite—approaching it from either side. He signalled Gabe and Gunner to jockey the mule wagon until the cannon was trained on the same spot.

Their invisible target crouched in the dark, alert to each of their maneuvers, uncertain in which direction to fire his drawn weapon first. Heff and Mody were circling in closer. And down below, a dim shape. Billy Roy was struggling to free himself.

"Vince!" he shouted now. "Billy Roy gets it the instant I do!"

"He's going to kill me, Vince!" Looking up from the gully, Billy Roy screamed.

Instantly, Vince bellowed an order. "Mody! Heff! Hold off!"

Belly flat to the rock, gun still trained on Billy Roy, Jess called across to the opposite rise. "Tell 'm to drop their rifles and lie face down. Vince."

"Heff! Mody!" The reply was instantaneous. "You heard him!"

Jess could see the shadows to his right and left obeying, dropping weapons, stretching flat. And from across the gully the hard, familiar voice rang out anew.

"All right, Jess, it's a stand-off. What've you got in mind?"

"Taking this cannon back where it came from!" Jess yelled back. "Moving it into town right now—if you want to keep Billy Roy alive." Having said it, he melted from the spot where he had spoken as if he were a black liquid flowing. Vince was calling.

"Anything wrong with us talking it over, Jess? How come so much money doesn't appeal to you? And you don't have to raise a hand to get it—"

At the same instant, the cannon spoke. Dynamite exploded among the boulders, creating havoc where Jess just had been crouching. The flare of light showed the helpless bodies of Heff and Mody being torn apart and hurtled high. But Vince had not put their survival ahead of his precious brother's. They had been expendable.

Sliding down the hillside, Jess took a long leap which carried him across to where the three remaining Hackett riders—Vince, Gunner, Gabe—were just regrouping. His

.45 snarled even as he landed, and Gunner sprawled across
the cannon lifeless.

Vince and Gabe opened instant fire. But Jess's weapon
yammered to keep them pinned down. As they scuttled
apart, and then veered in on him from opposite flanks,
Jess eeled into a fresh position and blazed away again.
One of his shots caught a mule hoof, and the animal reared
in panic. Suddenly the full team stampeded.

Swaying, lurching, the wagon was on the move. Jess was
still firing. A powder keg caught a bullet and exploded
deafeningly, igniting several more. The hillside shuddered
to the concussions, and Gabe was blown with them past
the gates of an earned Hell.

On the hillside the wagon lurched anew and the cannon's lashing began to snap as dislodged weight strained
them. The cannon burst free, rolled over and began to
slide into the gully. Still struggling down there, Billy Roy
saw it coming and shrieked.

"Vince! Vince!" But his handcuffs held him to the
mesquite where Jess had left him anchored. Over him
the heavy gun rolled pitilessly, and his cries cut off.

Staring down into the gully, Vince cried in disbelief.
"Billy Roy—?"

A sudden maniacal rage overwhelmed the gunslinger
then. Demented, wild, he flung toward the last spot from
which Jess had fired. "Wade! Good friend Jess Wade!" And
as he flayed about his gun was roaring senselessly, emptying itself into the night.

There was a sudden silence, broken by the futile click
of a hammer on nothing.

"What do you do now, Vince?" Jess demanded quietly,
rearing himself erect. As he emerged from behind his
rocky cover, his own gun covered Vince unmovingly. "I'll
tell you what you do now. You and the cannon go back to
Mexico with me."

All Rio Seco gathered in the street next morning to
watch the departure.

Sunlight glittered like fire on the golden barrel of the
cannon, no longer masked by its tarpaulin. Each man he
passed on his way to take the wagon's reins reached out

to shake Jess Wade's hand. But he ignored them all, keeping his gaze set ahead.

"Come back," urged someone. "You'll always be welcome, Jess."

"We want to say thank you," someone else spoke out. "Thank you, Mr. Wade."

Jess did not even glance at them as he mounted the driver's seat. In the place alongside, handcuffed and with his legs stoutly chained, Vince Hackett already waited. He flicked his reins without a word and the wagon started to roll.

But Tracy was running alongside it. "You won't be coming back, Jess, will you?"

"No," he said, and meant to say no more. But the stark grief of her lifted face got to him. And suddenly something in him came alive like the golden gun to the light.

"I'll send for you!" he called back. "You'll come when I say. It won't be long."

That was enough to keep a man happy in his heart all the way to Mexico. Because the look on her face as it fell behind and out of his view was a look that told him everything. She'd come to him. Any time. Any place. No matter what.

A NATIONAL GENERAL PICTURES PRESENTATION
    in TECHNICOLOR
Written, produced and directed by CHARLES MARQUIS
    WARREN
Story by FREDERIC LOUIS FOX
Adapted for SCREEN STORIES by JEAN FRANCIS WEBB